SCC Library

3 3065 00388 2952

Praise for *Wide Open Privacy*

Santiago Canyon College
Library

"Privacy is a shared responsibility. There is a role for laws and regulations; there is a role for self-regulation; and there is a role for consumers to exercise control. As the public policy debate continues about how best to protect personal data, *Wide Open Privacy* shows how consumers can exercise control of their digital identities effectively. Smith and MacDermott have provided an extremely important contribution to the privacy framework discussion. This is essential reading for tech-using consumers."

–Christopher Wolf, Founder and Co-Chair, Future of Privacy Forum and Global Director, Hogan Lovells Privacy and Information Management Practice

"New insights for a new digital age. Ratchets up the pace of solutions to address the ever increasing pace of the challenges."

–Major General Michael W. Davidson, author of Victory at Risk

"The authors write fluently about both the problems and possible solutions for the computer user—but also about the policy challenges confronting governments today in this well-written and up-to-the-minute account that offers important insights for anyone using computers today."

–Dr. George Conyne, Director-Designate, Center for American Studies, University of Kent and BBC Commentator on American Affairs.

"*Wide Open Privacy* shows how Internet users can take back control of their digital identities. Smith and MacDermott offer a compelling, and sober, analysis of the many threats to privacy in the modern age, but they don't view privacy as a lost cause. Instead, with a mix of policy analysis and useful tips, they advocate for a user-centric approach to personal data, equally relevant to consumers and business."

–Justin Brookman, Irector, Center for De****** **& Technology Project on Consumer Pri**

D1025995

KF
1263
.C65
565
2012

WIDE OPEN PRIVACY
Strategies For The Digital Life

J.R. Smith and Siobhan MacDermott

ocn 893098197

$15.00 Qg 5-17-15

Santiago Canyon College
Library

IT-Harvest Press

330 East Maple Rd, #406, Birmingham, MI 48009

www.it-harvest.com

Copyright © 2012 J.R. Smith and Siobhan MacDermott

All rights reserved.

ISBN-13: 978-0-9854607-3-0

For Blanka, Francesca, and Sofia.

–J.R.Smith

To Mom and Dad for everything. To A. and his
Magician.

–Siobhan MacDermott

[WIDE OPEN PRIVACY]

Table of Contents

INTRODUCTION
Digital Morning

Silver sunlight filters through the horse chestnuts, lengthening the soft pewter shadows of passersby along the north footpath of the Champs-Élysées. Among them, an American woman of twenty-five, inhaling the light of a sweet Parisian morning, walking toward the ascending sun, its rays steadily intensifying across the Arc de Triomphe in the distance ahead. This, she thinks, almost aloud, is bliss.

Among her fellow strollers she notes many who seem unable to take their eyes off her, some smiling, some gaping; although there are just as many who pass her by without so much as a glance. Like the scent of a subtle perfume, her bliss diminishes as she meets the eyes of those who gaze. At length, she looks away from them and down, down at her own two feet, which are bare. In fact, her downcast eyes tell her, she is naked.

The revelation pierces her—a high-pitched tone, rising in volume, rhythmically pulsating, relentless, even inhuman. The young woman's eyes open wide upon the eggshell vista of a popcorn ceiling typical of a suburban American condo bedroom. She turns her head, presses down her pillow to see the four tiny glowing faces of the "World Clock" app on her smartphone. There are clocks for New York, Los Angeles, Paris, and the city near which she lives. The faux analog hands of this little clock point to 6:45. The time is visible just above the pillow-linen hillock, beyond which, in her field of vision, are a window, a parking lot, and the windowed wall of a neighboring condominium building identical to hers. She takes the device in her hand to caress the touchscreen, silencing the alarm.

Promenading on the Champs-Élysées! She smiles to herself as she sits up, recalling first her dream and then a real, waking week spent in Paris two years ago. Wonder when I can get back there again? Gazing at the phone in her hand, she switches to her home screen, which is a view from the Place de la Concorde. Then it hits her—the real point of the dream: I was naked! A shiver of embarrassment is followed by a jolt of fear that quickly settles into a kind of mild thrill.

Just imagine that ...

She gets up, sets her phone on the indentation in her now-vacant pillow, throws on a robe, takes up the phone again, and, just as 75 percent of us report having done, carries it into the bathroom with her. There, she reads the morning's emails, answering those from people associated with work, including her boss, an assistant who reports to her, a girlfriend, a customer, and a young man who actually works at a competing firm, but with whom she has been enjoying a pleasant flirtation, entirely online. She does not think twice about responding in rapid succession to this diverse and not entirely compatible constituency of correspondents, even as she performs her morning ablutions. It certainly does not occur to her that anyone with the will and access to the right (generally accessible) technology could monitor her messages. "Anyone" includes her boss, her assistant, or the young man at the competing firm. Even less does

1

she consider that an individual or entity (corporate or governmental) possessed of a bit more technical savvy could remotely turn on the microphone in her smartphone or, for that matter, the video camera. Whatever she says and whatever is said to her, that remote eavesdropper will hear. What she sees, he, she, or it will see also.

(The potential for mobile device monitoring is quite routine, and does not require the practiced craft or nefarious motive of a criminal. Her email provider always has everything it needs, technically, to access all her email messages. Her phone carrier always knows where she has been, who she has called or texted, and who has called or texted her.)

And whoever reads her mail, listens to her speech, or looks at what her smartphone sees—even in the sanctity of her own bathroom—also knows exactly where she lives, thanks to the GPS in her mobile device. When she leaves her condo, smartphone tucked into her purse, she can be tracked throughout her day as the faithful GPS radio keeps broadcasting and the phone itself dutifully pings one cell tower after another.

It is quite possible, however, that she might not even leave her home today. Her smartphone, her laptop, and her high-speed Internet connection with a WiFi router enable her to work from home. When she first joined her current company straight out of college four years ago, "telecommuting," as it was then called, was more or less a novelty at the firm. Something of an experiment, managers were unsure about it. By now, however, it's really caught on. Nobody thinks twice about it anymore, and, on many days, the office is practically a ghost building, as two out of three employees work at home on any given day. Productivity? It's actually up. For one thing, people spend less time commuting to and from work, to and from lunch, and to and from meetings. For another, the water cooler and break room are no longer thronged by knots of employees engaged in what used to be called "idle office gossip." The people working from home really do work. Of course, they know the boss tracks the hour, minute, and second they log onto the corporate network. He can, if he wants, review just what they do when they're logged on, and he can pinpoint the moment they log off for the day. No old-school assembly-line time clock was ever more accurate or more detailed in the data it recorded.

The company's network gives every employee at a certain level access to everything stored in the company servers, or more accurately, in the chunk of "the cloud" that the company leases; the physical onsite servers were dumped last year. This means that every scrap of information our young woman needs to do her job—every report, every summary, every file, every figure—is available to her in very close to real time. No need to walk down the hall to "accounting." Filing cabinets were ditched long before the servers were shed. As for older documents, they used to be stored in the basement or, if really old, at an out-of-town archive facility. Now everything is digitized. No basement journey is required, and no offsite safari need be mounted.

After she finishes in the bathroom, fires up her laptop, goes online to check out the performance of her modest investment portfolio, clicks through some interesting emails from clothing retailers she likes, and skims the online editions of one local and one national newspaper, she downloads some confidential patent reports from the company's cloud space. After digesting these, she does some Internet searches related to them. It all moves very quickly, orders of magnitude more quickly than research in the days of paper files, brick-and-mortar archives, and shoe-leather excursions to the public library. She's not even changed out of her robe. It's her business suit these days.

She does all of this via the Internet access her employer has paid for and installed in her condo. Does she know that her bosses can find out what newspapers she reads and news sites she visits, if they care to? And that they can even track down what articles she reads in those newspapers? Does she know they can, if they wish, monitor where she shops online and what she buys, as well as how much she spends?

Maybe she does know, but sees it all as the price of working at home and getting Internet for "free." In any case, her bosses aren't the only parties privy to this information. Each time she visits a news site, an array of ad networks, her Internet Service Provider (ISP), providers of analytics, Twitter, and Facebook may also find out just what interests her.

Another unanswered question is whether her company's management knows that neither the ISP installer nor she ever bothered to create an access password for the wireless router that sits in her bedroom. Any passerby within three or four hundred feet can surf the Web on her employer's dime, perhaps monitor some of the company's data traffic, and maybe even make a lucky guess about a password or two and enjoy something approaching the same level of access to the very guts of the firm she (and the CEO, for that matter) enjoys. Or maybe a neighbor's got a hobby he'd rather nobody—like the police, for instance—knows about. Let's say it's collecting child abuse images. Download this stuff to his computer using her open WiFi network, and the cops, should they ever come calling, will be asking her and her bosses some very embarrassing, potentially very costly questions. But speaking of open networks, nobody at the firm complained when she, stuck in an airport during a March blizzard, logged onto the company cloud via the jam-packed terminal's free and open WiFi access to download one sensitive document after another. Complain? She was congratulated for having turned a miserable weather delay into a marathon work session. Her boss even sent her a thank you email.

That happened to be the same trip on which she nearly lost her phone when she accidentally left it next to her seat in the waiting room when she got up to ask the gate agent a question. When she returned to her seat a full fifteen minutes later, she was alternately stunned then relieved to see her $600 smartphone sitting there, safe and sound—though she could swear she had put it down on the seat to the left of hers, not the right. Could somebody have "borrowed" it? She made a mental note to review her bill very carefully when it came in, but she never got around to it. In any event, she soon became less concerned by the thought that somebody could have made calls from her phone than she was irritated by the sudden decline in performance of her phone's batteries. Nine in the morning, battery at 98 percent, then down to 60 by ten-thirty, and in the teens at lunchtime. This started happening right after that trip, along with an array of random buzzes and clicks during some phone calls and the weird SMS texts she received from time to time, always meaningless strings of numbers, punctuation marks, and symbols.

Someday, when I am actually at the office, I will have to take my phone down to IT. Let them figure it out. But "someday" never arrived.

After about two hours of hard work, she finishes a confidential report and transmits it. It will be saved to her company's cloud, but, because she considers herself a prudent and savvy computer user, it will also be automatically backed up onto the cloud service she uses: a confidential corporate document put into storage along with her personal emails, her photographs, some videos, a short story she's been noodling with, her private journal, a whole lot of personal financial information, and, indeed, all the ever-accumulating minutiae of an ordinary, active life. The company running the cloud service knows the contents of all this, at least in theory, at least if it cared to take a peek.

So now it's time for a break this morning: a second cup of coffee and a little online shopping. She clicks through some shoe offerings at her favorite sites, each click dutifully recorded by the site and advertising networks to which hundreds and even thousands of retailers subscribe. Each website and each ad network is silently compiling a dossier defined by her interests, her product preferences, her ideal price range, her browsing habits, and her buying habits. The dossier, ever growing, always up to date, fits her into a profile of similar consumers. This way, the online merchant can send her ads precisely tailored to her profile, and the ad networks can sell to their subscribers not ad space on some random website, but ads that will be opened right in front of the eyeballs of consumers who fit the target profile. Online advertisers need not buy ad space when they can buy audiences for their ads—more specifically, self-targeted audiences, who have revealed their retail sweet spots simply by browsing the web, clicking on links, and making purchases.

From our young woman's point of view, this is just fine. She is impressed that the online merchants she regularly visits always seem to know pretty much what she wants. A few years ago, window shopping on the Net could be pretty annoying, she reflects, as irrelevant banner ads stared her in the face, distracting her gaze with annoying animations, and pop-ups perpetually intruded. Lately, she's been pleasantly surprised that most of the ads on her screen actually interest her. It's as if they know what she wants.

(That's because "they" do. And when she actually buys an item, her credit card company knows what she's bought, too. That company makes a very nice living charging vendors a service fee and charging her interest, but some of its best revenue comes from selling information about her purchases—together with those of others who fit her profile—to retailers, advertising agencies, and ad networks.)

Third-party knowledge about this young woman extends beyond merchandise. In an election year, she's been getting a really annoying volume of robocalls and emails touting this or that candidate. That most of the communications promote the candidates she actually intends to vote for scarcely makes the intrusions more welcome. Where does it all come from? She has been reading more political news online lately, most of it on sites that tend to favor her own point of view, but she has been very careful to avoid filling out any forms, signing any petitions, or taking any surveys. Of course, she did register for "free" access to a number of the sites, providing her phone number and email address, but even if she had never disclosed this much information, the big online search providers have been relentlessly following the trail of her meanderings through the Web, day after day, night after night. That's what they do, and the information they collect is for sale: to merchants, to advertisers, to advertising networks, to political organizations, and, for that matter, under certain circumstances, to agencies of local, state, and federal government.

This young woman, who dreams of Paris and has a good job, is computer savvy. Born into the age of the personal computer and having come of age in the era of the Internet's ascendency and triumph, she is very comfortable with the technology. She understands (if rather vaguely) that merchants, advertisers, and others are tracking her. Often, the trackers even tell her this, sending emails that begin, "We noticed you were looking at sandals ... or flat-screen televisions, or flavored vodkas ... and we thought you'd want to see ..." At odd moments, this strikes her as snooping, maybe even stalking, and she feels a twinge of creepiness.

But the feeling never lasts. Certainly, it has not moved her to read the interminable privacy policy statements many of the websites she visits require her to click agreement to before they open their doors to her. (Very few users read these statements. According to a Carnegie Mellon study by Aleecia M. McDonald and Lorrie Faith Cranor, the average online consumer would have to devote between 181 and 304 hours annually to reading the privacy policies of each of the sites they visit. Extrapolated to a national figure for the United States, this would come to between 39 and 67 billion hours a year, representing an annual loss in national productivity of between 559 billion and 1.1 trillion dollars. Even if she and her fellow Americans did put in the requisite hours, the vast majority of privacy policy texts are so vague, obscure, and relentlessly legalistic in content that comprehension is a long shot at best [McDonald and Cranor, 2008]).

Shopping done—she didn't end up buying anything this morning, but she clicked through plenty of items—she returns to work, opening an email from a major employer in her field. Her eyes grow wide. It seems this guy read an opinion piece she wrote and posted in response to an article in an online forum. He was sufficiently impressed to go to her LinkedIn page, then followed up on links she'd included there to some other pieces she had posted online. He says he wants to set up an interview ...

She looks at the masthead on the email. This is a great company, she thinks. It's a great company, and it has an office in Paris ...

She congratulates herself on having contributed to the forum, having posted good stuff on websites relevant to her industry, and having kept her LinkedIn page up to date. But into her expectations intrudes the recollection of having posted a few "unprofessional" photos and comments on her personal Facebook page. (Like many users, she's never bothered to alter the default Facebook privacy settings, settings that make most content public.)

He'll never look at that stuff, she assures herself as she begins typing a response to the email.

She lifts her fingers from the keyboard. No, he'll never look at that stuff, and, anyway, it's not so bad. Everybody parties once in a while. But before she finishes the email, she logs onto her Facebook page and starts deleting. Finished, she asks herself: He won't have seen this yet, right?

Just as she hits send, her smartphone rings—it's a retro telephone ringer, the kind her grandparents, not her parents had. She answers; that young man from the other company is asking her to a high-end local café for lunch.

"Do you know where it is? Or do you want me to pick you up at your place?"

"No. I'll meet you there. Just give me the address, and I'll put it in the GPS."

Walking out her door, down the stairs, through the lobby, past the comforting presence of the surveillance cameras, out into the parking lot, past another surveillance camera or two or four, she opens her car door, and settles into the driver's seat. Near her left knee, inserted into the car's diagnostic port is the new device her auto insurance company has given her. "Rewards your safe driving," they said. "Significant savings for you."

The same Bluetooth fob in her purse that unlocked the car door on her approach lets her start the car with the press of a button. Before shifting into drive, she keys the café address into her car's GPS, touches the accelerator, and heads off to a place she does not know to eat lunch with a man she has met only online.

Not quite true.

The online review she glanced at before leaving her laptop gave the place four out of five stars and lauded its gazpacho. As for the man whose invitation she accepted, the people search "verification" website she checked out just before going out the door revealed nothing objectionable about him, except for a traffic ticket to two.

Turning out of her building's parking lot, she just makes it through the first intersection on a yellow light.

"Or was it red?" she wonders aloud. That damn stoplight camera. What a shame it would be to spoil a perfect morning.

.01

[*Brave Nude World*]

CHAPTER ONE
The Privacy Paradoxes

Daniel Defoe's novel *Robinson Crusoe* was a bestseller from the get-go, sailing through four editions in 1719, the year of its publication, and innumerable editions, iterations, and incarnations since. No book in the canon of Western literature has had wider distribution or has been more prodigiously translated (you can find Coptic, Maltese, Inuktitut texts). On the face of it, the story doesn't sound all that appealing. Crusoe is a seventeenth-century slave trader who is shipwrecked on an island near the mouth of the remote Orinoco River, the sole survivor of the catastrophe, but for the captain's dog and two cats. (Eventually he adopts a local parrot as well.) Appalled by the prospect of solitude, he calls his little scrap of land the Island of Despair.

At length, Crusoe scratches out a place to live, reads his Bible, becomes pious, thanks the Lord for his salvation, but continues to despair of the absence of human society. Years pass in isolation. He discovers that cannibals occasionally make use of the island to consume their captives. Of course, Crusoe wants no part of the cannibals' society, but he does dream of freeing one or two of their would-be meals to be his servants and companions. Eventually, he encounters an escapee, to whom he gives aid, shelter, and a name: "Friday," after the day of the week on which he discovered him.

About seven hundred alternate Crusoe versions, adaptions, and spin-offs have been counted since 1719, among these *Cast Away*, a film from 2000 in which a FedEx systems analyst played by perennial Everyman Tom Hanks crashes into the Pacific and washes up on a desolate and deserted island along with a few packages from his downed cargo plane. Unlike Crusoe, he never finds a Friday, but, while struggling to make a fire, he cuts his hand, explodes in a rage of frustration, and hurls various objects from one of the packages. Among these is a volleyball, which now bears his bloody handprint on one side and the name of the manufacturer, Wilson, on the other. Hanks soon recovers the ball, draws a crude face in the bloody print, and calls his new friend "Wilson."

Cast Away cost $90 million to make and grossed $429,632,142 in box office receipts—a success perhaps less sensational than that of *Robinson Crusoe*, but a solid showing nevertheless and a film still talked about. Whether in the eighteenth century or the twenty-first, the nineteenth century (think Alexandre Dumas' *The Count of Monte Cristo*, about a man wrongfully imprisoned for fourteen years) or the twentieth (the comic TV series *Gilligan's Island*, about a group of tourists marooned when a "three-hour tour" goes awry), humanity is fascinated by tales of the most extreme form of privacy: total isolation from society. The prospect is at once terrifying and tempting, a deep emotional paradox. Each of us craves company and companionship, but who of us hasn't wanted to get away from it all, to be alone, really alone, entirely free from prying eyes, from social constraints, mandates, and sanctions, free from all responsibility?

Indeed, the very pinnacle of enlightenment and the object of religion, knowledge of God, has always involved conflict between the ideals of a selfless identification with one's fellow beings ("No man is an island," John Donne wrote in his "Devotion XVII") and hermetic isolation. Christ and Mohammad were charismatic social beings; but the likes of Anthony of Egypt, the fourth-century founder of monastic Christianity, Gautama Buddha, founder of Buddhism, and Lao Tzu, founder of Taoism, were all celebrated hermits.

Isolation, solitude, privacy, society: the definitions of each have never been simple, and the attitudes toward each have always been tinged with ambivalence and paradox. In 1953, sociologists David Riesman, Nathan Glazer, and Reuel Denney published an iconic study of the American character, which, they said, had emerged from an early cultural orientation shaped by conformity to the past ("tradition-directed") and a later orientation in which people looked within themselves for direction rather than to social norms ("inner-directed"). This evolved—or devolved—into the modern "other-directed" American, who conformed neither to tradition nor to an inner voice, but to the way his neighbors lived, behaved, and consumed. The result was a nation that was neither a society of traditionalists nor individualists, but a collection of conformists: *The Lonely Crowd* (Riesman, 1953).

Digital Privacy
Almost certainly, every generation has struggled to define what is perhaps humanity's broadest social issue: the proper relation of the individual to the community. The enduring popularity of *Robinson Crusoe* and its pop culture progeny as well as the religious paradox of Donne's "continental" man versus the enlightened hermetic "islander" attests to the fact that this age-old issue remains essentially unsettled. Concern, anxiety, and debate over privacy are hardly unique products of the Internet age. As President Barack Obama stated in his introduction to the administration's proposal for a Consumer Privacy Bill of Rights (officially titled *Consumer Data Privacy in a Networked World: A Framework for Protecting Privacy and Promoting Innovation in the Global Digital Economy*), "Americans have always cherished our privacy." He alluded to the Fourth Amendment to the Constitution, which guarantees the "right of the people to be secure in their persons, houses, papers, and effects, against unreasonable searches and seizures." Yet, the president observed, "Never has privacy been more important than today, in the age of the Internet, the World

Wide Web and smart phones" (White House, February 2012).

When the Bill of Rights, which includes the first ten amendments to the Constitution, was ratified in 1791, and throughout most of the 221 years since, security in person, papers, and effects, like "searches and seizures," was defined by physical parameters. Soldiers, policemen, government agents, and others posed physical threats. They could accost you and pat you down, they could pick your pocket, they could break into your house, ransack your desk, crack your strongbox, peer under your mattress, cut into your pillows. They could pry, they could examine, they could take. Tools, crowbars, weapons, and hands were involved. If there was violence, you felt it, even if it was nothing more (or less) than the sensation of hot breath down your neck. Almost always, physical evidence of intrusion was left behind. There was visibility, there was proximity, there was sensation.

Moreover, searching and seizing took effort, consumed time, required significant manpower, called for the resources of organization and at least the veneer of authority, and was difficult to keep secret. If your colleague or compatriot had been searched, you were thereby alerted that official snoops were on the prowl, and you could take steps to hide your papers, your effects, even yourself. If you were truly prudent, you did all this preemptively. Privacy was mostly an issue of physical proximity, since proximity was a prerequisite for invading someone's privacy. Preserving privacy was therefore largely a matter of common sense.

In matters of privacy and much else, the "age of the Internet, the World Wide Web and smart phones" has, from the perspective of a digital eavesdropper or investigator, rendered physical proximity and presence unnecessary, circumvented authority, and radically reduced the need for organization and personnel. From the point of view of the ordinary digital citizen, our private effects are no longer represented by rag or wood-pulp papers but now by our ever-growing "data footprint," an accumulation of binary zeroes and ones stored God knows where yet accessible to God knows who.

As the introduction to this book is intended to illustrate, our digital age has exposed us all. Not only are we exposed in new ways, but the 360-degree extent and relentless 24/7 quality of the exposure are unprecedented. The word "exposure" is itself both positive and negative in connotation, perfectly expressing combined opportunity and threat. The Internet plugs us into the world, removing much of the physical friction of distance, time, and awareness that has traditionally separated us from knowledge and knowing. At the same time, the world is plugged into us, making search and seizure, reasonable or unreasonable, matters of routine—and, in contrast to those who are subject to the searches of physical papers contemplated in the Fourth Amendment, the subjects of online intrusions may never even know they've been searched or have had their data seized.

Our exposure is greater than most of us imagine. This is true for "exposure" in the positive sense. Unfortunately, it is also true for the word in its negative connotation. You may understand, as most of us do, that some rogue "hacker" might attack your computer by infecting it with a virus or a Trojan horse, thereby stealing access to data. That is a risk. But the fact is that most intrusions do not involve "hacking into" a machine. Your data is scattered across many places throughout the Internet. We each leave a digital footprint that spreads far and wide. Recently, the browser maker Mozilla released an "experimental" add-on to its popular Firefox browser called "Collusion," which "allows you to see which sites are using third-party cookies to track your movements across the Web." It shows graphically and "in real time, how that data creates a spider-web of interaction between companies and other trackers" (Mozilla, Collusion 0.16.3). The Collusion add-on doesn't identify who's interacting with your data at any particular time, but the growing web of nodes and edges sends an unmistakable message. With every stroke of the keyboard, you put some piece of yourself "out there," far beyond your desktop, laptop, or smartphone.

As the introduction suggests, our Web browsing is tracked and our online transactions recorded and sold many times over. The concept of "privacy" " must be interpreted in new ways in our interconnected digital world. Once you upload data to the Web—whether it is through a deliberate posting on a blog, a Twitter tweet, a comment on Facebook, an online purchase, an online news article you choose to read—it belongs to the Web. Each packet of data you commit to the Internet is a digital representation of some aspect of your privacy. In other words, there is far less "privacy" in cyberspace than there is data.

We have implied that the Fourth Amendment, written at a time when privacy was essentially an issue of physical security, is out of date in a digital era that has done away with so much of our ink, paper, safe-deposit boxes, strongboxes, vaults, and secret compartments. Looked at from another angle, however, the two-hundred-plus-year-old Fourth Amendment appears remarkably prescient precisely because it, in effect, defines privacy as data. Neither the amendment nor the body of the Constitution itself ever uses the word privacy, but the Fourth Amendment does speak of "persons, houses, papers, and effects," which are nothing less than vehicles or containers of privacy, serving in a physical environment the same function as bits and bytes in a digital environment. Data is neither an abstract concept nor a right, but a commodity that may be produced, modified, used, shared, sold, traded, adulterated, or stolen. It is property, like one's person, house, papers, or effects.

Since the ratification of the Fourth Amendment, Americans have largely defined privacy in terms of property (although this view has been modified in 1928 by Justice Brandeis's dissent in *Olmstead v United States* and in 1967 by the decision in *Katz v United States*, in which the Supreme Court held that physical intrusion was not necessary to constitute a search as defined by the Fourth

Amendment).

The tendency of Americans to treat privacy in terms of property is the crux of a debate currently raging between U.S. policymakers and European Union legislators over the protection of privacy online. Whereas Americans find it relatively easy to define privacy online as a commodity, subject to legal protections similar (though not completely aligned with) those accorded property, Europeans see it as an absolute right. "The European concept of a right to privacy is centered round preserving the individual's honor and dignity in the public sphere," Terence Craig and Mary Ludloff, the authors of *Privacy and Big Data* explain (Craig and Ludloff, 2011, loc. 660). Although U.S. law has long recognized certain "penumbral rights of privacy" implied by the First, Fourth, Fifth, and Ninth Amendments, "In general," the authors explain, "the American view of privacy is focused on the home and on the person. Our home and person is protected against intrusions . . . especially from the government" (Craig, T., and Ludloff, M., 2011, loc. 610). In this sense, privacy is protected much like property and, because it is property, it is subject to trade. In the European view, privacy, as honor, is an absolute right and must not be regarded as a commodity.

There are sound ethical arguments to be offered in support of both views, but two points must be made. First, the root of the difference between the EU and the American view of privacy online is neither legal nor ethical, but cultural. The EU's view, dominated by the continental nations, is founded in a Greco-Roman concept of honor. The American view is founded on the Bill of Rights. Unfortunately, cultural divides are far more difficult to bridge than legal or ethical gaps. Second, the American view is more compatible with a technology that transforms private information into data than is the European view. "Privacy" digitized is no longer a right or even a concept. It is an expression, a vehicle, a container—like it or not, a commodity.

Wide Open Privacy
This book makes no attempt to referee, let alone resolve, the cultural differences between Europe and the United States. With regard to privacy, an issue "never more important than today, in the age of the Internet, the World Wide Web and smart phones," we instead propose a third approach as an alternative to the clashing approaches of Europe and the United States. This third approach would place control of "privacy"—more accurately, personal data—neither in the hands of government nor commerce, but in those of each individual digital citizen, user, and consumer. We call this "wide open privacy," and we explain it in detail in Chapters 4 and 5. In preparation for this explanation, however, we need first to present and explore the four paradoxes of online privacy, each of which affects each of us who use the Internet, regardless of our nationality or cultural heritage and orientation.

The Invisibility Paradox

We know that the Internet exposes us and connects us to the world, and yet this unprecedented technology of exposure and connection, which should put us on our guard, tends to create and foster various forms of what psychologists call disinhibition. Although we are indeed exposed and connected, although we are broadcasting to and interacting with friends, family, authority figures, potential employers and current employers, potential allies and potential rivals, current allies and current rivals, not to mention perfect strangers, being online prompts many of us actually to loosen up, to express ourselves more openly, even carelessly. This can produce benign, pleasant, even laudable results, including expressions of generosity, kindness, and creativity. It can also be conducive to unpleasant, even rude expressions and behavior, explosions of anger and abuse, racial, ethnic, or other slurs, and even threats, including cyberbullying and worse.

Although you may realize on an intellectual level that you are exposed and connected online, you may very possibly feel anonymous, even invisible: "I can see you, but you can't see me."

The fact is that, in many online environments, some others really cannot "see" you. But this does not mean you cannot be tracked by webmasters, by users who have the software, technical know-how, and motivation to track you, by advertisers and advertising networks, by online merchants, by non-profit and for-profit organizations, by political parties, by government agencies, by banks, by credit bureaus, and by private or judicial investigators. Nevertheless, at any given time, you, as an individual, may indeed be practically and effectively invisible to most others. Indeed, for all our concern about being tracked online, as any of us moves around the Internet, most of the other users we encounter or who encounter us cannot easily tell who we are.

You may find the sensation of invisibility to be powerfully disinhibiting, giving you the courage and inclination to explore websites, engage in conversations, post comments, share images, or make revelations you would not dream of making in "real life." A potential positive outcome of such disinhibition is the possibility of genuinely creative and productive liberation, enlargement of knowledge and experience, and self-discovery, as a 2011 study of the therapeutic value of adolescent blogging suggests (Boniel-Nissim and Barak, 2011). Potential negative outcomes include hurting or even bullying others, getting others angry enough to take action against you—emotionally, legally, or even criminally—or damaging your reputation. Your online identity may not be immediately apparent, but it can, after all, be discovered, and what you say and post online cannot be retracted. Once you put your feelings and thoughts into the form of data, they are wholly or partially out of your control, potentially forever.

One of the first combat lessons both cops and soldiers learn is to never confuse concealment with cover. Concealment, such as behind a bush, may hide you, but it won't stop a bullet before it reaches you. Cover may or may not hide you, but at least it will keep you from being shot. The feeling of invisibility that Internet communication creates may feel like cover, but it is at best concealment, and it is most dangerously self-deceptive when you are engaged in such text communication as email, text messaging, chat, and blogging. You are still literally invisible, which confers an aura of anonymity, but those who read your texts may quickly discover quite a bit about you and your identity.   Even if you are intellectually aware of this potential for self-disclosure, however, in our minds, the fact of literal invisibility tends to trump the absence of actual anonymity, reinforcing that false sense of being anonymous. There are obvious social and psychological reasons for this sense. When we communicate in the physical presence of others, we are aware of how we look and sound and of how others look and sound. We are keenly attuned to tone of voice, to grunts and tsk-tsks, to exasperated or disapproving sighs. We pick up on such visual cues as a nodding or shaking of the head, a frown, a grimace, a sardonic smile, a yawn, hands placed on hips, arms crossed over the chest, and other aspects of body language.

In a famous study, the Iranian-born Armenian-American psychologist Albert Mehrabian concluded that three elements account for our "liking" of a person who puts forth a message concerning his or her feelings. Just 7 percent of our "liking" depends on the speaker's words; 38 percent depends on tone of voice; and 55 percent on body language (Mehrabian, 1971). If this study is any indication, it is no wonder that we feel anonymous and therefore disinhibited when we are literally invisible online. All but 7 percent of the emotional presence we project—and receive—is missing. We need not be concerned about our tone of voice or our body language, or about the tone of voice and body language of others. The grimace, the frown, the disapproving shake of the head, the groan—none of these cues are available to curb, shape, or stop our online verbal flow. Watch a child (or an adult, for that matter) admit to some wrongdoing or embarrassment. The child's natural, almost irresistible, tendency is to avert her eyes from those of the person to whom she speaks. By default, online text-only communication is communication with eyes averted.

The sensation of online invisibility provides the apparent opportunity for you to separate your words from 93 percent of the real world (assuming Mehrabian's figures are reliable). Not only are you invisible, so likewise are the receivers of your communication. Your words are not linked to their visible, physical responses, which means that they are hardly linked to either your offline life or theirs. To a large extent, you may not feel obliged or even motivated to take responsibility for what you say, because you and others are only about 7 percent real. The Invisibility Paradox may promote online behavior that, in a "real life" context, would be judged symptomatic of disassociation, a pathological detachment from emotional and physical reality. Online, the behavior is normal.

The Impulse Paradox

Taken to an extreme, the sensation of online invisibility may create what psychologists call solipsistic introjection. Without the physical, face-to-face presence of the person or persons with whom you are communicating—without, that is, perhaps 93 percent of the substance of the communication—you may identify with your correspondent so intensely that it seems as if your mind and his are one. It is even possible that, in reading the other's message, you will come to hear it in your head, as if the other's presence has been introjected into your consciousness. You may, in fact, imaginatively create the physicality of this person, the 93 percent that is missing in online text communication. This is not truly a psychotic break with reality, but it can be a powerful perception of your own imagination as the most significant form of reality. (In philosophy, solipsism is the view that self, as the only object of real knowledge, is the only thing that is real.) The result is that cyberspace becomes a fantasy world, much like the theatrical stage as Shakespeare portrayed it in *As You Like It*—"All the world's a stage, / And all the men and women merely players." To the degree that such solipsistic introjection operates, you may feel that you are merely playing a role, without real-life consequence, and therefore become increasingly disinhibited and liable to act on impulse.

If all the world's a stage, it may seem natural to conclude that you can say or do anything you want online. In his *Poetics*, the Greek philosopher Aristotle proposed the concept of catharsis—emotional cleansing or purging—as the great service a tragic play performs. Witnessing the unfolding drama, the audience experiences all the strong feelings of the characters, including sorrow, pity, and fear, yet does so with aesthetic pleasure instead of real-life pain, misery, and horror because, intense as these emotions are, associated as they are with catastrophe and loss, they are experienced vicariously in an environment ultimately separate from the reality of the audience and from which the audience members can (and will) escape.

A similar sensation may govern the online experience. The disinhibition fostered by the sense of invisibility and anonymity, possibly intensified by solipsistic introjection, is magnified even further by a feeling that cyberspace, like a theater, is ultimately escapable. Your online world may seem like a fantasy in which your persona and those of others are merely players in a play or a game, from which you can, at will, walk away without consequence in "real life." Indeed, this sense of online interaction as a game is reinforced by familiarity with a host of online games, from elaborate role-playing games to first-person shooters. For decades now, the online space has been for many children and adults a game-playing, role-playing, id-indulging space. Shut down the computer for the evening, and that space disappears as you return to your quotidian existence "in real life."

To the degree that existence online seems to you escapable, you may tend to act with exaggerated disinhibition—that is, you may routinely act on impulse when you are behind the monitor's screen.

The paradox? The digital environment that fosters impulse by appearing as a cathartic stage, an engrossing game, an intense fantasy space from which instant escape is nevertheless just a matter of logging off or pulling a plug is the very same environment that broadcasts, records, ramifies, magnifies, and propagates impulse and the consequences of impulse. Online, the thoughtless act of a moment may become the property of the world, creating a digital footprint that is as permanent as the one Neil Armstrong left in the dust of the moon, a place with neither the water nor the wind to erase it.

The Crowd Paradox

Online you may feel all-powerful even as you also see yourself as just one of a crowd of millions. This can have a paradoxical effect on your perception and attitude. You can present yourself as a billionaire living in opulence. No one will know that you are actually sitting in the basement laundry room of your parents' bungalow in the burbs. The person you are communicating with may actually be that billionaire, but, online, in the absence of your physical presence in his mansion or his penthouse office suite, he is on your level as you are on his. You may therefore be quite uninhibited in telling him what you think.

The Internet truly is a peer-to-peer network, and that can be a powerfully democratizing and liberating force. Yet the sense of being part of a crowd can also engender more potentially destructive and self-destructive assumptions and attitudes.

Perceiving yourself as part of the crowd may enhance your impression of anonymity—the notion of safety in numbers. The truth, however, is that computers love "big data." Even among billions, you can be picked out, tracked, followed, stalked, robbed, even ruined by people and entities you've never met and don't even know.

Identifying with the crowd may also reduce personal ethics to a mob mentality. In some groups, this may promote cyberbullying:

Don't you feel bad, treating so-and-so that way?
No. Absolutely everybody thinks she's a creep. He deserves what he gets.

Or the crowd may become both an ethical justification for some illegal activity and a perceived protection against punishment for engaging in it. Consider the many thousands who illegally share copyrighted software, music, and video on peer-to-peer networks every day. "Everyone does it," so it can't be wrong (or "can't be all that bad"), and, because "everyone does it," it is unlikely that I will get caught, let alone punished.

The Island Paradox

"No man is an island," John Donne wrote, and yet accessing the world via the Internet makes many of us feel very much like islands. Exposed and connected though we are, we may feel invisible, anonymous, and autonomous. There are those who regard the Internet as a dangerous place. It is not the Internet that is dangerous, however, but the all too common "island" attitude toward it. The illusionary product of distorted perception, the island view of the Internet leaves users vulnerable to exploitation by criminal as well as commercial predators and, potentially, by government agencies as well. This view also makes it nearly impossible to use the Internet to create and project to the world a strategically productive definition of yourself. Instead, it abandons your identity and reputation to fortune and misfortune and to the perception, will, and motives of others.

By way of introducing an alternative to online illusion and drift, consider the history of another island.

After surviving a childhood fraught with hazard—she was the outcast daughter of Henry VIII and Anne Boleyn, one of the two wives, of his half-dozen, the king beheaded—Elizabeth Tudor of the island nation England ascended the throne in 1558. On this occasion, one of her subjects summed up the status quo:

> The state of England lay now most afflicted, embroiled on the one side with the Scottish, on the other side with the French war; overcharged with debt ... the treasury exhausted; Calais ... lost, to the great dishonour of the English nation; the people distracted with different opinions in religion; the Queen bare of potent friends, and strengthened with no alliance of foreign princes.

At this time, England was an economic and cultural backwater, impoverished, burdened by runaway inflation, cursed with a debased currency, possessing neither an army nor a navy to speak of, torn internally by religious dissension propelling the country toward civil war, faced with enemies in Scotland (at the time a foreign country), plagued by rebellion in Ireland (only nominally an English realm), eyed greedily by the French, the Spanish, and the Holy Roman Empire, its pitiful throne still contested by more than a few pretenders. England was an island, economically, politically, militarily, and intellectually insular, cut off from the rest of Europe. Cut off, yet exposed. Isolated from the cultural and material riches of the Renaissance under way on the continental mainland, England was nevertheless vulnerable to any major power that might at any time decide to invade and conquer.

Elizabeth the survivor came to the throne no longer willing merely to survive. She resolved to transform survival into triumph and her kingdom from a vulnerable island, positioned for no more than isolation and conquest, into a nexus poised to create the most powerful empire since ancient Rome. Over the course of a forty-five year reign, from 1558 until her death in 1603, Elizabeth I reshaped the identity of England, leading it through crisis and confrontation with foreign powers in Scotland and on the continent; through economic disaster to economic success; from insular isolation to the exploration of the New World; from foreign threat to decisive victory over Spain; and from medieval kingdom to Renaissance empire, not only in geographic extent but of incomparable cultural influence in world literature, art, learning, and enduringly sound government.

At its height in 1922, the British Empire that had originated in the reign of Elizabeth I nearly four centuries earlier was the foremost global power and commanded the allegiance of 458 million people, at the time one fifth of the planet's population, who lived on more than thirteen million square miles, about a quarter of the Earth's total land area. At the center of it, an island of some 42 million people living on 50,346 square miles, a place considered so central to the world that international time was measured from its Prime Meridian running through the town of Greenwich just outside of London.

Elizabeth I understood the Island Paradox and used it to her advantage and to the enduring advantage of her realm, ending isolation while turning exposure into opportunity and converting connectedness from an avenue of threatened invasion to a highway of influence and empire. In *Wide Open Privacy*, we ask you to take inspiration from her precedent to effect a like growth and transformation in your own relation to the world via the World Wide Web and other digital technologies.

There is no shortage of how-to guides to Internet "safety" and "security." These cover such topics as defending against malware, viruses, Trojan horses, password compromise, phishing, spoofing, and online predators. Any number of books address safety and security on e-commerce sites and the social web. And it is well that they do, because all of these topics are important. We will certainly not ignore them. Nevertheless, defensive and precautionary measures are tactical in approach. In contrast to them, the Elizabethan offering we bring in *Wide Open Privacy* is strategic in emphasis.

Instead of deploying a kit of miscellaneous "Internet security tools and tips," we have set out to deliver a comprehensive understanding of digital privacy and to develop a commensurately comprehensive suite of affirmative strategies for a productive life online. Unlike "Internet safety" books, *Wide Open Privacy* is not about defending against threats to security, but is a comprehensive guide to playing offense online by developing an individual brand, reputation, and identity. It lays out a strategy that turns the concept of privacy inside out, much as England's Elizabeth turned the concept of an island realm inside out. Our approach is intended to take full advantage of the Internet by opening the world to you and you to the world, but strictly on terms you define and you control.

Whereas the majority of technologists, psychologists, media gurus, cultural commentators, and the makers of policy and law speak of protecting privacy – a form of defense, we focus on strategies to control personal data not merely to "protect privacy" but to go on the offensive, to fully realize the power of privacy in a digital world.

The digital revolution is yesterday's news. We hope to lead you to the revolution that is just beginning, an all-consuming contest to create, claim, and control our digital data—our very selves—online.

CHAPTER TWO
From Private Person to Data Subject

We think of ourselves in a wide variety of ways: as fathers, mothers, sons, daughters, teachers, lawyers, doctors, football heroes, racecar drivers, citizens, taxpayers, voters, shoppers, and on and on. All of us, of course, think of ourselves as men, women, human beings, people, folks, individuals. We do not, at least not naturally or easily, think of ourselves as what the European Union's European Commission recently called us: data subjects. Yet that is precisely how corporations, advertisers, marketers, charities, research institutions, and even governments think of us. That is how these entities first meet us, get to know us, track us, and study each one of us. Not as a person, let alone a "private person," but as a data subject.

Want evidence?

In a 2010 article, the *Wall Street Journal* reported that the top fifty U.S. websites were each installing an average of sixty-four pieces of tracking technology, usually without notice, on each computer that visited their sites (Angwin, July 30, 2010). These software programs are the instruments of online behavioral targeting, better known in the Internet advertising and marketing industry as online behavioral advertising—OBA for short. The tracking software works like this: You visit a web site, and the OBA software tracks the pages you visit, the amount of time you view each page, the links you click on, the searches you make, and the items you interact with. The software allows the website to collect this data, which may be collated with other factors to create a "profile" linked to your web browser. The owner or publisher of the website can use such data, tracked from thousands of visitors, to define audience "segments," each segment composed of visitors with similar profiles. When you return to a specific site or a specific network of sites (provided you use the same web browser to do so), advertisers can use your profile information to position their online ads in front of you (and other visitors with similar profiles) on the assumption that you will likely be interested in the advertiser's particular merchandise or service.

Instead of randomly placing ads, the advertiser is able to target you based on the interests your profile reveals. OBA becomes increasingly accurate over time, as your profile accretes more data and becomes more complete. Companies called "advertising networks" or "ad nets" deliver ads to and track users across not a single website but networks of sites. This enables them to assemble rather detailed pictures of the demographic makeup of a large swath of Internet users.

This means that an ad net can sell advertisers exposure to specific audiences rather than merely a spot on specific websites.

If this explanation of OBA is not sufficient to explain why the leading websites embrace it so passionately, the results are certainly compelling. According to a 2009 study, OBA can increase click-through rates by as much as 670 percent. The click-through rate—what insiders call CTR—is a common yardstick for measuring the success of an online advertising campaign at a particular website. CTR is defined as the number of clicks on an ad divided by the number of times the ad is shown. This number is referred to as "impressions." The quotient is expressed as a percentage. That is, if an ad is shown 100 times (delivers 100 "impressions") and users are sufficiently intrigued to click on it 25 times, the CTR of that particular ad is 0.25, or 25 percent (Yan et al, 2009; Chen and Stallaert, September 15, 2010).

So now imagine how online advertisers and marketers would respond if they opened up the morning "paper" (figuratively speaking, since they're opening it online, of course) and were greeted by a headline like this:

Web Users Cheer Online Behavioral Advertising
They Clamor to Be Tracked

How to describe the reaction? Joy? Ecstasy? Unfortunately for the purveyors of e-commerce, the headline is total fantasy. Recent real headlines about OBA and online tracking have all been quite different:

Consumers Union, April 7, 2012—
Consumers Concerned About Their Online Privacy
Consumer Reports survey: Most consumers "very concerned" about online companies selling, sharing personal data without permission

Center for Digital Democracy, April 4, 2012—
Massive Scale "30 billion audience data" archive linked to real-time targeting of consumers

J. Melik in *BBC News Business*, March 25, 2012—
Internet privacy: Genuine concerns or paranoia?
However unwittingly, you share personal information with complete strangers every single day—via the internet

Consumer Reports, June 28, 2011—

CU Poll: Consumers want government to protect Internet privacy

Smart, Useful, Scary, Creepy

Look behind the headlines, and it seems only to get worse. In an April 2012 paper titled "Smart, Useful, Scary, Creepy," researchers at Carnegie Mellon University published findings on "Perceptions of Online Behavioral Advertising" based on interviews they conducted with "ordinary" Internet users (Ur, B., et al., April 2, 2012). When the researchers asked, "Are there any negative aspects of behavioral advertising?" study participants answered:

> "I don't really like the idea of someone looking at what I am looking at, and that kind of freaks me out. Also, I do not like the idea of them putting stuff on my computer without me knowing about it."

> "It is a little creepy... because I feel that I should get to decide what is going in and out
> of my computer."

> "It's scary. It makes me nervous. I was thinking about it last night when I was searching for stuff. Like I thought how do they know all this, how do they keep track of this, how do they do this?"

> "It makes me want to go home and delete all my cookies, but then I know that's not gonna help much. It makes me mad."

> "They are gathering information ...without you knowing it, maybe even giving that data to another party."

> "It is kind of a creepy thought that you are being followed and monitored."
>
> (Ur, B., et al., April 2, 2012: 5-6)

The Carnegie Mellon study interviewed just forty-eight Internet users, the majority of whom expressed either full or partial opposition to being tracked by e-commerce providers. A much larger study, based on 1,004 interviews conducted between May 26 and June 2, 2011 by TRUSTe Research and Harris Interactive, found first and foremost that 75 percent of the study sample believed the Internet "is not well regulated and naïve users can easily be taken advantage of" (TRUSTe, July 25, 2011).

- 59 percent felt that "online tracking" was either a strongly or somewhat negative term.
- 43 percent also felt this way about "online behavioral advertising."
- 52 percent believed that websites share "demographic information" as well as information on "online browsing behavior" without users' permission.
- 30 to 43 percent believed that Personal Identifying Information ("PII," which can include current location, name, and contact information) was being shared without users' permission.
- 25 percent of those interviewed believed unauthorized sharing extended to "health-related information."
- 22 percent believed that personal "financial information" was being surreptitiously shared.

Financial information was a real sore point. Understandably, interviewees had a particularly strong aversion to sharing it with advertisers: 66 percent said they "definitely would not consent" to such sharing if given a real choice in the matter, and 14 percent said they "probably would not consent." Most were also either dead set against sharing other types of information with advertisers or, at least, disinclined to share—

- Contact information: 49 percent "definitely would not consent"; 22 percent "probably would not consent"
- Health-related information: 52 percent; 18 percent
- Their current location: 46 percent; 20 percent
- Their name: 45 percent; 19 percent
- Their "online browsing behavior": 34 percent; 21 percent
- Their profession: 32 percent; 19 percent
- Their demographic information: 27 percent; 15 percent

Twenty-six percent of respondents "definitely would not consent" (and 14 percent "probably would not consent") to sharing with advertisers even such apparently innocuous data as information about their hobbies and interests.

Deliver Us from Dinner

As the Carnegie Mellon and TRUSTe/Harris studies reveal, if you feel stalked by ravenous advertisers online, you are not alone. Most Internet users see e-commerce providers as predators and themselves as prey. Headlines, in the popular press as well as in professional and academic publications, both reflect and reinforce this feeling, so that we consumers begin to wonder not if we will be consumed, but when, how, and by whom. Little wonder, then, that governments are scrambling to devise approaches to "protect" privacy online and to regulate e-commerce providers to stop them from dining upon consumers.

In Chapter 3, we will briefly consider the regulatory initiatives emerging from the European Union and in the United States. For now it is sufficient to note that the EU, operating in a culture that places great confidence in government, is demanding strict legislative regulation of Internet privacy, especially OBA and other Internet tracking, whereas the United States, whose citizens and legislators profess more faith in private enterprise than in government, is calling largely for industry self-regulation. It is yet to be seen just how much friction the profound differences between the EU and U.S. approaches will create. There is very real reason to fear that these sharply different approaches will create a crisis of what policy makers call "global interoperability." That is, U.S.-based companies operating online under U.S. law might be restricted in or even barred from doing business online within the EU.

The biggest bone of contention is the issue of tracking. The EU proposes to forbid any given website from tracking any user who has not affirmatively opted in by giving his or her express permission to be tracked by that particular site. That is, the EU wants to mandate a system in which users are opted out of tracking by default. In the sharpest possible contrast, the U.S. is calling for a system in which users are opted in by default – a system in which any user may be tracked by any website unless that user withholds his or her permission by expressly opting out. (EU-U.S., March 19, 2012; White House, February 2012).

Make no mistake, the EU-U.S. dispute is serious, but where OBA and tracking are concerned, the differences between the European and American positions are actually more a matter of degree than of kind. EU administrators assume that left unregulated, companies will *certainly* invade and destroy individual privacy. Their U.S. counterparts assume that they *might* invade and destroy individual privacy.

The EU regards e-commerce providers as inevitably predatory. The U.S. sees them as capable of being predatory. Both European and American officials do agree that Internet users, online consumers, require protection. That is, both define consumers as helpless victims—and the headlines and the study data suggest that most consumers would not argue with being defined this way. By and large, we really do feel helpless, as if a bull's eye has been painted on our backs in bright digital colors.

Predator and Prey: Must It Be?

Are we justified in feeling like dinner? Are we destined to be prey to digital merchants who are (according to the EU) dead set or (as American regulators see it) inclined to be predatory? A deeper look into the study results suggests that destiny may not be absolute.

25

The same Carnegie Mellon researchers who so vividly reported consumer fears point out that "OBA presents both benefits and downsides to users":

> If their interests have been accurately profiled, users will receive more relevant advertising. However, collecting data about users' online activities can potentially violate their privacy. Previous research has found that users have substantial privacy concerns about OBA ... while marketing surveys have found that consumers like OBA and that discomfort with OBA is reduced when users are properly informed that non-personally identifiable information is used for OBA (Ur, B., et al., April 2, 2012:1).

In fact, the Carnegie Mellon researchers discovered that most of their respondents did not simply dismiss OBA as intrusively predatory, but found it to be "simultaneously useful and privacy-invasive" (Ur, B., et al., April 2, 2012:1). Taking the hint, then, we should stop focusing exclusively on the negative aspects of consumer response and instead investigate why users, wary of OBA as they certainly are, nevertheless find it "useful."

When the researchers asked, "What is the first thing that comes to your mind when you hear 'Internet Advertising'? 21 of the 48 study participants responded with "pop-ups," which all of them found "annoying" because (as one respondent put it) they "kind of pop up out of nowhere, and I just wanna get rid of them and block them, and they don't go away." Other interviewees called Internet advertising "bothersome, not needed, distracting, potentially harmful or dangerous" and still others found it "irrelevant" and "not worth paying attention to." But when the researchers asked, "Is it useful for you to see ads that are tailored to your interests?" the respondents answered much more positively. Thirty-one of the 48 said yes, even though some continued to express fear that "it might be an invasion of privacy" (Ur, B., et al., April 2, 2012:3-4).

Researchers conducting the larger TRUSTe/Harris study found that "consumers feel ads have become increasingly relevant over the years." In 2008, only 12 percent had judged them relevant to their "wants or needs," whereas 32 percent found them relevant in 2011. So what happened between 2008 and 2011? During that period, non-targeted banner and pop-up ads increasingly gave way to targeted OBA, thereby populating the Internet with more relevant ads. Not that this drew a loud consumer cheer for OBA. Forty-three percent of the TRUSTe/Harris group responded negatively to the phrase "online behavioral advertising." Yet this was more an objection to the term itself than to the concept of targeted ads. When researchers used the phrase *interest-based advertising* instead of *online behavioral advertising*, only 24 percent felt negatively about it (TRUSTe, July 25, 2011:21).

Does this mean that advertisers could erase the negatives—maybe even actually realize their fantasy headline—just by calling OBA something else?

Of course not, but the two studies do suggest a glimmer of hope that online advertisers and online consumers are not natural and inevitable enemies.

The Carnegie Mellon researchers found that their respondents feared and distrusted OBA and tracking not because they knew these were bad things but because they assumed they were. "Since OBA is not visible on its own . . . participants felt that OBA was a hidden practice," the researchers concluded (Ur, B., et al., April 2, 2012: 9). Because the study participants were unable to "accurately determine what information is collected for OBA purposes, or by whom, . . . they assumed the worst, leading them to oppose strongly a practice they expected would involve the collection of personally identifiable and financial information" (Ur, B., et al., April 2, 2012: 2). The researchers came to believe that if users had "understood the profiling technologies that underpin most behavioral advertising strategies, they would have realized that some of their worst fears about the collection of personal information were unfounded" (Ur, B., et al., April 2, 2012: 9).

So there is a lesson here for e-commerce providers. Come clean. Explain what you're doing and what you are not doing. Transparency is undeniably one way to move the indicator needle away from distrust of OBA and toward the perception that OBA ads are actually "useful" to us.

From Transparency to Control

Yet if an understanding of profiling technologies would make most users more receptive to OBA and tracking, it is impractical for us all to become educated in this highly technical area. It is far more feasible for those involved in the e-commerce supply chain—advertisers, advertising network owners, and website operators—to provide us with simple tools to enable each of us, individually, to selectively or entirely opt out of OBA. The TRUSTe/Harris researchers found that 22 percent of study participants *strongly agreed* and 33 percent *somewhat agreed* with the statement, "I would be inclined to do more business with an advertiser or publisher who gives me the option to opt out of Online Behavioral Advertising." Even more significantly, 16 percent *strongly agreed* and 35 percent *somewhat agreed* with, "I would be more inclined to click on an advertisement that gives me the option to opt out of Online Behavioral Advertising" (TRUSTe, July 25, 2011: 32).

Transparency is important, but by far the stronger basis for consumer acceptance of OBA would be individual control. Combine control with a basic level of transparency, and acceptance increases even further. Only 11 percent of consumers approve of OBA if they believe that personally identifiable information (PII) is attached, whereas approval doubles, to 22 percent, if they are assured that PII is not attached (TRUSTe, July 25, 2011:31).

If e-commerce providers would combine transparency with consumer control, far more of us would see online behavioral advertising as interest-based advertising. That is, we would see it as advertising based on *our* interests. It would be advertising of clear value to us, not just to the advertisers.

The e-commerce industry has an opportunity to stop all of us consumers from assuming the worst about OBA and tracking. Let them come clean about OBA and let them provide us all with the tools to control our individual participation in OBA, and we will no longer see advertisers as predators and ourselves as prey. Instead, consumers and marketers may realize that both have a shared interest in discovering the same information. The e-commerce provider wants to make his advertising more effective by tailoring it to the interests of the individual consumer and we know from the studies (and doubtless from our own feelings as well) that the individual Internet user does not want to be annoyed by intrusive ads of no interest to him or her. Most users actually prefer to see ads for items that interest them. If Internet advertisers lift the curtain on OBA and at the same time give consumers the means of controlling their participation in it, these internet advertisers will, in effect, recruit us to become empowered customers. If we control who tracks us, then we are able to tell advertisers what we want them to sell us.

Any college undergrad who takes Marketing 101 learns that "segmentation"—the identification and classification of potential customers for a given product—is a critical step in building an effective marketing campaign. Segmentation is the ultimate purpose of OBA. By giving consumers control over tracking, advertisers prompt them to announce their own interest in certain categories of products and services. By yielding control, advertisers actually recruit consumers to voluntarily segment themselves. This, of course, amplifies and multiplies the accuracy and effectiveness of OBA. Sellers sell more. Consumers buy more. Everyone is a lot happier.

The Tipping Point

If increasing both the acceptance and effectiveness of OBA is not sufficient to persuade the e-commerce industry to become transparent and to surrender the steering wheel to consumers, the industry needs to recognize that we've finally reached a tipping point. Refusing to be transparent and stubbornly withholding opt-in/opt-out control from consumers are both destructive strategies that will compel governments to continue to brand e-commerce providers, online advertisers, and Internet companies as the consumer's enemy. And the result of this negative branding will be an increasingly relentless regulatory push by the EU as well as the United States. Provisions in the EU's new, extraordinarily strict privacy regulation make Europe's position crystal clear: advertisers prey upon consumers and therefore must be policed—harshly. Even the U.S. proposal for voluntary industry self-regulation includes calls for Congress to pass broad privacy legislation that allows consumers to see how their online data is collected, used, and sold and gives them controls to opt out of OBA and tracking.

Online marketers, merchants, website owners, and advertising network operators can voluntarily reach out to consumers with honesty, openness, and the means of control. Or they can hold back and wait for government to force them to be honest and open and give up control—but that won't be pretty for them.

What To Do Now

We consumers don't have to wait for everyone in e-commerce to do the right thing. As things stand right now, we can't have complete control over OBA and online tracking, but we can educate ourselves about them, and we can take much more control of our digital fate than most of us now even realize is possible. Recently, *Consumer Reports* noted that while most Facebook users changed default privacy settings, 13 million (7.69 percent of U.S. Facebook users) did not (*Consumer Reports*, June 28, 2011). This means they either are not aware of privacy risks, are not aware that they can change default privacy settings, or they just don't care about one or the other. Even if the percentage is relatively small, thirteen million folks adrift on the digital ocean is a big number. We should all be aware of the risks and the controls.

Your AdChoices Icon

In 2010, the Digital Advertising Alliance (DAA), a coalition of leading media and marketing trade associations, introduced the "Advertising Option Icon" to identify OBA advertisements and to link to enhanced information about them (DAA, "The Self-Regulatory Program for Online Behavioral Advertising"). It was an industry gesture toward transparency, yet the icon was so poorly recognized by consumers that it not only failed to provide transparency—it was often mistaken for an opt-in button (by which, the user believed, she gave permission to be tracked!) or even the instrument of some sort of hacker scam. The Carnegie Mellon researchers found that fewer than 5 percent of Internet users recognized the Advertising Option Icon for what it is (Ur, B., et al., April 2, 2012: 9). In January 2012, the DAA announced the launch of the "Your AdChoices" public education campaign. As of this writing, it is too early to judge the effectiveness of the campaign. Certainly, it has not stilled the clamor for government regulation in Europe or the United States.

The icon is easy enough to spot. Companies that have signed onto the DAA program place in the upper right corner of an OBA ad a blue triangle with a lower-case *i* in the middle and the phrase "Your AdChoices." The icon identifies the ad as an OBA ad.

When you visit a website and see an ad bearing the Your AdChoices icon, you are unmistakably alerted that you have encountered an OBA ad. If you do nothing, you should know that, by your visiting this web page, the advertiser has tracked you, recording your visit, likely by storing a small text file known as a "cookie" in your Web browser. This information will allow advertising service providers to attempt to predict your interest in various merchandise, products, or services and to further predict which ads may be most relevant to you when you next visit this website or others.

If, instead of doing nothing when you see the icon, you click on it, you will be given information about OBA and how interest-based ads are delivered to you. You will also be given access to controls that will allow you to opt out of the OBA advertising that you receive from companies participating in the DAA program. Note that in many cases, however, users can only opt out of receiving targeted advertisements; the icon does not allow them to opt out of the tracking that underlies these advertisements (Davis, July 12, 2011). Nevertheless, these important controls and are a huge step forward, signifying that many OBA advertisers are already providing both transparency and user control. It's just that most Internet users don't know about this.

Other Controls Available Now
Most current web browsers offer controls that give users the ability to make many choices about privacy online. These controls include ways to limit or block cookies. To learn about these, consult the "Help" tab in your browser or look at the following:

> For Internet Explorer: http://windows.microsoft.com/en-US/windows-vista/Change-Internet-Explorer-Privacy-settings
> For Mozilla Firefox: http://support.mozilla.org/en-US/kb/Options%20window%20-%20Privacy%20panel
> For Google Chrome: http://www.google.com/chrome/intl/en/more/privacy.html
> For Apple Safari: http://www.apple.com/safari/features.html#security
> For Opera: http://www.opera.com/browser/tutorials/security/privacy/

Some major industry players are going beyond browser basics to give users even more advanced and thorough control. Google recently announced that its Chrome browser will join Internet Explorer 9 (IE9) and Mozilla's Firefox in adding full do-not-track (DNT) support. (IE 10, released in October 2012, set DNT by default. Users who *want* to allow tracking must change the default setting.) Apple's newest version of the Safari browser, which is included in OS X Mountain Lion, makes its current DNT provisions easier for users to access. Other browser makers, including those used on mobile devices, seem poised to follow suit, and Yahoo! rolled out a DNT tool across all of its platforms in the summer of 2012.

For those of us who want the most comprehensive DNT control options, AVG (www.avg.com) offers a comprehensive DNT tool as part of its AVG Anti-Virus Free Edition 2012 downloadable package, and at least two other firms, Abine (www.abine.com) and Ghostery (www.ghostery.com), offer standalone DNT software. The DAA itself has a beta version of an "Opt Out from Online Behavioral Advertising" online tool, which allows you to selectively opt out of receiving OBA ads delivered by 79 of 98 DAA-participating companies. Check this out at http://www.aboutads.info/choices/#completed.

Before You Choose to Opt Out

You may decide that you want to use the current DAA opt-out controls to the full extent they allow, opting out of tracking whenever and wherever it is possible to do so. That's fine, but before you make this decision, consider this:

    1. Ads are information.

    2. Information that is useful to you (delivers data concerning things in which you have an interest) is generally desirable.

    3. OBA is designed to deliver ads likely to interest you, based on tracking of websites you visit.

    4. You may actually want to receive these ads.

For real: there are identity thieves and other criminals stalking the web. The chapters in Part II of this book, "Outright Threats and Obvious Opportunities," contain a comprehensive discussion of online hazards. Some people find OBA creepy and intrusive. Some people find it objectionable on principle and just don't want it. Nevertheless, OBA does not present a malicious threat to your computer or your privacy.

OBA does not typically track or use information that is personally identifiable to you, such as bank account numbers, credit card numbers, email addresses, street addresses, phone numbers, photographs, and so on.

The Carnegie Mellon and TRUSTe/Harris studies both reveal that a majority of Internet users fear cookies, believe they track personally identifying information (PII), financial information, and other information that may aid identify thieves. The cookies typically used to facilitate OBA may minimally compromise privacy, but they are not in any way enabling, or related to, identity theft. You may be tempted to delete all your cookies. If you do, you may have trouble logging into certain web sites.

All modern web browsers allow you to block cookies, but blocking all cookies is generally not practical. Most browsers allow you to choose whether to block so-called 'first party cookies' and/or so-called 'third party cookies.' Blocking first party cookies will lead to a loss of certain interactive features or even basic site functionality. We do not suggest you do this. Blocking third-party cookies, on the other hand, will rarely affect your experience on a website but will prevent much (but not all) online tracking. If you decide that you do not want to be tracked online and you do not want to receive targeted advertisements, one step you can take to minimize tracking is to block third-party cookies.

None of us wants to trade our personhood for the status of data subject. This said, any trace of ourselves we leave online, intentionally or unintentionally, is neither more nor less than data. Privacy is a moral, cultural, spiritual, and emotional attribute. To the infrastructure of the Internet, to the bytes and bits and the equipment that facilitates their movement, "privacy" has no meaning. Privacy does, however, have a digital equivalent, which may be called "data security," but that, more accurately, should be called data control.

Online, we protect our privacy by controlling our data. This does not mean simply pulling the plug. Disconnecting from the Internet does not wipe out the personal data that has already accumulated online. On the contrary, by unplugging we relinquish any control over that data. The far more secure choice is always to act online in ways that enhance our control over our personal data. This means making productive choices about tracking where possible and, in all cases, actively, vigilantly, thoughtfully, and strategically deciding what data to share and what data to hold close.

CHAPTER THREE

The End of One-Way Media

"Americans have always cherished our privacy," President Barack Obama wrote in his introduction to *Consumer Data Privacy in a Networked World*, which includes The Consumer Privacy Bill of Rights. "From the birth of our republic, we assured ourselves protection against unlawful intrusion into our homes and our personal papers," the president wrote. "Never has privacy been more important than today, in the age of the Internet, the World Wide Web and smart phones." He went on to declare it "incumbent on us to do what we have done throughout history: apply our timeless privacy values to the new technologies and circumstances of our times" (White House, February 2012).

President Obama's introduction is dated February 23, 2012. Less than a month later, on March 15, intelligence journalist James Bamford published in Wired.com a story about a massive $2 billion National Security Agency (NSA) facility under construction in the shadow of Utah's Wasatch Range: "Once built, it will be more than five times the size of the U.S. Capitol." The facility's mission will be "to intercept, decipher, analyze, and store vast swaths of the world's communications as they zap down from satellites and zip through the underground and undersea cables of international, foreign, and domestic networks." Bamford continued:

> Flowing through its servers and routers and stored in near-bottomless databases will be all forms of communication, including the complete contents of private emails, cell phone calls, and Google searches, as well as all sorts of personal data trails—parking receipts, travel itineraries, bookstore purchases, and other digital "pocket litter." It is, in some measure, the realization of the "total information awareness" program created during the first term of the Bush administration—an effort that was killed by Congress in 2003 after it caused an outcry over its potential for invading Americans' privacy (Bamford, March 15, 2012).

Let's take a moment to digest. Having proclaimed privacy a "timeless" American value and having asserted digital privacy as never more important, the nation's chief executive presides over the building of a facility dedicated to rendering digital privacy impossible. Can you say "cognitive dissonance?" After a collective shake of the head, we should at least be able to agree on one inescapable conclusion: the fate and future of privacy is a defining issue of our era.

The New Celebrities: Us

Government is a significant source of digital surveillance and intrusion, but hardly the only one. Like it or not, we are all celebrities today. We are all famous or notorious—or may become so at any moment—because everything we do is observable by some government or corporate entity or even by an individual, a friend, family member, enemy, or stranger. We each of us publish an extraordinary volume of financial, intellectual, and political personal data, voluntarily if unthinkingly, on e-commerce websites, financial websites, media sharing sites, and social media sites. With even less conscious volition, we also leave our digital footprints everywhere we travel on the web, as well as in emails, instant messages, texts, and cell phone conversations.

Some of this self-exposure is so self-destructive as to defy easy explanation. On May 27, 2011, Anthony Weiner, at the time a Democratic U.S. Representative from New York's 9th District, used his public Twitter account to send a link to a photo he had posted on the image-hosting service yfrog. The image was of his erect penis concealed by boxer briefs. The recipient was a twenty-one-year-old female college student who had been following the Congressman's Twitter posts. Unknown to both Weiner and his intended recipient, another Twitter user captured screen shots of the image and sent them to conservative blogger Andrew Breitbart, who published them on his popular BigJournalism website the very next day. When the story broke, Weiner initially claimed he was a victim of a hacker/hoaxer presumably bent on political sabotage. Ultimately, however, Weiner was forced to admit having taken, posted, and tweeted the photograph himself, and he further confessed to having "exchanged messages and photos of an explicit nature with about six women over the last three years." On June 16, he announced that he would resign from Congress, and five days later he did just that. A special election in the traditionally Democratic district replaced him with a Republican (*Wikipedia*, "Anthony Weiner sexting scandal").

Yet even if we aren't foolish or bent on self-destruction, even if we take great care to avoid revealing ourselves online, we may be revealed. Friends or enemies may post our private emails, pictures, or videos on their blogs or other publicly accessible websites. Or a perfect stranger may snap a cell phone picture or a smartphone video and serve it up to the world. In most cases, this is harmless enough, but not always.

In 2005, for instance, in Seoul, South Korea, a young woman was riding the subway with her small dog, which defecated on the floor of the subway car. When other passengers insisted that the woman clean up the mess, she refused, indignantly telling fellow riders to mind their own business. A commuter snapped a cell phone picture showing the woman, her dog, and the offending pile, then posted the image on a much-visited South Korean website over a caption that has been translated as "Dog Poop Girl." Not only did the image go viral, but what can only be termed "Internet vigilantes" were soon able to identify the woman in the photograph and, in a self-appointed campaign of digital shaming, used Internet sources to obtain a wealth of personal information about her, including her name and address, which they duly posted. The story was picked up by mainstream media in South Korea and elsewhere, and Dog Poop Girl became widely recognized and was so relentlessly hounded (how else can one put it?) that she dropped out of her university. Although some commentators in Korea and elsewhere decried the episode as what law professor and privacy scholar Daniel J. Solove called victimization by "cyber-posse, tracking down norm violators and branding them with digital Scarlet Letters," many others held that the rude woman had gotten precisely what was coming to her (Solve, 2007, pp. 1-4).

But say you lead an exemplary life, which includes scrupulously picking up after Fido. Even so, your smartphone is a location-tracking device (whether by GPS, cell phone tower pinging, or both) and also provides data on your movements, your communications, and your social proximity to others (by means of Bluetooth monitoring). Remote surveillance can monitor your calls, SMS transmissions and browser use, as well as the data logs for all of these. Apps, both those actually running and those merely installed, are subject to monitoring, as are your contacts, personal information, and music, image, and video files (funf.org).

So you turn off your smartphone. Even this provides no guarantee of privacy. According to the U.S. Commerce Department, "a cellular telephone can be turned into a microphone and transmitter for the purpose of listening to conversations in the vicinity of the phone." Software remotely installed by a cell phone service provider can, without your knowledge, activate the device's microphone, even when no call is being made or received. Some phones can be remotely accessed and made to transmit room audio continually. The FBI reportedly used such remote cell phone microphone activation to create "roving bugs" against "members of a New York organized crime family who were wary of conventional surveillance techniques" (McCullagh and Broache, December 1, 2006). Indeed, today's smartphones offer not only a microphone, but extraordinarily sophisticated video camera features, which can be remotely activated without your being any the wiser. It is also possible to remotely activate the webcam of your laptop or desktop computer, again without your knowledge, let alone permission (Magid, February 22, 2010).

So what if you hurl your smartphone into the dumpster and rip your PC's Ethernet cable out of the wall socket? You are still subject to satellite surveillance, pilotless drones, and fixed-location surveillance cameras that are ubiquitous in buildings and on the streets. It sounds like science fiction, but it's not fiction anymore.

The Facebook Example

Privacy and its future are urgent issues, yet seemingly so vast as to defy cogent let alone productive discussion. Let's focus then on a single website, albeit one with extraordinary reach: Facebook.

To talk about the particular topic of "Facebook privacy" is in many ways to address the general topic of privacy online. Facebook's business, after all, is founded entirely on the user's willingness to share information. This means that Facebook's business is founded on the very core of the Internet, which is, first and last, an information-sharing platform. Ideologically, culturally, and commercially, Facebook may be regarded as the "flagship" Internet site. We could call it a microcosm of the Web, except that there is nothing "micro" about it. With one billion users, the company earned a profit of $668 million in 2011 and booked $3.7 billion in revenue. Its much-anticipated IPO of May 18, 2012 was valued at $104 billion. This stratospheric valuation is what happens when nearly a billion people freely volunteer so much information (Associated Press, March 23, 2012). Despite a retreat from its IPO stock valuation, Facebook is a combination gold, platinum, and diamond mine for online behavioral advertising (OBA): those ads that target users based on data-rich user profiles.

Even the most casual user of Facebook must be stunned by the level of personal, financial, intellectual, and professional information many willingly divulge (in many instances) to thousands of "friends" and (also in many cases) to potentially one billion total strangers. This individual willingness goes to the heart of Internet privacy, and yet recent efforts by the United States government and the European Union to plan how to regulate, manage, and protect online privacy do not even address it. Instead, they propose (in the words of a EU-US "Joint Statement" issued on March 19, 2012) to promote "the rights of individuals to have their personal data protected" (EU-U.S., March 19, 2012).

Read that closely, because something's missing. It is the word *privacy*. The EU-US Joint Statement does not commit the governments to promoting rights of protection of personal privacy, but of personal data.

What's in a Name?

The EU-U.S. word choice—*personal data*, not *personal privacy*—speaks volumes. Keep it in mind as we return to the case of Facebook.

The company has a history of wrestling with privacy issues. In November 2011, it settled with the United States Federal Trade Commission (FTC) over allegations that it had misled users about how it handled their personal information, and on March 22, 2012, Facebook posted a draft of its revised "Statement of Rights and Responsibilities" (SRR). One of the revisions was the renaming of its "privacy policy" a "data use policy" (Allan, March 24, 2012). This, among other so-called "tweaks" to the SRR language, unexpectedly triggered a torrent of user protests, including Facebook postings by more than 30,000 German users who rejected the proposed changes en masse.

Arguably—and paradoxically—what the disgruntled users were unwittingly protesting was Facebook's earnest efforts to be honest, straightforward, and transparent. The revised language may well have been an attempt to avoid any more charges of misleading users. The language change could be interpreted as an admission that, like any other Internet site based on sharing information, Facebook could not sincerely promise to protect "privacy" because privacy depends on what users choose to share and what users choose to withhold. All the company could in good faith pledge was to undertake to protect "data." Unfortunately for both Facebook's public image and the naïveté of many users, this close attention to choosing the right word exposed an unavoidable gap between privacy (which is a moral construct that can be created or destroyed by individual actions) and data (a morally neutral arrangement of digital bits and bytes). When we commit our private thoughts, feelings, or facts to paper, to silicon, or to the cloud, they are no longer thoughts, or feelings, or facts. They are data.

Like the governments of the EU and the U.S., Facebook proposes to promote the protection of personal data, but it is data nevertheless, no matter how much many of us wish it would remain special, individual, human, and private, which is to say sacred. Silicon is not a sanctuary, however, and the cloud is not heaven. On the web, all is data.

Guarding the Treasure

Like other for-profit websites, Facebook monetizes data. Because Facebook has a billion users, so many of whom divulge detailed data about themselves, it monetizes more data more profitably than just about anybody else.

In a recent article, Alexis Madrigal, a senior editor at *The Atlantic*, pointed out that online user "profiles"—essentially portraits of what individual Internet users (i.e., consumers) are interested in—are sold to advertisers and marketers for half a cent per profile (at the high end). For Facebook and Google, who deliver many ads from many different advertisers and marketers to each of their users, this translates into roughly $5 for each Facebook user and $20 for each Google user. The whole of the "Internet advertising ecosystem," according to Madrigal, generates something like $1,200 per user per year (Madrigal, March 19, 2012). From an individual perspective, privacy, even when represented as data, is of inestimable emotional, intellectual, and moral value. From the perspective of the Internet advertising ecosystem, however, this same data costs just half a penny but ultimately goes for $1,200 a pop.

The bottom line online is that privacy, represented as data, is a treasure. For Facebook and the other constituents of the Internet advertising ecosystem, the treasure is virtually infinite, provided that users remain willing to share personal information. This means websites that collect and use such information have an urgent interest in guarding the treasure both for its value to the individual and for its value to commerce. In fact, they need to guard it with their lives—for the simple reason that their treasure *is* their lives. Without it, they're belly up.

Certainly, Facebook acted in just such a spirit when, on March 23, 2012, Erin Egan, the company's "chief privacy officer, policy," issued a statement concerning "a distressing increase in reports of employers or others seeking to gain inappropriate access to people's Facebook profiles or private information."

> The most alarming of these practices is the reported incidents of employers asking prospective or actual employees to reveal their passwords. If you are a Facebook user, you should never have to share your password, let anyone access your account, or do anything that might jeopardize the security of your account or violate the privacy of your friends. We have worked really hard at Facebook to give you the tools to control who sees your information
> ...
> We don't think employers should be asking prospective employees to provide their passwords because we don't think it's the right thing to do. But it also may cause problems for the employers that they are not anticipating. For example, if an employer sees on Facebook that someone is a member of a protected group (e.g. over a certain age, etc.) that employer may open themselves up to claims of discrimination if they don't hire that person (Egan, March 23, 2012).

Egan's statement went on to promise, "We'll take action to protect the privacy and security of our users, whether by engaging policymakers or, where appropriate, by initiating legal action, including by shutting down applications that abuse their privileges" (Egan, March 23, 2012). As Matt Brian of *The Next Web* reported, the company was "willing to go to bat for users that feel they have been wronged by an employer, which could go as far as filing lawsuits against the companies involved" (Brian, March 23, 2012).

Facebook's stand has been praised both as a brilliant PR move and as a noble blow struck in the defense of online ethics and individual freedom. What Facebook did is also, of course, an act of enlightened self-interest, and, as such, has another basis in the precise meaning of words. Facebook took heat for being honest about the use of the word *data* in preference to *privacy*. Clearly, Facebook's leadership also understands the meaning of the word *share*. The verb implies free will, decision, and choice. It is emphatically not a synonym for *relinquish, lose, give up*, or *abandon*—which is what employers and others who would extort a user's password demand. (Recently, some employers have reportedly sought to circumvent Facebook's ire by "shoulder surfing"—demanding that an employee or prospective employee open up his or Facebook page while the bosses look on. After all, it is unsavory personal information they're after. The password was only a means to that end.) Allow user data to be extorted or stolen or otherwise forcibly surrendered, and who will continue to willingly share? Stop sharing, and Facebook closes up shop. If the flagship sinks, what will happen to the rest of the fleet?

Let's Party Like It's 1934

Before interactive media began to eclipse mass broadcast media during the mid-1990s, government regulation of "communications" was relatively simple. The central regulatory authority was the Federal Communications Commission (FCC), which had been established by the Communications Act of 1934, signed into law on June 19 of that year by President Franklin D. Roosevelt. The FCC was charged with "regulating interstate and foreign commerce in communication by wire and radio so as to make available, so far as possible, to all the people of the United States a rapid, efficient, nationwide, and worldwide wire and radio communication service with adequate facilities at reasonable charges."

So far as radio communication was concerned, the authority of the FCC rested on the principle that the "airwaves" were a public interest and that the limited availability of broadcast bandwidth, a public resource, therefore had to be federally administered to protect and to serve the public good. Until nearly the end of the twentieth century, local broadcast television channels were relatively few, and truly national TV networks were only three. FCC monitoring of so compact a group was feasible, so feasible, in fact, that broadcasters created organizations to avoid government intervention by neatly policing themselves.

While the relatively contained scope of mass-media broadcasting helped make government and industry oversight practical and effective, even more important was the fact that radio and television were one-way media. Broadcasters were the producers, and viewers were the consumers. End of story. Only the producers were seen as requiring regulatory attention, whether by government, industry organizations, or the corporate sponsors who ultimately financed all programming.

In contrast to broadcast radio and television, the Internet is interactive and therefore by definition a two-way medium. Every entity that uses the Internet is both a producer and a consumer. Even if as an individual you do not create a website, offer anything for sale online, or write a blog, you still produce data—by some calculations (as we have just seen) at least $1,200 worth.

Whereas three fully national networks exclusively plied the broadcast television airwaves during the second half of the twentieth century, today the Internet hosts billions of consumer-producers. Everything from basic communication, to commerce, to entertainment, to government administration, to social interaction, to the creation, sharing, and dissemination of knowledge takes place on the Internet platform. As recent events in the Arab world and elsewhere have demonstrated, entire governments rise and fall by dint of the Internet.

The value at stake—the "public good"—is certainly incalculable, but just as surely has never been higher. We do have tangible statistics on the cost of identity theft. At present, one out of ten U.S. consumers has been a victim. In 2008, more than 35 million corporate and government data records were compromised by security breaches. Phishing—using the Internet and email to dupe people into revealing personal, especially financial, information—has cost consumers an estimated $1.2 billion to date (VentureBeat, February 2012).

The cost of non-criminal analogues of identity theft—that is, the collection and use of personal data without our knowledge or permission—probably cannot be calculated. But just consider that, until it reached an agreement with the FTC in 2010, Facebook routinely compiled user information even from people who were not members of Facebook. This occurred whenever a non-member user visited a website that featured the familiar Facebook thumbs-up "Like" button. It was not even necessary for that visitor to click the button. As Rob Shavell, cofounder of the online security company Abine, commented, the buttons worked "like a dark video camera—you see them, they see you." By 2010, these buttons were on nearly a million websites (VentureBeat, February 2012).

While the "dark video camera" functionality of Facebook "Like" buttons has been discontinued for Facebook non-members, Internet users are still exposed to data mining by cookies, which function to exchange information between the user's computer and a website. About half of the Web's most popular sites use cookies and at many sites they are required to enable user interaction. As we saw in Chapter 2, third parties such as advertisers, advertising networks, and marketers, place cookies on some websites to enable them to track browsing information through other websites. While most cookies store user and browsing information for only the duration of the browsing session, 18.5 percent are termed "persistent cookies" and store information indefinitely (VentureBeat, February 2012).

The value of Internet data may be incalculably great and at least some of the threats commensurately sinister, yet the growth and volume of Internet traffic, the varied nature of that traffic, and the expectation of freedom and openness among users have all outpaced government efforts at regulation.

On February 8, 1996, in recognition of the fact that the nation could no longer party like it was 1934 when it came to regulating communications, President Bill Clinton signed into law the Telecommunications Act of 1996. Its principal thrust was the deregulation of the broadcasting market, but it also represented a change in both telecommunications and related laws by including the Internet, which was then just emerging from infancy into toddlerhood, in the broadcasting and spectrum allotment. An advance over 1934, to be sure, the 1996 legislation was nevertheless obsolescent before the ink had dried on the president's signature.

Trusted Under Penalty of Law

Let's fast forward to January 25, 2012, when the European Commission's Directorate-General for Justice (DG JUST) presented its proposal for a regulation to replace the EU's existing 1995 Data Protection Directive. Aimed at strengthening the rights of "data subjects" (a.k.a. Internet users), the proposed new legislation would require "data controllers" (a.k.a mostly website owners) to provide more transparent and accessible information to data subjects and to be more responsive to individual requests for personal information. The proposal asserts a right of EU citizens "to be forgotten," thereby obliging data controllers to delete personal data on request. It would also prohibit any data controller from collecting data from a subject unless the subject gives express consent, which the subject may subsequently withdraw at any time. A strict opt-in approach for consumers to expressly allow the placement of every tracking cookie is part of the proposed legislation.

The EU's government-centered approach raises serious questions of public and corporate costs, feasibility, and the prospect of cumbersome regulations inhibiting the overall growth of the Internet. In particular, businesses that rely on OBA, including consumer profiling and targeted advertising, are likely to suffer widespread, possibly profound, disruption.

There is another problem. In contrast to the EU's government-centered approach to regulation, the United States has proposed precisely what the EU has already rejected: industry self-regulation. As it stands, this difference of approach threatens the global interoperability of Internet commerce, perhaps of the Internet itself, since companies operating in ways that satisfy U.S. privacy laws will very likely fail to satisfy EU privacy laws and will therefore be prohibited from doing business online in the nations of the EU.

A month behind the EU's actions, in February 2012, the White House released the Consumer Bill of Rights (White House, February 2012). The framework consists of four elements:

1. A Consumer Privacy Bill of Rights
2. "A multistakeholder process to specify how the principles in the Consumer Privacy Bill of Rights apply in particular business contexts"
3. Proposals for strengthening FTC enforcement
4. A "commitment to increase interoperability with the privacy frameworks of our international partners."

Despite its grandiose name, echoing the popular title of the first ten amendments to the United States Constitution, the Consumer Bill of Rights is not legally prescriptive, but instead is meant only to provide "general principles that afford companies discretion in how they implement [the Bill of Rights]." This flexibility is intended to promote innovation and "encourage effective privacy protections by allowing companies, informed by input from consumers and other stakeholders, to address the privacy issues that are likely to be most important to their customers and users, rather than requiring companies to adhere to a single, rigid set of requirements." What the framework refers to as the "multistakeholder process" is aimed at producing "enforceable codes of conduct that implement the Consumer Privacy Bill of Rights." Industry participation in the multistakeholder process will be voluntary, and companies will choose whether or not to adopt a given code of conduct; however, the FTC will enforce whatever "privacy commitments" a company voluntarily makes when it adopts a given code of conduct (White House, February 2012).

It does sound odd, but the White House proposal works like this. A company's commitment to the Consumer Privacy Bill of Rights is voluntary, but once a company volunteers to commit to a particular policy, the FTC will enforce that commitment under penalty of law.

The Obama administration acknowledges that the proposed U.S. industry-centered approach is radically different from the EU's government-centered approach and, therefore, includes in the framework a commitment to "developing codes of conduct that simplify companies' compliance obligations" globally. Unfortunately, however, the EU has already signaled that it is quite unimpressed. In an article posted on NetChoice, Carl Szabo quoted European Commission (EC) representative Françoise Le Bail as warning the United States that it "cannot escape" the EU privacy rules. When asked if the EU representatives would respect the outcome of the proposed U.S. "multistakeholder process," Jacob Kohnstamm of the Dutch Protection Data Protection Authority replied bluntly that even if the stakeholders agreed that consumers would be opted out of interest-based advertising by default (and would have to opt in to receive such advertising), the EU would reject the U.S. approach. Szabo also reported that the EC's Paul Nemitz "would dismiss" the results of the U.S. multistakeholder process since such a process "is not necessarily a product of the people" (Szabo, March 26, 2012).

Media Unmediated: The Third Approach

If the EU's government-centered approach to protecting personal data raises grave doubts as to the economic impact of impediments to trade, potential inhibition of innovation, and difficulties with global interoperability, the White House framework surely seems more like an aspiration than a realistically executable plan, especially with its combination of voluntary codes and FTC enforcement. Still, as *New York Times* technology reporter Steve Lohr recently observed, an "individual's actions ... are rarely enough to protect privacy in the interconnected world of the Internet" (VentureBeat, February 2012). So, clearly, good governments need to find new ways to do in the digital realm what good governments have always sought to do elsewhere: protect the rights, lives, and property of citizens while simultaneously promoting their welfare, which means (in part) enacting laws that facilitate rather than impede economic and cultural development. But neither the EU "regulation" nor the U.S. "framework" seem anywhere close to practical readiness for effective implementation, and it is difficult to say how long it will be before the governments evolve effective legislation that also harmonizes the differing approaches on both sides of the Atlantic.

Fortunately, something can be done now. We can take a third approach, one that is truly global precisely because it is most diverse in its application. Instead of vesting regulation either in government or in commercial corporate entities, we propose a strategy that puts it in the hands of individual users of the Internet. This is neither to cynically assert that corporations are incapable of acting ethically even in their own self-interest nor to abandon government. Industry will have to work the common ground between ethics and profitability, and government regulation will almost certainly have to play a role in something as all-encompassing as the conduct of human affairs on the Internet. But this is precisely the point. The Internet is a platform for human affairs, and it is therefore with the individual, with each human node on the vast network, that effective and practical Internet regulation must both commence and culminate.

It is easy to be swamped by issues of online privacy, security, and safety. We should not, however, let ourselves become so overwhelmed by these considerations that we forget that no technology is more liberating than that of the Internet. It has entered into and opened up virtually every social, creative, intellectual, political, and economic activity. Yet as all people accustomed to democratic government understand, with liberty for all comes the necessity for discipline of the self. Put another way, the greater the freedom, the greater the need for a disciplined approach to that freedom. No technology in the history of civilization has demanded a greater degree of self-regulation than the Internet.

Basic Tools and Broader Strategy

In the heyday of one-way media, the individual had few threats to defend against: broadcast lies, perhaps, and deceptive commercials for bad products. What the FCC couldn't police, individual common sense generally could.

The effective regulation of two-way media requires more individual vigilance, knowledge, judgment, and initiative. It begins with thoroughly informed self-defense, and the chapters in Part II of this book, "Outright Threats and Obvious Opportunities," provide the essential information and tools you need not only to acquire a realistic understanding of the hazards of the web but to secure yourself against these online.

Software tools and simple safety precautions are essential, but not sufficient, to achieve for yourself what the White House hopes to achieve for all users of the Internet: protecting privacy while making the most of the global digital economy. In addition to providing for self-defense, we advise equipping yourself to play offense in the universe online. Specifically, we recommend following the centuries-old example of great and successful businesses by consciously and thoughtfully creating for yourself a "brand." In the case of the Internet, this means crafting an online identity that is designed to present you to the world as you want to be seen by it, as you want it to deal with you.

For a company, a brand is proprietary—private—yet also public. The more widely it is recognized, the more successful it is. We believe that the most effective and productive individual users of the Internet present themselves in much the same way, as privately public or publicly private. They achieve what we call wide-open privacy. It is a concept we will explain in greater detail in Chapter 13: a strategy for becoming fully connected to all of the Internet's frictionless freedom, yet also for exercising sufficient self-discipline to preserve as sacred whatever data you choose not to share.

We are convinced that all of us would benefit from proactively and strategically building and protecting our own personal online brands. The problem is that if you don't craft your own digital brand, someone else will do it for you—or it will be thrown together accidentally, haphazardly, inconsistently. Allowing your identity, as you want others to understand it, to be defined by those others is the ultimate threat to privacy. Over the next decade, people will discover that they must do what the managers of successful companies and products do: prioritize, invest in, and discipline their own brand building. This means playing offense in constructing your own digital profiles and in all your online communications. Figuratively, this means building and maintaining your own "website" in every interaction on the Internet. The objectives are these:

Define Yourself: If you don't define yourself others will. What is especially important is to create your own "web" presence, in all online communications as well as with respect to more trusted people in your network, in which you continually and consistently define the values and character that go into your work and life.

Define Your Space: What do you stand for? What's important to you? And why? Best that you define this in your own publicly private/privately public "branded" digital space so that you can communicate this when and where you wish—and on your own terms.

Define the Future: This is what great leaders must do and, more and more, it is what everyday citizens must also do around the world. Define your own "destination"—where you see the future and where you are contributing to make this vision a reality.

The age of one-way media is ending and the era of two-way media is already well upon us. It presents threats and complex hazards, which nevertheless are far outweighed by benefits unprecedented in the history of civilization. For all its complex risks and rich rewards, life online is first and last a dialogue—with individuals, customers, clients, bosses, colleagues, family, friends, strangers, the world. The cardinal rule of building an online personal brand is the cardinal rule of all productive conversation: The person who controls the dialogue wins.

.02

[*Outright Threats and*
  Obvious Opportunities]

CHAPTER FOUR
In the Hot Zone

Our aim in this book is strategic rather than tactical. We've sought to turn the concept of digital privacy inside out with a discussion of how users of digital technology can take full advantage of the Internet by opening the wired world to themselves and themselves to that world, albeit on strategically self-defined, self-regulated terms. That is our strategic aim. But it would be foolish to ignore in the name of strategy the tactical threats that are, alas, quite real. This chapter provides a comprehensive survey of the most critical online security issues and how to address them, including malware, cracked passwords, the hazards of wireless networks, and physical security. We also provide an overview of phishing and social engineering scams, which are treated in detail in Chapters 6 and 8.

Tactical Hazards Online: The Major Threats

The major hazards to the security of your data online come from malware infection—which includes viruses, Trojan horses, and rootkits, among other threats—compromised passwords, unsecured WiFi networks, and physical theft or loss (theft of a computer, theft of a flash drive, theft of a smartphone or tablet device). In addition, you may fall victim to online scams, chief among which are—

> Phishing: The scammer uses a fake website or fake emails to pose as a legitimate, typically large and well-recognized, business in an effort to prompt you to click on an option button or otherwise download malware. Or a fake website or email is used to solicit confidential information from you, typically credit card or bank account information, passwords, Social Security number, address, phone number, date of birth, and so on. Phishing is sometimes called spoofing.
> Social engineering: The scammer persuades you to divulge confidential information (as in phishing) or to perform some action authorizing the release of confidential information for the purpose, usually, of larceny. Social engineering may involve the actual use of phishing, or it may consist of a convincing phone call, letter, or even a face-to-face encounter.

We will explore phishing and social engineering in detail in Chapters 6 and 8. In this chapter, we will confine ourselves to malware threats, compromised passwords, compromised WiFi networks, and physical theft or loss.

Malware Threats

Malicious software—malware—may infect your computer when you click on a link or open up an attachment included in an email, when you visit a malicious website, or when you unwittingly download a piece of malicious code that masquerades as something fun (wallpaper, a free game) or useful.

Some malware is neither more nor less than sociopathic vandalism. Infection may produce such annoyances as taunting or even threatening messages that pop up randomly or bizarre responses from ordinary computer operations. Some viruses may attack your hard drive, deleting data. Some may make your data inaccessible. Some may not allow your computer to boot up. Another class of malware is designed to spy on you or to steal your data, including passwords and banking and credit account information. Other malware programs can hijack your email account, using it to send bogus messages to everyone in your contact list or address book while making it appear as if the messages have originated with you. (In the majority of these cases, such hijacking does not involve malware that physically infects your computer, but is the work of someone who has managed to obtain or guess the password to your email account and has used it to hack into your account via your email provider. See "If Your Email Is Hacked," later in this chapter.) Some of the most sophisticated malware can turn your computer into a zombie, taking it over by remote control and using it for just about any purpose—legal, illegal, or simply embarrassing—just as if each keystroke were coming from your own fingers.

Viruses

A virus is a program designed to infect multiple computers. Once it enters your system, it attaches itself to a file, macro, or program and then replicates itself when that program is run, infecting other programs on your computer and spreading to other computers that may be networked with it. The damage viruses do may include annoying acts of vandalism, deletion or corruption of data, hijacking of your email system, degrading of computer performance resulting in crashes, slow execution of processes, and even the inability to operate the computer at all.

In the early days of the personal computer, most virus infection came from users who thoughtlessly installed a free program—typically a screensaver or a game—from a diskette. These days, PCs still get infected by USB thumb drives or flash drives, but, more typically, viruses are propagated via the Internet, most often when an unsuspecting user clicks on an email attachment, which may open a greeting card, a video, an audio, a still image, or a simple game that is infected.

Although the makers of antivirus software products continually identify new threats and meticulously catalogue them, it is very difficult to make an accurate estimate of the number of viruses in circulation at any given time. Some estimates reach well into the millions. The major types include:

Boot sector viruses: These infect the boot record of your boot drive. Boot up, and the virus then spreads to all removable media.

File infector viruses: These infect executable files and are propagated upon execution of the infected file.

Macro viruses: These infect program-specific data files, such as those produced by word processing programs, database programs, spreadsheet programs, and so on.

Multipartite viruses: These combine one or more of the properties listed above.

Worms

A worm may be considered a type of virus because it replicates itself to infect the host computer and others; however, unlike a generic virus, it is a standalone program that does not need to attach itself to an existing executable or other file. Once installed, the worm typically exploits the host computer's address book and sends an email to every contact, each email bearing a link to the worm. The worm may wreak the same havoc as a virus—deleting files, stealing data—and it may go even further, opening a "backdoor" to the infected computer, which will allow a remote computer, via the Internet, to take control of it, thereby transforming it into a zombie. When zombies are surreptitiously networked, they become botnets, and are harnessed by professional spammers to send massive amounts of spam email into the world.

At the very least, worms steal network bandwidth and processor power. They can slow a company's network and servers to a crawl. This is known as a denial of service (DoS or DDos) attack, and cyber criminals use the mere threat of such an assault to extort money from companies.

Trojan Horses (Trojans)

Like a virus and like a worm, the Trojan Horse is an alien presence on the host computer and can do damage to files and steal data. It can also spy on the user, create a zombie, and even neutralize antimalware software present on the computer. Unlike viruses and worms, the Trojan cannot replicate itself or infect other files. It enters the host computer via an email attachment or other software download. Like the Trojan Horse the Greeks used to penetrate the defenses of Troy, the Trojan poses as a "gift," something fun or useful—a game, a video, a piece of music, even an antimalware program! Install it, however, and you have installed a Trojan Horse.

Keylogging Trojans "log" (record) your keystrokes, creating a log file and then automatically emailing it surreptitiously to a remote attacker, who can obtain passwords, account numbers and names, and other personal data.

RATs, or Remote Access Trojans, create another kind of portal into the host machine. Through it, a remote attacker can access any non-password-protected file on the computer and may even take the computer over as a zombie.

IRC Trojans use Internet Relay Chat servers to send remote commands to any number of Trojan-infected computers.

Destructive Trojans behave more like certain viruses in that their function is not control or spying, but destruction of files on the host.

Finally, Software Detection Killer Trojans are designed to seek out and neutralize antivirus/antimalware software on the host computer, rendering it vulnerable to multiple attacks by viruses and worms and other malware.

<u>Rootkits</u>

Like a virus, a rootkit attaches to legitimate-looking software and is installed on the host machine when that software is installed. Unlike a virus or worm or Trojan, the rootkit is not a single program, but a collection of programs that, together, directly modify the computer's operating system, becoming part of it, so that the rootkit is almost completely undetectable.

The purpose of a rootkit is almost always to open up a backdoor to the host machine, through which an attacker can introduce other malware or simply enjoy administrator-level access to the machine, allowing her to do anything a legitimate user could do, and do it remotely and surreptitiously. The most sophisticated rootkits, called kernel mode rootkits, operate on the very core of the computer's operating system and thereby achieve full stealth mode. They are virtually impossible to detect. As for removal, the only way is to fully reformat the machine's hard drive.

Symptoms of Infection

Symptoms of a malware infection range from none to the total non-functionality of a computer that refuses to boot up to a useful level. In between these extremes, you may notice a significantly increased rate of errors and crashes, including, for Windows users, the so-called Blue Screen of Death (BSOD), which appears whenever that operating system encounters a major system-halting error. You may notice subtler problems, especially markedly slower operation and signs of continual activity, such as a hard disk whirring away fiercely even when you are doing nothing at all with the machine. Note, of course, that the occurrence of any of these errors or conditions does not warrant a certain diagnosis of infection. If, however, these problems are recurrent—and especially if you notice a great deal of unexplained disk activity—you should be suspicious.

The surest way to diagnose a malware infection is also the second surest way to prevent one to begin with (we'll get to the first surest defense in a moment): use an updated antimalware program to perform a full scan of all your hard drives and any attached outboard storage devices. Even if you don't have antimalware software installed, you can download the free Microsoft Safety

Scanner, which is available at http://www.microsoft.com/security/scanner/en-us/default.aspx.

If Your Email Is Hacked

The following is a distressingly common occurrence: A friend emails you or calls to tell you that she has been getting a "lot of weird emails" from you advertising a 100-percent-guaranteed high-yield investment in precious metals or free trials of a "male enhancement" product. This is often the only warning you get when a spammer has hijacked your email account and is using it to send spam messages to all your contacts—as if the messages have come from you. Usually, these invasions are embarrassing and annoying rather than destructive; however, the spam emails may contain harmful attachments or links that spread the infection or do worse.

If you discover that your email has been hijacked, you should run a full antimalware scan. The chances are, however, that it will turn up nothing—for the simple reason that your computer itself has not been penetrated. Most email hijackings are the work of an attacker who has either obtained or successfully guessed the password to your account and has signed onto it remotely. Fortunately, this type of invasion is easy to repel. All you need to do is change the password to your account. This usually requires nothing more than signing on to your account via the website of your ISP and making the changes. Choose a strong password (see "About Passwords," below), and note that you will have to make the same changes on all your devices that send and receive mail from the account. A good preventive measure is to routinely change your email account password every few months.

Antimalware Software

As executives with AVG Technologies, we are confident in recommending AVG Anti-Virus Free Edition, which is not only very popular and very good, but also free. In addition, we invite you to go online and consult descriptions, reviews, and ratings of other major antimalware programs. Windows users should also check out Microsoft's own Microsoft Security Essentials, which is a free antivirus add-on for Windows. Whatever software solution you choose, the most important thing is to actually use it: set it to run automatically in the background so that it can detect threats as they arise, set it to perform regular scans, and keep it up to date. Most programs include an automatic updating option. Take advantage of this, as threats continually change.

Firewalls

Firewall software provides a layer of security between your computer and the outside world. Generally, firewall software analyzes incoming data to determine if it is either data you requested or data that originates from a trusted source.

Windows comes with a firewall, which you should ensure is activated. (Go to Control Panel and click on System and Security.) Alternatively, you can install a firewall from a third-party Internet security software suite.

Preventive Measures

Antimalware and firewall software will enable you to detect and neutralize most threats and will prevent many others. Using these, we have said, is the second strongest defense against malware infection. The strongest defense is to avoid threats in the first place by employing safe computing practices. Here are the basics:

1. Do not download software from unfamiliar sources. Whenever you are tempted to do so, perform a Web search to check out the item before you download it.

2. Do not download or use pirated software. Not only is this illegal, the software is often used as a vector of infection.

3. Do not click on email attachments unless you are certain of the sender and the content of the attachment. Be especially cautious about opening executable attachments. This is the primary mode of spreading infection.

4. Do not click on links you encounter on unfamiliar websites. These are also common vectors of infection.

5. If your email program has a provision that prevents automatically downloading pictures in messages you receive, enable this provision. It will help protect your privacy and may prevent an infection.

6. Some authorities suggest that, when you surf the Web, do not do so as an Administrator, but instead log on with a non-administrator account. Doing so gives you limited access privileges, which will in turn limit the damage of any malware infection you may encounter.

By default, Windows hides file extensions (such as .doc or .exe). This makes for a less cluttered screen appearance in file listings, but it can be a dangerous practice because it makes it easy for attackers to disguise the malware files they send as email attachments. For instance, you may be tempted to open hothothot.jpg, because you know that the "jpg" extension indicates a non-executable jpeg file, which, because it is not executable, should be harmless. Had you enabled the visibility of file extensions, however, you would have seen that the file is really hothothot.jpg.exe, an executable file with all the earmarks of malware. (In addition to .exe, other common extensions that indicate files that can potentially deploy malware are .bat, .com, .pif, .scr, .reg, .vb, and .vbs.) To enable visibility of extensions, open Windows Explorer and select Tools > Folder Options. In the Folder Options dialogue box, click on the View tab, then deselect "Hide extension for known file types." After clearing the checkbox, click OK. Now all extensions will be visible.

A Word about the Macintosh

One of the reasons Mac users can be so annoying to users of PCs is their tendency to boast about how they are invulnerable to the viruses that perpetually plague the PC. Most annoying of all is the fact that there is considerable truth to this claim. The closed and highly regulated Mac operating system—currently some iteration of OS X—employs "sandboxing," a way of sequestering key system files that significantly restricts the global actions that can be performed by third-party (non-Apple or non-Apple-approved) applications or utilities. Should you download an infected program, chances are that it will be blocked from attacking the system.

Contrary to your Mac friends' claims, this does not mean that Macintosh computers are absolutely immune from viruses and other malware. For one thing, even if infected files don't harm the Mac, that machine may still act as a carrier, a Typhoid Mary that passes the malware infection along to PCs networked with it or via email. The Sophos security firm estimated that one in every five Mac computers "harbors malware" (Sophos, April 24, 2012). Moreover, even Apple warns that although the Mac OS is specifically designed to "provide protection ... right out of the box ... no system can be 100 percent immune from every threat." This means, according to the folks at Apple, that "antivirus software may offer additional protection" (Apple, "Safety. Built right in."), and the company itself recently released a fix for a widespread infection called "Flashback" (Sherr, April 6, 2012).

About Passwords

The most important thing to know about passwords is that, in order to make them effective, you need to use them wherever there is an opportunity to do so. Like locks on the doors of your house, passwords are a basic defense of your security and privacy—provided they are used.

The second most important thing to know is the difference between a weak password (one easily guessed and therefore readily compromised) and a strong one. To create a strong password, you need to be able to recognize a weak one. The following are characteristics of a weak password:

1. It is the unchanged default. Some software and hardware ships with default passwords such as user, admin, or even password. An attacker will usually try these first, knowing that many people never bother to change the default. If the attacker guesses correctly, his attack will succeed.

2. A password that is shorter than seven characters.

3. A password containing your name, a pet's name, or any proper nouns

4. A password that fails to combine at least three types of characters. (At

minimum, the password should mix uppercase and lowercase letters plus numbers. Even better is to add such symbols as -, +, =, !, and ? or others your software or hardware may permit.)

5. A password based on anything readily identifiable with you, such as your name, your license plate number, a credit card PIN number, hometown, favorite movie, birthdate, child's name, nickname, and the like.

To create a strong password, avoid the pitfalls inventoried above. The strongest passwords are the most random and meaningless. In fact, consider using a random passphrase generator to create a password for you. You can check one out PCTools.com.

Use different passwords for different accounts or, at the very least, use different passwords for your critical files and accounts and your less important ones. This will limit the damage should an attacker succeed in cracking one of your passwords.

It is also crucial that you protect the physical security of your passwords. If you can memorize them and avoid writing them down, do so. If not, keep the information at a distance from your computer. As convenient as "autofill" browser options are, avoid them. Indeed, never store passwords on your computer, and don't put them on a USB flash drive or the equivalent unless you strongly encrypt the storage device (see the next section).

A convenient way to keep track a multiplicity of passwords is to use password management software. These programs allow you to access any number of passwords with just a single master password. Because the master is encrypted, it is secure. This means that you can get the ease-of-use of a single password without sacrificing the security of separate passwords for your most important accounts, data, and functions. Moreover, because the manager is Internet based, you can access it anywhere.

There are several password management software products on the market. The leading standalone programs are RoboForm Everywhere, Sticky Password, DataVault, Kaspersky Password Manager, Hand Password Manager, SplashID Safe, Aurora Password Manager, TK8 Safe Pro, AnyPassword, and Password Agent. A number of Internet security suites include a password manager among their features. Not surprisingly, the authors' favorite is AVG Internet Security, but BitDefender Internet Security, Kaspersky Internet Security, Panda Internet Security, Norton Internet Security, F-Secure Interent Security, Avast Internet Security, and ESET Internet Security all include password management solutions. Whatever software you use, make certain that it is fully trusted and secure. If it is vulnerable to being hacked, all of the keys to your castle will be forfeit.

Encryption

Strong passwords provide an important level of protection, but also consider taking the next step: encryption. Even if an attacker breaks your password or passwords and gains access to your computer, he will find whatever files you have encrypted inaccessible. Encryption is the very best defense against the most dire consequences of a stolen computer.

The best and most convenient encryption solution is on-the-fly data encryption that creates a "container file" on your hard drive, a portable drive, USB flash drive, or other storage device. The container file acts like a virtual drive (known as an encrypted virtual drive, or EVD), which shows up on your system just as if it were a physical hard drive, designated by its own letter. The critical difference is that everything saved to the EVD is inaccessible except to those who use a password you create.

Encryption does not require a degree in cryptography. It does require encryption software that is available from a variety of vendors. The most popular programs include Folder Lock, Advanced Encryption Package Pro, BestCrypt, SensiGuard, Safe House Personal Edition, SecureIT, CryptoForge, and SafeBit Disk Encryption. In addition, TrueCrypt is a free, open-source program that is well worth checking out at www.truecrypt.org before you purchase a commercial program.

Although encryption is not foolproof, it does make your encrypted data safe from all but the most sophisticated, most determined, and most adequately funded attackers. This class of criminal is not likely to invest effort in striking against individuals and small businesses, but will carefully choose high-value targets. The legendary safecracker Willie Sutton did not squander his prodigious talent on candy store strongboxes, but went for bank vaults. Asked by a reporter why he robbed banks, he replied quite directly, "That's where they keep the money."

WiFi Security

If you have a smartphone or laptop with built-in wireless capability or a wireless card, you have doubtless noticed that you can pick up signals from any number of wireless networks wherever you happen to be. If you live in a suburb or city, you will see networks belonging to your neighbors. If you are working in an office, you will detect networks belonging to other departments in your company and other companies in your building or across the street or down the block. Some network names will appear onscreen with a little padlock icon. Some will show either no icon or an icon with an unlocked padlock. The closed padlocks denote networks protected by a password. Without knowing the password, you cannot access them. All the others are open. Anyone within range—and, these days, WiFi routers tend to have a range radius of 300 to 600 feet—can log on to use free

WiFi on the registered user's dime and in the registered user's name. If a free rider decides to transact illegal business via the open network—to download or upload child pornography, for instance—the activity will appear to the outside world, including police investigators, to be coming from the network and computer of the legitimately registered user. Moreover, once on the open network, a free rider may be able to gain access to the legitimate user's computer or computers.

The first rule of WiFi security is simple: Do not leave your wireless connection open. Password-encrypt it.   Most currently available routers make this encryption quite simple. Consult your manual, and if you don't have one, look it up on the Internet, or go to the website of your ISP (if the ISP supplied your wireless router). It is important to use the latest encryption method, known as WPA or WPA2, either of which is superior to the old standby, WEP, an easily penetrated encryption.

In addition to password-encrypting your wireless network, be sure to change the default username and password that allow access to the settings on the router itself. Most routers for home and small office use employ a Web interface for purposes of configuration. By default, the interface allows access to the router settings when you type in the username "admin" and the password "admin." Change both to prevent unauthorized access to your router.

When you access your router's settings, you should also change the option that allows broadcast of the Set Identifier (SSID) number. By default, a wireless router will broadcast its unique SSID, thereby proclaiming itself to the world. Change the default by turning off the SSID broadcast.

In addition to password protecting router access and turning off SSID broadcast, you should make some changes to the setting in Windows. Most important is to turn off public printer and file sharing. Go to the Network and Sharing Center, click on Advanced sharing settings, and then click the button next to "Turn off file and printer sharing." If you fail to do this, anyone who gains access to your WiFi network can access your shared files.

One of main benefits WiFi offers is that a laptop or mobile device (such as a smartphone; see Chapter 8) can connect to the Internet wherever WiFi service is offered, which, these days, is almost anywhere. In many public places—airports, hotel lobbies, waiting rooms, coffee shops, and so on—WiFi access is wide open and requires no password to log on. Even those that do require a sign-on password are hardly secure, because many people obtain the password and use the network. Just about all of these users, presumably, are strangers to you. Protect your security and privacy when using public WiFi by doing the following:

1. Be sure you have antimalware software and a firewall installed, updated, and activated.

2. Be sure that all sensitive and critical information on your laptop or mobile device is password protected.

3. Encrypt sensitive data – this is your best form of defense.

4. Avoid accessing, downloading, or uploading critical, sensitive, or important information and documents over publicly accessible WiFi hotspots. Receiving and sending confidential business files via a public network, for example, is a high-risk proposition.

5. When you log onto a public WiFi hotspot, make absolutely sure that you are in fact connecting to the genuine hotspot and not a "spoofed" (counterfeited) site. A reasonably sophisticated criminal can position herself within range of your laptop's wireless signal and convincingly counterfeit a WiFi hotspot login page. If the hotspot requires you to register and pay for access, the spoofer will acquire any identifying information or passwords you type in, as well as your credit card information.

6. Before logging on, look at the sign-in page very carefully. The URL should be specific to the WiFi provider, and it should be preceded by https (not simply http), which indicates a secure site. In Internet Explorer and some other browsers, you should also see a locked padlock icon to the right of the URL, indicating a secure connection.

Physical Security

The physical security of desktop and laptop computers, as well as smartphones, is one of those security considerations that is so obvious it is often taken for granted and overlooked. The loss of any of these devices, either to careless accident or theft, can be expensive, running into the hundreds or thousands of dollars for the equipment alone. The loss of the data contained on this equipment can carry catastrophic costs.

Lock down your equipment. Many laptop and even desktop computers are equipped with hardware that allows them to be cable-chained to some immovable object: a permanently installed desk, a pipe, or other fixture. Office and study doors should be locked. Your home should be secure. In public, keep track of your laptop and smartphone. Never trust them to the kindness of strangers.

In an office environment or any environment in which printers and photocopiers are connected to a computer network, especially if they are connected wirelessly, these devices, vulnerable to theft, contain network access information and may even contain file information from material printed or copied.

And don't forget to physically secure software media, including portable hard drives, USB flash drives, microcards, CD-ROMs, DVD-ROMS, and any obsolescent (but still present) diskettes. Any of these may have sensitive or identifying data on them.

Beyond Basic Security

Beyond basic security—those vulnerabilities that can be addressed with antimalware software, passwords, encryption, physical locks and keys, and wide-awake common sense—are threats to security and privacy produced by bad actors on social media sites (Chapter 5), by cyber criminals (Chapter 6), by predatory e-commerce providers (Chapter 7), by vulnerabilities specific to the mobile sphere (Chapter 8), and by official and quasi-official agencies of government (Chapter 9). After dealing with these tactical hazards, Part II concludes with affirmative strategies for creating productive privacy online (Chapter 10).

CHAPTER FIVE
Antisocial Behavior

Nicholas A. Christakis and James H. Fowler, authors of *Connected: How Your Friends' Friends' Friends Affect Everything You Feel, Think, and Do* (Christakis and Fowler, 2009), propose that the traditional phylogenetic name for human beings, Homo sapiens ("knowing man"), be updated to more accurately reflect what the authors believe is the true evolutionary status of modern humanity. The name they suggest is Homo dictyous ("network man"). They argue that our species has evolved to care about others and that social networks have become so central to human existence that they are now "a kind of human superorganism," which vastly expands the range of human capability. "Just as brains can do things no single neuron can do, so can social networks do things no single person can do" (Christakis and Fowler, 2009, xvi).

As Christakis and Fowler see it, the emergence of Homo dictyous from Homo sapiens is relatively recent on the timeline of human evolution, which, however, still means that it is a development many thousands of years old. During those millennia, social networks have been of immeasurable value in our cultural evolution and (if Christakis and Fowler are correct) even in our biological evolution. Over the centuries, various milestone inventions have enabled human beings to expand their social networks. The invention of writing in a reasonably portable form made it possible to convey messages over distances. The invention of various vehicles—from ships, to wagons, to railroads, to automobiles and trucks, to aircraft—both extended the distance of written communication and the speed of its transmission, thereby enhancing humanity's networking capacity.

Samuel Morse's invention of the telegraph in 1837 enabled virtually instantaneous communication, quickly spawning an electric signaling network that enabled a vast human network. Indeed, in 1998, Tom Sandage, science correspondent for *The Economist*, published *The Victorian Internet: The Remarkable Story of the Telegraph and the Nineteenth Century's On-Line Pioneers.* (Sandage, 1998). This first "internet" was expanded even farther, from continent to continent, with the Atlantic cable, which began operation in 1858. Radio came into being late in the nineteenth century, and the Irish-Italian inventor Guglielmo Marconi made the first long-distance overland transmissions before the century ended. He sent the first trans-Atlantic message on December 12, 1901.

Throughout the twentieth century, improvements in radio, the development of television, and the invention of the telephone (including long-distance transmission via landlines, satellites, and cellular relays) steadily increased the range and scope of human networking. But it was the emergence of the Internet at the very end of the twentieth century that provided the electronic platform capable of creating digital-human networks theoretically limited only by the finite nature of the planet's human population. The creation of social networking websites, which (according to Internet historians Danah M. Boyd and Nicole B. Ellison) commenced in 1997 with SixDegrees.com, started to exploit the potential of this platform, and, as of 2012, the most popular social website, Facebook, is a network of more than 900,000 human beings among a global population of just over seven billion (Boyd and Ellison, 2007).

How important are social networks? Christakis and Fowler see them in evolutionary terms and declare, "When we lose our connections, we lose everything" (Christakis and Fowler, 303). All inventions have been, in one way or another, extensions of our natural human faculties. If Christakis and Fowler are right, Internet-enabled social networking is a technology as fundamental to humanity as the wheel. Its potential in just about every area of endeavor is extraordinary: communication, collaboration, sharing of knowledge, development of knowledge, debate, coordination of local and global social, political, aesthetic, intellectual, creative, and emergency action, commerce, commerce, and more commerce. The list is probably as long as any list of productive human activity one might care to compile. For any one of us, networking online not only can mirror, but also can enlarge and amplify the social networking of the offline world. By any measure, online social networking is a liberating technology, which means that it frees us to take risks. As a liberating technology, online social networking is therefore also a technology freighted with hazards.

The Cyberscape of Risk

In his *Complete Guide to Internet Privacy, Anonymity and Security*, author Matthew Bailey observes, "It is often said that if an Internet service is free, you are not the customer, you are the product" (Bailey, 2011). Memorizing the gist of this sentence may well be the single most useful thing you can do to begin playing offense with your privacy and security on the social web. While social networking may be a force of human evolution—and, what is more, a force toward empathy and altruism rather than the dog-eat-dog evolution the poet Tennyson painted as "nature red in tooth and claw"—and while many founding figures of the Internet and even the social web were and remain idealistic champions of open-source free access, websites like MySpace, Facebook, and Google+ are unabashedly for-profit enterprises. You may not think of yourself as a "customer" of these websites, but the myriad merchants, advertisers, marketers, and advertising networks who pay these sites billions of dollars for access to the data each user generates and the consumer profile each user represents are most certainly customers, highly valued, highly sought-after. The product they pay for is you: a targeted consumer, a potential node of profit.

If all of us members of Homo dictyous are participants and potential participants in some network or networks, we are also representatives of capitalist humanity and therefore likewise consumers or potential consumers. Unless you rigorously observe such ideological orthodoxies as Marxism, you should find nothing inherently evil in this. It is good to be a producer, and it can also be good to be a consumer. Purchasing a product you really desire will cost you money, but to the degree that you benefit from it, the purchase will actually make you richer. Nevertheless, your presence on the social web does have a privacy cost, and the use to which the web's paying customers put your privacy—your personal data—may sometimes seem to you unacceptably intrusive or even predatory (see Chapter 7).

For example, in a press release of June 12, 2012, the U.S. Fair Trade Commission (FTC) announced that the data broker Spokeo, Inc. had paid $800,000 to settle FTC charges that it marketed and used personal data from social media sites in violation of the Fair Credit Reporting Act (FCRA). Spokeo used the personal data to create profiles that included contact information, marital status and age range, and in some cases a person's hobbies, ethnicity, religion, participation on social networking sites and photos. These profiles were then marketed to companies in the human resources, background screening, and recruiting industries for use in making decisions on whether to interview or hire a job candidate. The FTC alleged that Spokeo violated the FCRA by failing to ensure the consumer reports were used for legally permissible purposes, by failing to ensure that the information was accurate, and by failing to inform users of the reports that they had obligations under the FCRA (FTC, June 12, 2012).

Not everyone or every entity who sees or makes use of your private data on the social web is a paying customer. As disturbing as the transgressions of legitimate practitioners of e-commerce are, criminal predators may do far worse. The moment you walk out your front door, you expose yourself to the potential for reward and the potential for risk: the possibility of harm. (Indeed, you don't even have to leave your house.) Put yourself or some portion of yourself online in the form of personal data, especially via a social website, and you may increase the potential for reward, but you certainly increase the possibility of harm. The technology of the social web does not create malice, but it does potentially facilitate and amplify it just as it potentially facilitates and amplifies any other human networking encounter or relationship.

The Wider Vulnerability

On June 6, 2012, Gregory S. Saikin of the Baker Hostetler law firm reported that the FBI had issued a warning to users of internet-based social networking concerning hackers—"ranging from con artists to foreign government spies"—who were "looking for every opportunity to exploit the users' identifying and related personal information." The FBI reported that social networking hackers were "carrying out two general tactics, which are often combined." They acted as "social engineers," exploiting personal connections through social networks, and they wrote and manipulated software code "to gain access or install unwanted software on your computer or phone." The FBI was particularly concerned about a trend in which "hackers are impersonating social networking users with the intent to target the user's workplace." In spear phishing aimed at a workplace, the hacker poses as the user in an email to the user's co-workers. The hacker's email contains a link or file with malware that, if opened, launches the malware into the firm's network. Depending on the nature of malware, the assault could provide the hacker access to the firm's data, including trade secrets, security measures, and employee files (Saikin, June 6, 2012).

Out of Control

In Chapters 2 and 3, we considered the nature of Internet privacy and reached the conclusion that, in a digital context, where your presence is translated into a set of data, "privacy" does not so much cease to exist as it ceases to have practical meaning. At best, privacy is represented online as the way a particular collection of personal data is treated. This data set can be viewed, in turn, as a possession, property (private property), a commodity, merchandise, or some combination of all these. As such, it can be controlled, at least to a certain degree, but it is also available for or vulnerable to trade, sharing, sale, misappropriation, and theft.

Understand that your presence—your "privacy" and the presentation of your "self"—is never completely within your control on the social web. What you disclose about yourself may be available to a huge number of strangers now and possibly for years to come. Once your name or your picture is a presence on Facebook or some other social site, you relinquish at least some degree of control over it. Another user may choose to tag a picture with your name, announcing to the world that you are spending time with so-and-so, whether you want that fact known or not. Someone may choose to post that tagged picture on their Facebook timeline, along with an embarrassing story (true or fictitious) about you. Of course, it's just as possible that the post might be accompanied by a wonderful story about you. The point is that you have no control over which it will be.

For many people, relinquishing a degree of control over their image and presence is a minimal cost of creating what they regard as valuable online social connections. For others, it represents a painful intrusion. In a small minority of cases, the intrusion can rise to the level of cyberbullying or cyberstalking. In addition, any personally identifying information (PII) you disclose on the social web may be picked up by companies (such as data aggregators like Spokeo) and exploited by fraudsters, scammers, and identity thieves. Your interaction online, even within Facebook and similar sites, is also subject to malware attacks expressly designed to target social networking sites.

How to Play Offense with Your Personal Data

Understand that adopting the most extreme posture of control toward the social web—staying off Facebook, MySpace, Google+, LinkedIn, Twitter, and the like—does not guarantee that your likeness, name, or presence will not be misused or abused by others. Anyone, for example, can post and tag your photo if it is available somewhere online, even if you have no social website accounts. In fact, you arguably sacrifice more control if you opt out of the social web, because you will not know how others are using or abusing your data until someone happens to tell you about it.

Your privacy—your identity, your "brand," your presence—is valuable. Approach it, therefore, as an asset. There are two circumstances in which an asset will do you absolutely no good. One is if it is lost or stolen. The other is if it is hoarded and never used. The most productive use to be made of an asset is to thoughtfully invest it.

1. Withhold what privacy experts refer to as sensitive unclassified information, which includes PII. Never post on any social website your middle name, your address, or your phone number. If the website requires your date of birth to register, make certain you apply the maximum privacy settings to it. Not that you would do this, but just in case: Never post your Social Security Number, student ID, banking information of any kind, or credit card information. Do not post any such information about other people either, including friends and family members.

2. People share a lot of "routine" information on social websites, quite commonly including vacation and other travel plans. Do not do this. A proclamation of your absence from home is an invitation to burglary. (You don't think burglars have Facebook accounts?) Again, also refrain from posting similar information about others.

3. The majority of Facebook users and users of other social websites post pictures of themselves. That is part of the fun of a social website. It is, however, a far more strategic move to avoid posting any pictures of yourself. Advances in facial recognition software make it possible for strangers of all sorts to match your unidentified photo to your name and, potentially, to a database of information about you. In fact, Facebook recently acquired a facial recognition software company and turned on facial recognition by default. If this makes you uncomfortable, opt out of the default by opening Facebook privacy settings, selecting "Edit Settings" next to "Timeline and Tagging," then selecting "No one" next to "Who sees tag suggestions when photos that look like you are uploaded?" Be sure to click "OK" to finalize the change you made. We'll have more to say

about privacy settings shortly.

4. Post information strategically, not impulsively.

5. Before you post, imagine your family, your parents, your kids, your friends, your boss, your clients, you coworkers, your employees, future potential employers, future potential clients, and future potential spouse(s). Are you perfectly comfortable with each of them seeing or reading what you are about to post?

6. Whatever you post can be copied and reposted by people, organizations, and agencies you do not know and in contexts you never imagined.

7. Whatever you post is very sticky. It might remain on the Internet and accessible to others just about forever. This means it can haunt you and everything you do.

8. Avoid the pitfall of TMI: too much information. Gossip around the office watercooler can be destructive—who's been hired for a new "secret" project, who's sleeping with the boss, and so on. People have been fired for such loose talk, or they have seen their climb up the corporate ladder interrupted or stopped by it. Now imagine the six coworkers clustered around the watercooler multiplied by a factor of several hundred or thousand—among this mob your boss, her husband, the client planning to entrust your firm with the new and no-longer-so-secret project. Before you post, picture yourself onstage, behind a huge microphone, the long lens of a television camera pointed right between your eyes, thick cables running from the mic and the camera to a control room that relays your image and your every word to an audience in every nation of the world and also makes an indelible recording of the whole thing.

9. Be aware of and take time to understand the privacy settings of the social websites you use. On Facebook, for example, anyone can see your so-called "public information," which includes your name, picture (if you post one) or other "profile" image, gender, username, user ID (account number), and networks. Other than these basics, you can make use of the "audience selector" to choose who sees each piece of additional information you post. By using the "View As" tool, you can see how your Facebook profile (timeline) appears to others.

10. Share information cautiously and selectively.

11. Many people believe that the more "friends" they have on a social networking site, the better. Consider instead the strategic advantage of being highly selective.

12. Remember that social websites are subject to the same kind of malware and phishing attacks that afflict the Internet as a whole. Arguably, the laid-back, seemingly benevolent social website environment makes users even more vulnerable to attacks than they would be elsewhere on the web. (Hey, it's a party!) Hackers, phishers, and fraudsters can invade social networking accounts and send fake messages entreating you to disclose PII and financial information or

enticing you to click on an executable file or link, thereby deploying malware. Don't let your guard down.

Damage Control

You recall the fate of Humpty Dumpty. All the king's horses and all the king's men could not put him back together again. In many of life's activities and episodes, once the egg is broken, it stays broken, the spilled beans are spilled for good, and the cat, let out of the bag, does not meekly return to it. This may or may not be the case with damaging items posted by you or others on Facebook and similar social websites.

If you have second thoughts about a post on your wall, go on a wall-scrubbing mission. Remove compromising or questionable photos, delete unsavory or embarrassing comments, purge profanity. If you are preparing for job interviews or college-admission interviews, be aware that as many as 90 percent of interviewers will look you up on the social web. Scrub hard, very hard. Remove anything you would not say or show in the interview itself. If your "like" of an X-rated movie risks giving offense to a prospective employer, scrub it out. Consider taking the time to rethink and reset your privacy controls to exclude any outspoken or out-of-control friends who might post questionable items on your wall.

Be thorough, but also be aware that some or all of what you scrub may already have been picked up, copied, and reposted by others. In some cases, search engines may have cached various items, which could then show up on a Google or other search. The web is a very big place. You can't expect to clean it all.

Privacy: A Communal Affair

On social networks, privacy, as *Atlantic* writer Megan Garber explains, is a "communal affair ... something that all of us, as individuals and as a group, are responsible for." Privacy "concerns ... expand with network effects." Photos, in particular, "can reveal not only a user's favorite places, vacation spots, and closest friends and family members, but also that same information for the other members of the user's network. For those who have an interest, commercial or otherwise, in figuring out users' identities and interests and overall persona on Facebook, your data can reveal your friends' data—and vice versa." Citing a study from the University of Minas Gerais, Brazil, Garber points out that "photo tags can work effectively as pieces of the identity puzzle, helping 'malicious attackers' ... to augment the picture painted by friends and photos alone." The University of Minas Gerais researchers concluded that attackers "who possess privacy-attacking algorithms" may use the tagged photos to pinpoint an individual's position among others in his network, thereby extracting information about identity, affiliations, likes, and dislikes of everyone in that network. Garber concludes that members of social networks will need to conceive "of themselves not simply as users sharing their own information, but as actors and influencers who are responsible for the network at large" (Garber, April 26, 2012). In other words, protecting privacy in online social networks must be seen as the collaborative—networked—responsibility of those networks.

Cyberbullying and Cyberstalking

Cyberbullying may be broadly defined as using the Internet and other digital communications technologies to harass, intimidate, or otherwise harm others in a deliberate and repeated manner. Cyberbullying can be a criminal offense and is currently subject to some forty-five separate state laws throughout the United States.

The term *cyberbullying* is generally applied to cases involving minors, whereas *cyberstalking* is usually used in cases involving adults; however, in practice, there are some other distinctions between these categories of behavior. According to the National Crime Prevention Council, cyberbullying occurs "when the Internet, cell phones or other devices are used to send or post text or images intended to hurt or embarrass another person" (National Crime Prevention Council, "Cyberbullying"). Cyberstalking against adults is typically even more malicious, carrying with it what most people would consider a sharper criminal intent or, at least, an intent that reaches beyond mere harassment. Cyberstalkers generally use social media and online information sites to damage or destroy their victim's reputation, deliberately threatening his or her career, employment, and even physical safety. The objective is to turn public opinion against the victim. Specific cyberstalking actions include making false accusations, making threats, engaging in identity theft, causing damage to data, framing the victim (for example, by faking solicitation of minors for sex), and illegally monitoring and eavesdropping to gather damaging information for purposes of harassment.

Social networking sites are particularly fertile fields for cyberbullying and cyberstalking. Users of the sites disclose large amounts of personal, even intimate information. They often "confide" to their Facebook page as if they were writing in a secret diary kept under lock and key. They also post pictures of themselves and their friends, disclose contact details (email, SMS, phone numbers), geographical information (home, school, office), and a wealth of biographical information. Users often comment freely and even provocatively. Relationships and issues of sexual behavior and sexual identity are major topics of discussion. Users also casually "like" books, music, and movies – thereby publicly linking their entertainment preferences to their profiles. In short, social networks provide both the ammunition and the battlefield for cyberbullying and cyberstalking.

Social websites also give the bullies and stalkers an unfair advantage. Attackers can be anonymous and they can strike 24/7. Social networks and blogs

68

make it quite easy for an aggressor to—

- Post nasty messages or threats
- Pointedly invade the victim's privacy
- Upload compromising or embarrassing images, both authentic and "photoshopped"
- Use personal information and "secrets" to out or otherwise expose the victim publicly
- Defame the victim
- Frame the victim with false information, "evidence," and accusations
- Create a bogus Facebook page (or its equivalent on some other site) for the purpose of ostracizing the victim, excluding her from a circle of friends
- Create a page or even a blog posing as the victim and posting inflammatory messages as if they originated with the victim
- Create a page purporting to present the results of a poll or survey that insults, degrades, or condemns the victim
- Use the social networking site to post compromising photos and videos obtained surreptitiously with webcams and similar technology

There are significant criminal and civil liabilities associated both with cyberbullying and cyberstalking, but by the time the issue reaches a courtroom, the victim has certainly suffered damage, perhaps irreversible. As individual users, we can all learn to play offense with our personal data, as outlined in this chapter. Social networking sites are intended to be fun. They therefore strive to create a non-threatening environment. The unintended consequence of this is that users are invited to let down their public guard. The situation is analogous to the manner in which some vacationers transform themselves from streetwise citizens into soft targets for crime by allowing their good judgment and self-preservation instincts to take a holiday. Social networking is all about exposure. On the positive, productive side, we expose ourselves to all that the outside world has to offer. On the downside, we expose ourselves to attack and victimization.

Beyond practicing commonsense caution and prudence as individual users of the social network, we must insist that these networks themselves discourage cyberbullying and cyberstalking. None of us should pass along cyberbullying messages. All of us—not just victims—should block communication with cyberbullies and cyberstalkers. Responsible users should use the social networks to discuss and actively discourage cyberbullying and cyberstalking. Facebook and other social websites provide the means for each of us to "report abuse." In the case of Facebook, a user can report abuse by selecting the "Report" link that is located near any photos, videos, or posting that the user judges to be offensive or inappropriate. The report link provides categories to classify the content, and reports are reviewed by a "user operations team." In this way, Facebook seeks to support the standards it has created in its Statement of Rights and Responsibilities. As in society itself, social websites offer the potential for abuse as well as efficient self-policing of behavior and actions. The same technologies and social structures that create the hazards provide the means of condemning, curbing, and even eliminating them.

CHAPTER SIX
Criminal Predators

In everyday language we often speak of doing things online versus doing things "in real life" (sometimes shorthanded to "IRL"). The distinction is of course misleading, since, for a long time now, life mediated by electronic devices and life unmediated by them are equally aspects of "real life." Whether mediated or unmediated by electronic devices, the communications and other transactions we engage in are real and have real-life results and consequences. Better, perhaps, to distinguish between digital and physical activities, recognizing that both classes of action and behavior are equally real in their effects.

In Chapter 5, we discussed what we have classified as antisocial online crimes, including stalking, sexual predation, and cyberbullying. In this chapter, we will consider two classes of online crime that are even more common: identity theft and fraud.

The Digital Master Crimes
In the physical realm, larceny comes in a dazzling variety. These crimes encompass such forms of "the wrongful acquisition of personal property from another person" (the generic definition of larceny) as theft by taking, theft by trickery or deceit, burglary, robbery, armed robbery, mugging, pickpocketing, purse snatching, shoplifting, breaking and entering, smash-and-grab, auto theft, and on and on.

In the digital world, the range of larceny is more limited. It is typically either the result of identity theft or other fraud—or of some mixture of the two. From these two crimes, a whole catalog of larceny events opens up.

Identity Theft versus Identity Fraud
Strictly speaking, identity theft might be better described as identity fraud, since the crimes involved are those of impersonation and misrepresentation. If you become a victim, your identity is not literally stolen; rather, sufficient personally identifiable information (PII) is compromised to allow a criminal to misrepresent himself or herself as you, almost always for the purpose of larceny. Because "identity theft" has been the common term for the crime since the phrase was coined in 1964, however, we will use it here.

Scope of Identity Theft

According to the *2011 Identity Fraud Survey Report* (Javelin, 2011), 8.1 million American adults were victims of identity theft in 2010. Although this actually represented a 28 percent decrease from 2009, the average out-of-pocket loss per consumer increased dramatically: in 2010 it was up 63 percent from 2009, to $631 per incident in 2010 from $387 per incident in 2009. It may well be that fraudsters are becoming more selective and more efficient.

Types of Identity Theft

The most widespread identity theft involves compromise of your financial identity. This results when an identity thief obtains such personal identifying information (PII) as a Social Security number, driver's license number, date of birth, credit card account numbers, bank account numbers, and the like. With some or all of these, your financial accounts, including bank accounts and credit accounts, are at grave risk, as are your good name and credit.

An increasingly common subtype of financial identity theft is governmental identity theft. Typically, this crime is committed to obtain a fraudulent federal income tax refund. A perpetrator who obtains your Social Security Number can create a fraudulent return that shows a refund due. Your first indication that this may have occurred is usually an IRS notice that "you" have filed more than one tax return in a single year or that IRS records show wages from an employer unknown to you.

In medical identity theft, a perpetrator may obtain medical services using your PII, so that you, not the fraudster, is billed. In government benefit fraud, someone uses your PII to apply for and receive government benefits (Social Security, Medicare, Medicaid, and so on). Typically, you, the victim, discover this crime when you apply for benefits, only to be turned down because you have "used up" your benefits for the month.

Even more devastating may be criminal medical identity theft, in which you may be held responsible for the criminal acts of another. For example, a female drug addict, having entered a hospital using your PII, gives birth to an addicted infant and flees the hospital, abandoning the infant. The police knock on your door, arrest you, and consign your children to the safekeeping of Child Protective Services. How long will it take you and an attorney to straighten this out? What hardship (on you and your family) and costs will it involve?

Child identity theft occurs when a fraudster uses a child's PII to obtain something of benefit—often, a credit card, loan, or line of credit. The primary identifier misappropriated is the Social Security Number. Some fraudsters go far beyond using the child's PII to obtain credit. They actually assume the child's identity (commit "identity assumption") in order to disappear from creditors or the law, restart their financial lives after defaulting on major loans, or, in the case of undocumented alien workers, secure employment and evade deportation.

Some of these fraudsters acquire the PII of deceased children, searching for and obtaining death certificates on the Internet. When they find someone who matches the impostor's age, they go about either obtaining counterfeit documents, including a forged birth certificate, or they may even be able to obtain a genuine birth certificate via online channels.

Although the discovery of most identity theft takes some time—typically weeks or even months—the discovery of child identity theft may take years. A parent may not discover it until he or she attempts to open a savings account or college fund for the child. A teenager might be refused a driver's license because one has already been issued to a person holding his Social Security Number. The police may even knock on the door with an arrest warrant—for your toddler.

Consequences of Identity Theft

On average, a victim of identity theft spends 330 hours resolving the problem—a loss of more than forty-one eight-hour working days. In the meantime, loan applications may be denied, the victim may endure harassment from debt collectors, merchants, and even law enforcement. Job and college applications may be jeopardized. In testimony before the U.S. Senate Committee Hearing on the Judiciary Subcommittee on Technology, Terrorism and Government Information, identity theft victim Michelle Brown reported that "over a year and a half from January 1998 through July 1999, one individual impersonated me to procure over $50,000 in goods and services. Not only did she damage my credit, but she escalated her crimes to a level that I never truly expected: she engaged in drug trafficking. The crime resulted in my erroneous arrest record, a warrant out for my arrest, and eventually, a prison record when she was booked under my name as an inmate in the Chicago Federal Prison" (Brown, 2000).

Offline Vulnerabilities

Identity theft is hardly unique to the age of the Internet. Ancient and classical literature is full of mistaken identity and impersonation, and the term identity theft itself dates to 1964, well before the advent of the personal computer, let alone the Internet. Even today, much identity theft takes place—or begins—offline. It is important to understand that safe computing habits, while a crucial defense against identity theft, are no guarantee of immunity. Identity theft, like commerce, research, and communication, is not a product of the Internet; however, as it does with commerce, research, and communication, the Internet removes friction, amplifying, broadening, and accelerating the possibilities, the extent, the reach, the speed, and the consequences of fraud.

Before you even sit down at your computer, understand the most common offline methods fraudsters use to compromise your identity:

Dumpster diving—rummaging through your trash to recover personal information.
Countermeasures: Shred all bills, credit card solicitations, discarded credit cards, and the like before discarding them. Use a cross-cut shredder, which will make it virtually impossible to reassemble the documents.

Dumpster diving—for discarded electronics, including computers and cell phones that still have hard drives or SIM cards on board and intact.
Countermeasures: Before you discard or recycle your old electronics, wipe out all data. The easiest way is to "zero-fill" discarded hard disks, a procedure that overwrites the entire hard disk with zeroes, thereby obliterating all trace of other data. The major hard disk vendors offer software tools, online for free, to do this. Wiping memory cards, USB flash drives, and solid state drives (SSDs) requires other software, such as DiskWipe (available free at www.roadkil.net) and special utilities often included by vendors of SSDs. As for smartphone and cell phone SIM cards, cut them up into little tiny pieces before discarding them.

Exploiting public records—fraudsters may be able to find out a lot about you by visiting City Hall and the like or by using perfectly legal people-search sites, such as BeenVerified.Com. In combination with other information, these sources can facilitate identity theft.
Countermeasure: See "Playing Offense," below.

Pickpocketing, burglary, mail theft—these and similar crimes may yield debit and credit cards, identification cards, passports, and the like.
Countermeasures: Secure your person, secure your house, collect your mail every day—and consider renting a post office box for added security. Also see "Playing Offense," below.

Stealing checks—often out of a mailbox—to acquire banking information, including account numbers, and routing numbers.
Countermeasures: Secure your checks carefully. Use paperless statements, so that neither statements nor canceled checks end up in your mailbox.

Shoulder surfing—A fraudster looks over your shoulder as you type in your ATM PIN number, credit card PIN, or other password. This is low-tech, but quite efficient.
Countermeasure: Watch your back (literally).

Skimming—Criminals can readily obtain "skimmers," hand-held card readers, with which they can clone debit and credit cards. This is a common

problem in restaurants. You give your credit card to a waiter, he takes it away —pausing, before he gets to the cashier, to skim it—then returns it to you. More than likely, you'll include a generous tip.
Countermeasure: Use cash whenever possible.

ATM skimming—Sophisticated and determined criminals have actually installed card skimmers that masquerade as ATM machines, gas pump card readers, and the like, stealing card data from unsuspecting users. The fraudulent devices are often virtually impossible to distinguish from legitimate debit/credit card readers.
Countermeasures: Use ATMs at the bank. Avoid small, freestanding machines installed in convenience stores, gas stations, and the like. Do not use any device that appears strange or questionable.

Contactless skimming—A new generation of sophisticated credit card readers can acquire data wirelessly from any RFID (radio-frequency identification) card, RFID-enabled passport, or mobile phone with an RFID microSD card.
Countermeasure: Use shielded envelopes, wallets, or carrying cases.

Advertising bogus jobs in newspapers, neighborhood flyers, and the like—in print or online—that solicit and obtain applicant PII, including entire resumes or social security numbers.
Countermeasures: Check out any potential employer thoroughly before you respond to an employment ad or other offer. Remember what your mother or uncle or somebody somewhere, sometime told you: If it looks too good to be true, it is.

Pretexting—In what is something of an art, a fraudster—receptionist, customer service rep, hotel desk clerk, or the like—tricks individuals into disclosing PII relating to his or her target. The hit Steven Spielberg film *Catch Me If You Can* (2002) featured Leonardo DiCaprio as the youthful forger and master of pretexting Frank Abagnale Jr. You can also find detailed pretexting examples in Frank M. Ahearn's *How to Disappear: Erase Your Digital Footprint, Leave False Trails, and Vanish without a Trace* (Guilford, CT: Lyon's Press, 2010).
Countermeasure(s): Reveal to strangers as little about yourself as possible.

Online Vulnerabilities
Online attacks fall into two major categories:

1. Privacy breaches at government agencies, financial institutions, credit bureaus, corporations, and other entities that have files of your data. We can call these third-party breaches.

2. Direct attacks against you—your computer, your home or office network, your data.

Third-Party Breaches

We hear or read news reports about "third-party breaches" with distressing regularity. For example, on March 30, 2012, Reuters reported that "four giant card-payment processors and large U.S. banks that issue debit and credit cards were hit by a data-security breach after third-party services provider Global Payments Inc. discovered its systems were compromised by unauthorized access." At the time of the report, it was "not immediately clear how many cardholders became victims of the breach," which affected all the major card companies and the banks and other franchises associated with them. In the short run, the big losers were the card companies, merchants, card issuers, and Global Payments Inc. Card companies lost share value on the stock exchanges, and merchants, card issuers, and Global Payments were on the hook for any financial losses consumers might suffer. Nevertheless, any consumers whose accounts had been compromised would be faced with having to clean up the mess—typically a tedious, time-consuming, and expensive process.

Early in 2012, in cooperation with international law-enforcement agencies including the U.S. Secret Service, Verizon made public a Data Breach Investigations Report (Verizon, 2012), which detailed 855 major incidents involving 174 million compromised records worldwide—the second-highest data loss since 2004, when Verizon started tracking incidents. What accounts for these massive data breaches? The 2012 report summarized their nature this way:

98 percent stemmed from external agents (some of whom may have colluded with internal employees).

4 percent implicated internal employees (some of whom may have colluded with external agents).

Fewer than 1 percent of the breaches were committed by business partners.

58 percent of all data theft in 2011 was tied to "activist groups."

Breaches were carried out by means of—
Hacking: 81 percent
Malware: 69 percent
Physical attacks: 10 percent
"Social tactics" (social engineering, deception): 7 percent
"Privilege misuse": 5 percent

From the statistics above, it is clear that many breaches involved more than one of the listed methods. Common among the breaches were the following characteristics—

79 percent of victims were targets of opportunity; they presented some obvious weakness or vulnerability.

96 percent of attacks "were not highly difficult."

94 percent of data compromised involved servers.

85 percent of breaches took weeks or more to discover.

92 percent of incidents were discovered by a third party.

97 percent of breaches "were avoidable through simple or intermediate controls."

96 percent of victims that were subject to PCI DSS (the Payment Card Industry Data Security Standard, the information security standard for organizations that handle consumer cardholder information) "had not achieved compliance" with those standards.

Even a layperson glancing at these statistics can recognize some obvious vulnerabilities as well as the commonsense precautions that would have likely addressed them. The Verizon report specifically suggests that data managers, among other things, "eliminate unnecessary data" and "keep tabs on the rest," and that they ensure that "essential controls are met" and "regularly check that they remain so." The report also advises monitoring "event logs" to detect unusual or unauthorized activity. The point is that a very large number of data breaches are readily preventable. That should be good news—except that, as a consumer, how much can you do to prevent these breaches of third-party security that affect your personal data? The answer is, not very much.

1. You can go to the websites of the cardholders and banks you deal with, read about their commitment to security, and you can ask questions about how they protect your security.

2. You can make a point of dealing only with companies that promote security and privacy protection, and you can deliver feedback telling them that security and privacy played a big part in your decision to do business with them.

While you cannot do much to increase security at the firms that hold your data, you can take steps to minimize your exposure within these firms:

1. Make it a practice to provide companies and other organizations with only the minimum of data necessary to do business with them. You may want to think twice before filling out survey or market research forms, for example.

2. Keep an accurate and thorough record of all of your credit lines, loans, and credit card accounts, including date opened, account numbers, and customer service contact numbers.

3. Hold credit and credit card accounts to a minimum.

4. Keep physical control of all your credit cards and statements.

5. Rigorously coordinate credit use with members of your family.

6. Carefully review each and every credit card and bank statement you receive.

7. If any transaction seems strange or out of place, call customer service immediately.

Direct Attacks against You

We have already reviewed the major direct malware and network security threats in Chapter 4. Beyond these software- and hardware-based threats are those founded on the human element and that therefore resemble "traditional" larceny more closely. The main types of attacks include phishing and social engineering.

Phishing

Phishing is the impersonation of trusted organizations in emails, SMS text messages, phone calls, or other forms of communication in order to dupe victims into disclosing their personal information or login credentials, typically on a fake corporate website or data collection form. The act of counterfeiting a legitimate-looking email or website is often called spoofing.

We trust the legitimacy of big, brand-name corporations, especially banks and credit card companies. We trust them even more if we regularly do business with them. The very sight of a familiar logo and website lulls us into comfortable compliance. Requests for "verification" of account information, Social Security numbers, account numbers, birthdates, addresses, and the like seem legitimate, even matter-of-fact, when framed by the familiar logos and website trappings we have seen a hundred times. This is precisely what phishing fraudsters rely on. Counterfeiting currency takes a lot of talent. Forging a check is a genuine skill. Faking—or "spoofing"—a legitimate-looking email or website requires only a basic knowledge of the web markup language known as HTML. As scams go, phishing is quite easy and quite convincing.

A fraudster may send out mass faked emails, knowing that a certain percentage of recipients will indeed have an account with ABC Bank or the MyCredit credit card company. These recipients are especially vulnerable to the appeal in the email. But these days, when so many of us have so many accounts, a fake email posing as a communication from any major company may be sufficiently persuasive to dupe a victim. Of course, the most sophisticated phishers do not rely on random chance, but instead engage in spear phishing: phishing expeditions based on some information about you and targeting you specifically, by name. These scams naturally appear most legitimate.

Despite the veneer of legitimacy a phishing email may have, certain hallmarks betray it as a scam. These include:

1. A strange email address. A legitimate email should come from an email address that reflects the name of the legitimate corporation, not some cryptic arrangement of letters and numbers or a first name, or a nickname. Some faked addresses will actually include some part of a legitimate or legitimate-looking name. Move your cursor over the address, without clicking, and an entirely different name may show up.

2. A legitimate-looking website with a strange URL. As with emails, a legitimate corporate website usually has a recognizable URL. The ABC Bank website will have a URL that is something like www.abcbank.com, not www.nickandtony123.com and not www.abeeseebank.com. If you get an email with an HTML-based message that contains a link to even a legitimate-looking URL, examine the URL closely. Let your cursor hover over the link. Don't click, but do look at what pops up. Chances are it will be a strange-looking link that is obviously not from ABC Bank.

3. Trick links. Sophisticated scammers will make an effort to spoof a legitimate link. Let's say you actually do business with IOU Loan Company, which has a website with the URL www.IOU.com. A phishing scammer's email may link to www.IoU.com, substituting the numeral zero for the letter O.

4. Message content. Most phishing emails have an urgent or threatening message and tone, typically warning that your account will be deactivated or suspended if you do not click on the link, go to the website, and validate or confirm or update your account information. Be aware that, for this very reason, most banks and credit card firms will not send emails with links to a website. Instead, they will ask you to make a phone call or to go to your browser to log onto the corporate website.

5. Message tone, grammar, and literacy. Some phishing emails are very sophisticated. Most, however, can't quite pull off the professional tone of a legitimate message. Many originate offshore and are therefore less than fluent in the English language or idiom. They often appear as if a non-native speaker has composed them.

6. The request. Phishing emails usually request a great deal of confidential account information and PII. No legitimate firm will make such a request.

One preemptive way to avoid being phished is to make use of the phishing filters your web browser, email client, webmail service, or Internet security suite may offer (often, your spam filter will also serve as a phishing filter). Like anti-spam filters, phishing filters work to screen out email identified as phishing email and send it into your spam or junk mail folder. No phishing filter is foolproof, but most will stop many, perhaps even most, phishing emails from ever reaching your inbox.

If you do run across a phishing email, don't panic—but also do not click on any links, even out of curiosity. Generally, the phisher wants you to click on the link, then fill out the forms on the webpage that opens up. This will give him all the information he needs to compromise some or all of your accounts. Usually, if you don't fill in the information, the phishing expedition ends in failure; however, some phishing emails double as vehicles to deploy malware (see Chapter 4), which means that simply clicking on the link may result in a virus or Trojan infection.

If you are taken in and do enter your account information on a fake website, act immediately to change whatever passwords you supplied. You need to be quick. An alert hacker can log on to your own account or accounts before you do and lock you out of them. This is called hijacking.

And it gets worse. If a hacker can use the information you provide to compromise your email account before you can change its password, she can gain control of your contact list. Even if you change your password quickly, the hacker may have sufficient time to gather enough PII on you to submit successful "forgotten password" and "forgotten username" requests using your information and, in this way, crack any new password you may have set.

The key is not to get phished in in the first place and, if you are, to change all passwords immediately, beginning with your email account password. Once you have taken all the urgent steps, consider reporting the phishing attempt to the Anti-Phishing Working Group (APWG) at www.antiphishing.org, which will at least alert others to the scam and possibly make life a little more difficult for the fraudster.

Social Engineering

Phishing is often classified as a specific variety of social engineering, which is the art of persuading or manipulating people into divulging confidential information or performing other acts inimical to their security and beneficial to the interests of the scammer. Most of the time, social engineering, whatever specific form it may take, has as its objective obtaining a computer system password, an account password, a PIN, and other account access information. Hackers hailed as geek geniuses—people such as Kevin Mitnick, at the time of his arrest in 1995 America's "most-wanted" computer criminal—often observe that it is much easier to trick someone into revealing a password than it is to "hack into" a system by technological means.

The most widely used form of social engineering is pretexting, which involves inventing a persuasive story or scenario—the "pretext"—to deceive the victim into divulging the desired information. A pretexter may impersonate the police, a tax authority, a debt collector, or an accounts payable manager (who just wants to contact so-and-so to pay him the $10,000 he is owed). The objective of these impersonations is to convey sufficient legitimacy, authority, and urgency to overcome the victim's natural suspicions and thereby give him a motive to divulge information he would otherwise closely guard.

In another common social engineering attack, known as quid pro quo (something for something), an attacker calls random numbers at a company or organization he has targeted, claiming to be calling back from "tech support." If the organization is sufficiently large and diverse, the probability is high that the attacker will eventually encounter somebody who has actually called tech support with a problem. When he scores such a hit, the attacker will then walk the victim through a putative problem-solving process, which is actually a process of typing commands that give the attacker access to the computer system or allow him to install some piece of malware.

In another version of quid pro quo, employees at a target firm are persuaded to divulge a password or account number in answer to a fake survey. As inducement to take the survey, the victim may be offered a modest gift or token of some sort.

Another version of phishing takes advantage of our familiarity with Interactive Voice Response (IVR) phone systems. In IVR phishing, the victim responds to a request—usually sent via a legitimate-looking email—to call his bank or credit card company at a toll-free number for the purpose of verifying account information. The call is answered by an official-sounding IVR system, which requires the victim to log in using his PIN number. Often, the PIN is deliberately rejected (but recorded!), and the IVR requests an account number, followed by the Social Security Number "associated with the account for verification." By the end of the call, all of the victim's account and authorizing information has been collected. In even more sophisticated schemes, the IVR portion of the call may be followed by transfer to a "live operator," who, impersonating a customer service representative, asks questions that further compromise the victim's identity.

Chapter 8 includes discussion of another social engineering technique, baiting, in which the scammer leaves a provocatively labeled CD ROM or USB flash drive in a public location within (for example) a building housing the offices of a major corporation. Sooner or later, an employee will notice the item, see the label ("Executive Salaries, XYZ Corp. CONFIDENTIAL"), and, unable to fight down his rising curiosity, will pop the drive into the USB port on his desktop computer. In this way, the computer and the entire corporate network will become infected with a Trojan or other piece of malware that will give the attacker remote access to confidential corporate files.

Most social engineering schemes involve at least a certain level of con-artist skill and, at the very least, an ability to think on one's feet. One of the simplest forms of social engineering requires nothing more than the ability to walk inconspicuously behind another human being. In tailgating, an unauthorized person gains access to a restricted area by walking close behind someone who has a legitimate passcard, passkey, or passcode. If the tailgater is sufficiently nonchalant, chances are the person ahead of him will not question his presence. And even if he should question it, the tailgater may quickly flash some item, as if it were a legitimate ID. Once inside the restricted area, the tailgater may physically steal data (folders, USB drives, etc.), may shoulder surf employees at their computers, or may log into an idle computer on a vacant desktop.

Not surprisingly, the social web—and such sites as Facebook and LinkedIn—are often used to carry out social engineering scams. These vulnerabilities are discussed in Chapter 5.

Playing Offense

Identity theft can be a costly, time-consuming problem to deal with. It is far better to play offense with your personal data than merely respond defensively to threats or clean up after attacks. Playing offense requires you to take the preventative steps outlined in Chapters 4 and 5. In addition to these, it calls for the exercise of common sense and a strategically stingy, even miserly, attitude toward your data.

Make the minimum number of disclosures necessary to do business.

Avoid responding to requests for information in an automatic, kneejerk manner. Ponder before you disclose.

Beware of responding to requests for information from individuals, companies, and organizations you don't recognize or with whom you don't regularly do business.

Respond to queries concerning business you initiate. If someone else makes contact with you and seeks information, be circumspect.

Banks, credit card companies, and merchants are not likely ever to ask you to "verify" account information unless you yourself have initiated the call or the contact for a specific reason.

Banks, credit card companies, and merchants are not likely ever to ask you to reveal your password or PIN, unless you yourself have initiated a transaction requiring such identification.

Know your employer's security policy. Abide by it rigorously. Make no exceptions.

Be more than willing to cause inconvenience to others. Require others to follow the rules. Obtain satisfactory verification before agreeing to disclose any sensitive information. Do no "favors" and make no exceptions.

Playing offense with your personal data also means keeping thorough and accurate records of all your financial accounts, personal and business:

Review all financial statements as soon as you receive them.

Record all expenditures and payments. Know what comes in, what goes out, from whom, to whom, and when.

Obtain and review your major credit bureau reports regularly, at least yearly. Erroneous, inaccurate, and outdated information is common on these reports. Whether the misinformation is the result of error or criminal conduct, it can prove costly. Immediately challenge anything that looks wrong to you. The "big three" bureaus are Equifax (www.equifax.com), Experian (www.experian.com), and TransUnion (www.transunion.com). Reports from all three should be reviewed annually—or immediately, if you suspect a problem. By law, each of these big three bureaus must provide you with one free credit report each year. You can find out how to get your free credit reports by visiting www.ftc.gov/bcp/edu/microsites/freereports/index.shtml. To be even more thorough, also check your credit report at Innovis (www.innovis.com) and MicroBilt (www.microbilt.com). Health-related and health insurance-related data is the specialty of MIB Group. Request your file free of charge at www.mib.com. You may also want to keep tabs on at least one other data broker, LexisNexis, a major data supplier to attorneys and the legal profession. Unlike the credit-reporting agencies, LexisNexis generally permits you to opt out from its databases through a "request for suppression." Log onto www.lexisnexis.com or call 1-888-AT-LEXIS to submit such a request.

Bear this in mind: In 2011, 37 percent of data breach cases involved malicious attacks, but 39 percent were the direct result of user negligence (Symantec).

Close to Home

Most discussions of data breaches and assaults on online privacy and security focus on the misdeeds of outside agents and agencies—essentially actors who are total strangers to us. Difficult as it may be for many of us to accept, however, some threats may come from much closer to home:

If you work with data you want to keep strictly confidential, use passwords and encryption to protect it. Do not reveal the password to anyone, family and friends included. Curiosity need not be malicious, but family and friends do have disputes, do sometimes fight, do sometimes seek power over one another. Even more often, they can be just plain careless with confidences and secrets.

If you don't want others in your family or in your place of business to have direct access to your computer, protect the log-on with a password—and keep it secret.

If your computer is accessible to others in your home or office, make it your practice to check the "most recently used" (MRU) items in Windows. This will show you what files and documents have been accessed recently by you or by others—unless the last person to use the computer has deliberately cleared his or her MRU history. You might also want to look at the "history" section of your Internet browser and even try out search terms of interest by typing them into the browser's search bar and seeing how the autofill feature (if it is active) completes the search word. Finally, consider rummaging around in the Trash or Recycle Bin. Unless a previous user has been careful to empty it, you will have a record of recently deleted items.

The best defense against privacy and security attacks that originate from close to home is to secure access to your computer with a login password and encryption of sensitive files. Beyond this, you may want to install monitoring software. The most highly reviewed popular packages include Spytech SpyAgent, WebWatcher, Spector Pro, SniperSpy, eBlaster, PC Pandora Pro, Elite Keylogger Pro, IamBigBrother, and XPCSpy Pro. Most of these provide a combination of Web monitoring, monitoring of user activity, and reporting—including keyword logging. Most also allow you to selectively filter and block websites and social network use.

Despite the names of some monitoring programs, the software cannot be used legally as spyware. To legitimately monitor a computer, you must either own the machine or have written consent to monitor from all adult users of the monitored computer. (You may, however, legally install monitoring software on your minor child's computer.) In most cases, employers may legally deploy monitoring software on all business-owned computers. But stop to think. Even if you are acting within the law, the relationship cost of stealthily deploying monitoring software can be high, even destructive. Neither family members, friends, nor employees and business associates are likely to feel good about being spied on. Most experts agree that clearly informing users that the computer they are using is monitored may, if anything, prevent inappropriate, non-secure, or even criminal behavior. In the end, the best strategic moves are to restrict the use of your computer to yourself and other thoroughly trusted users, employ strong password protection, encrypt all sensitive files, and, if necessary, block access to selected websites. The prevention of a breach is the only absolutely effective step you can take to escape the consequences of a breach.

CHAPTER SEVEN
Commercial Predators

On June 28, 2012, Senator Jay Rockefeller (D-WV), chairman of the Committee on Commerce, Science, and Transportation, issued a statement on e-commerce industry self-regulation and privacy protections online. He did not paint a pretty picture for consumers, pointing out that both "the Obama Administration and the Federal Trade Commission (FTC) testified [before his committee] that Americans have very few rights to protect their information online." Unlike many of his legislative and regulatory counterparts on the European Union's European Commission (EC), Rockefeller took pains to "recognize that consumer information is the currency of the web." He expressed understanding and appreciation that advertising revenue makes it possible to supply "much of the rich content of the Internet ... to consumers for free." He also appreciated "that advertising is more effective and valuable to companies when it is tailored to match consumers' individual interests and tastes." He should have added that such advertising is also more "effective and valuable" for consumers, who thereby receive information they can actually use to make informed purchasing decisions. However, even if the senator had added this, he would have been justified in doing precisely what he did: call for consumers to be accorded "some degree of control over their personal, often sensitive, online information" (Rockefeller, June 28, 2012).

Bad News
One thing is for certain: There never seems to be a shortage of news stories about some new predatory e-commerce threat to online privacy. Senator Rockefeller was able to cite the "story we heard this week about Orbitz targeting more expensive hotel rooms to Mac users," a market segment that tends to have more disposable income than PC users. The senator commented that the story "should remind all of us that companies will always be tempted to misuse the consumer information they collect" (Rockefeller, June 28, 2012). But did Orbitz really "misuse" the information? The travel site did not actually withhold less expensive offerings from Mac users; it simply put the more expensive offerings higher on the list that the Mac-owning consumer's search returned. It surely could be argued that a consumer willing to pay a premium (some actually call it an "Apple tax") to own a Mac rather than a roughly equivalent PC is a consumer interested in paying for deluxe travel accommodations. If this is the case, Orbitz is seeking

to serve its customers' likely wishes by listing luxury above economy in its offerings. Arguably, the Orbitz practice is not so much predatory as it is good customer service in the digital age. To be sure, by "upselling," the company receives more revenue at the expense of the consumer, but the consumer likely receives more satisfaction: for greater cost he gains greater value. If a product creates customer satisfaction, both the producer and the consumer win.

Yet Orbitz failed to present its value proposition this way, and so the news story came across as a tale of a sneaky, insidious, unfair, and even predatory business practice. Senator Rockefeller's remarks did include a hopeful mention of an announcement by the Digital Advertising Alliance (DAA) "that its member online companies will stop collecting personal information from those consumers who tell them to stop doing so." Giving consumers this kind of control would go a long way toward avoiding the kind of impression Orbitz had created; however, Senator Rockefeller continued, "DAA also states that companies will still collect information on these very same consumers for 'market research' and 'product development.'" He pointed out that "These exceptions are so broad, they could swallow the rule. 'Market research' and 'product development' could encompass almost anything" (Rockefeller, June 28, 2012). In neither the Orbitz story, nor the DAA announcement, Senator Rockefeller said, is it certain that the consumer is actually being victimized

Take a look at more news from the summer of 2012.

On June 26, the Associated Press reported that Facebook "upset users" by deleting subscribers' preferred email addresses and replacing them with "@Facebook.com" email addresses. The social media giant did not ask subscribers' permission before making the change to the content of their Facebook pages. Even worse, the motive for the move is not difficult to discern. If subscribers are compelled to use Facebook email addresses to communicate with each other, Facebook positions itself to gather even more commercially valuable data about its subscribers (AP, June 26, 2012).

On June 28, an *InfoWorld* headline warned, "Top sites are covertly cramming cookies down users' throats." Reporter Ted Samson revealed that a Keynote survey "found that 86 percent of the 269 leading news, financial, travel, and retail websites install third-party tracking cookies on users' machines, and 60 percent of the sites have at least one tracker that violates good industry privacy practices" (Samson, June 28, 2012).

On the same day, June 28, in an article published in *PC World* and *InfoWorld*, reporter Mark Sullivan warned that when "you update your Facebook page, 'Like' something on a website, apply for a credit card, click on an ad, listen to an MP3, or comment on a YouTube video, you are feeding a huge and growing beast with an insatiable appetite for your personal data, a beast that always craves more. Virtually every piece of personal information that you provide online (and much that you provide offline) will end up being bought and sold, segmented, packaged, analyzed, repackaged, and sold again" to "a menagerie of advertisers, marketers, ad networks, data brokers, website publishers, social networks, and online tracking and targeting companies, for all of which the main currency—what they buy, sell, and trade—is personal data" (Sullivan, June 28, 2012).

The databases, Sullivan explains, "pull user information from a long list of sources—everything from birth certificates to browsing history to Facebook 'Likes.'—and they're becoming better at finding patterns in the data that predict what you might do or buy in the future." Sullivan claims that a "child born in 2012 will leave a data footprint detailed enough to assemble a day-by-day, even a minute-by-minute, account of his or her entire life, online and offline, from birth until death." That is because the databases "are increasingly hyperconnected; they can trade data about you in milliseconds." Privacy attorney Sarah Downey of the Abine security products company believes that we accept "more privacy intrusions each day, sometimes because we don't realize what we're giving out, other times because we don't feel we have a choice, other times because the harm of this isolated transaction seems so remote." The greatest problem, she believes, is that once our data is collected, it "ends up in unexpected—and unwanted—places, and spam emails, inclusion in harmful information databases, and even identity theft can follow" (Sullivan, June 28, 2012).

Sullivan catalogues the state of the art in personal data collection by companies associated with e-commerce providers. A "whole industry of public records data companies" aggregates public records from every city, county, and state, making the data easily available online." Companies like Spokeo and Intelius combine public data records (originally created offline) with the personal data we ourselves create online, mostly on social networks. The data these and other companies aggregate can easily be used by landlords, insurers, employers, or creditors to screen applicants—although the data collection companies disavow such uses as violations of the Fair Credit Reporting Act (FCRA) (Sullivan, June 28, 2012). FCRA recently showed its teeth. On June 12, 2012, the U.S. Fair Trade Commission announced that Spokeo, Inc., had paid $800,000 to settle FTC charges that the company had obtained personal data from social media sites in violation of the Fair Credit FCRA (see Chapter 5).

E-commerce providers aren't the only "sellers" tracking us online. Political campaigns are now making use of combined offline and online data to create voter profiles to help them craft targeted ads. Leaders in this field are Aristotle, CampaignGrid, Rapleaf, and TargetedVictory. Sullivan reports that these firms combine data compiled from public records, including party affiliation, frequency of voting, and real estate records, with online information they judge relevant. In the end, the methods for targeting voters for campaign ads and consumers for product ads are quite similar, with the array of personal data becoming both broader and deeper with regard to sheer volume as well as the quality of analysis.

Moreover, because the "traditional" method of tracking users via cookies is not foolproof—a cookie associated with a given browser may contain browsing histories from several users of that particular PC—a company called BlueCava has created a "device ID technology" that does not require cookies but can identify site visitors through the unique combination of settings on their Web browser. Whereas cookies can be purged, "device ID" is a permanent means of identification. You have no direct control over it, so that you can't escape it. BlueCava, however, promises that it will remove the device ID if a consumer requests this at the company website. Of course, one problem remains: most users have no idea that a device ID exists for them (Sullivan, June 28, 2012).

Sullivan reports that the increasing volume and quality of data aggregation— the gathering and analysis of "big data" (see Chapter 2)—"will define technology and culture in the first part of the 21st century." Big data can be analyzed for its predictive value. For example, the Target retail chain was able to use customer data to predict pregnancies and thereby predict future needs for baby products. While it can readily be argued that accurately and adequately stocking a store with the products consumers will need and want is a service to consumers and surely does them no harm, many privacy advocates fear that the "warehousing" of predictive data could enable third parties to predict future behaviors users do not want to share with anybody. For example, Target, which compiles and analyzes predictive data, mailed a teenager coupons for baby goods. Her father, coupons in hand, visited the local Target store and complained to the manager. "She's still in high school, and you're sending her coupons for baby clothes and cribs? Are you trying to encourage her to get pregnant?" The manager apologized in person, then telephoned a few days later to apologize again. The irate father, now abashed, explained that he had had a talk with his daughter. "It turns out there's been some activities in my house I haven't been completely aware of. She's due in August . . . ." (Duhigg, February 16, 2012). Target had outed the girl.

In the context of a political campaign, Sullivan warns, the candidate whose campaign possesses "the best personal data and the best analysts may win. That seems like a very undemocratic way to choose our policies and leaders" (Sullivan, June 28, 2012). (Or, unappealing though it may be, is it actually the most democratic way, reflecting, as it does, the attitude and orientation of the electorate?)

On June 27, CNET reported on UC Berkeley Law School's first Internet privacy survey, which concluded that websites are far more aggressive in scooping up users' data than most users suspect. The survey found that Google had cookies on 105 of the top 1,000 sites, and its ad tracking network, doubleclick.net, had cookies on 685. In total (there was some overlap between the sites), Google had a tracking presence (cookies) on 712 of the top 1,000 websites. Other heavy-hitting trackers listed were BlueKai, whose clients include six of the Fortune 20 companies, Quantserve (Quantcast), ScoreCardResearch (ComScore), and Adnxs, which the survey calls "a seeming vector for malware." Abine analyst Sarah Downey commented that the "harms of online tracking are real and growing." She believes that this is not all "about targeted advertising, like the ad industry wants everyone to believe. This is about the collection and use of your personal information in ways you can't even imagine." She lists the "real, demonstrated harms" as price discrimination (citing how Orbitz targets Mac users with more expensive hotels), lowered credit scores, lost job opportunities, identity theft, and more expensive insurance rates or denial of coverage (Violet Blue, June 27, 2012). (Insurance companies' testing of data profiles to identify risky clients was discussed in a 2010 *Wall Street Journal* article [Scism and Maremont, November 18, 2010].)

Bad News for Whom?

It is no wonder that we consumers see ourselves as the helpless prey of advertisers, e-merchants, and data brokers. As for our supposed defenders, *Wired Magazine*, in cooperation with the public interest journalism site Propublica.org, recently concluded that the FTC "privacy watchdogs" are "low-tech, defensive, [and] toothless." Hobbled by a lack of funding and authority, the FTC, they report, is simply no match for multinationals like Google and Facebook. How was this conclusion reached? *Wired* pointed to the research of computer science graduate student Jonathan Mayer, who singlehandedly was able to reveal instance after instance of large-scale privacy invasion that had simply escaped FTC notice (Maass, June 28, 2012).

And yet, for all their seeming omnipotence, consumer tracking and the customized ads, personalized product recommendations, and individually targeted deals frequently backfire on merchants. Natasha Turner of the *New York Times* recently reported on a failed program launched by Urban Outfitters to "make it easier for female shoppers to peruse women's apparel and for men to concentrate on men's clothing by altering the site's product displays to match a user's gender." Former Urban Outfitters marketing exec Dimitri Siegel observed, "If you could just stop marketing dresses to men, it would be amazing." When he experimented with gender personalization on the Urban Outfitters site, however, he discovered that "many female Urban Outfitters customers regularly bought men's items and ... took offense at being subjected to gender-based marketing." Hyper-customization, overly personal personalization, can turn customers off, sending them away from the website. When covert tracking erodes trust or when the results of tracking are perceived as intrusive or creepy instead of helpful, "customer frustration [will] outweigh any benefit," according to Siegel. "If you got it wrong once, it outweighed getting it right 10 times" (Singer, June 23, 2012).

What the FTC and other regulators may be too feeble to accomplish, consumers themselves can achieve by voting with their wallets—or PayPal accounts. Like the consumer, the overreaching merchant can become a victim of intrusive tracking and heavy-handed online behavioral advertising (OBA). The more you, the individual digital user and consumer, educate yourself about tracking, data collection, and targeted advertising, the more powerful you become and the less you need to look to inadequate regulatory and legislative bodies for protection. In the end, the very imperative driving e-commerce providers to target you—the competition for customers—makes you the most important stakeholder on the Internet. You are what it's all about. The first step toward acquiring the empowerment of digital literacy is realizing your own supreme importance online.

Do Not Track

As we have seen in Chapter 2, the issue of online behavioral advertising (OBA) along with the user tracking on which it relies is at the heart of the current digital privacy controversy. We have seen that OBA is very profitable for e-commerce providers and that there is also an argument to be made that it provides a valuable benefit to consumers by delivering ads (information) that are most likely of interest to particular consumers instead of indiscriminately deluging everyone with the same random ads. In this way, OBA fully exploits a key advantage of interactive technology over broadcast technology. Your computer, a fully interactive device, can deliver ads of interest, whereas ordinary one-way broadcast TV just heaps commercial after commercial on everyone. Nevertheless, the idea of being "stalked" online by anonymous third parties seems to many of us the very definition of invasion of privacy. This said, the actual threats posed are for the most part more vague than concretely imminent. Consider this article posted on lifehacker.com: "What's so bad about ad tracking on the web, a.k.a. behavioral targeting? Nothing, if you don't mind being a living stereotype.... Ad companies watch what you do online, and they make bold assumptions about you." The article concludes, "How you feel about that is up to you," but the implication seems to be that if you have no objection, there must be something wrong with you (*Lifehacker,* February 22, 2011).

In fact, deciding how to manage online tracking is a strategic decision that you, a powerful consumer, should make thoughtfully. Face it, all large-scale merchants and advertisers treat consumers as "living stereotypes." They aggregate—stereotype—individuals into markets and market segments, then design, offer, and advertise products and services tailored to those markets and market segments. They do this offline (and have been doing so for centuries) as well as online. If you believe that receiving ads—information—tailored to you as a member of particular markets and market segments is valuable to you, then the price you pay is to allow yourself to be tracked. If you do not find this service sufficiently valuable, then you should make the strategic decision to opt out of tracking as much as possible (and all companies should give you the chance to do so). The choice really is—or should be—"up to you."

May I Offer You a Red Herring?

Before we proceed to the do-not-track (DNT) options consumers have, let us step back to put the issue in perspective. As we saw earlier in the chapter, advocates such as Abine's Sarah Downey ascribe to tracking the potential for such abuses as price discrimination, lowered credit scores, denial of insurance coverage or higher pricing of coverage, lost job opportunities, and identity theft. There are, however, no comprehensive statistics on how significantly OBA tracking causes, leads to, enables, or facilitates these adverse outcomes. Instead, repeatedly, we are told that OBA targeting invades privacy, is "creepy," or turns us into "living stereotypes." Overwhelmingly, the harms alleged are vague and inadequately supported. Yet OBA tracking is the principal driver of the great global controversy over digital privacy (see Chapters 2 and 3).

The governments of the European Union, which advocate strong central regulation of e-commerce tracking practices, and that of the United States, which calls for industry self-regulation enforced to a limited degree by the FTC, all routinely engage in widespread monitoring of cyberspace, including the activities of individual users (see Chapter 9). Similar monitoring is routinely used by political campaigns, but neither Congress nor the White House has called for regulation or self-regulation of this activity.

DNT Options

As mentioned in Chapter 4, all of the latest versions of the major browsers today —including Internet Explorer, Chrome, Firefox, and Safari—include so-called do-not-track (DNT) user preference controls. In addition, the Internet security suites listed in Chapter 4 include DNT tools, and tools like Abine's DNT+ provide extensive standalone DNT control.

The DNT settings included on browsers send a signal (usually in the form of a "header" data block) to third-party websites that tells them not to track your Internet activity. The setting conveys the user's request and does not actually "block" tracking. Moreover, third-party compliance with the DNT is voluntary. While many e-commerce providers, advertisers, and ad networks have pledged to honor DNT requests, many remain recalcitrant. AVG Do-Not-Track, a feature of AVG Anti-virus Free Edition, provides extensive information on tracking cookies on your browser and gives the user a greater degree of selective control over opting in or opting out of tracking on a site-by-site basis. Like the AVG tool, Abine's DNT+ provides information on who is attempting to track you, but it also provides actual blocking of at least some tracking in addition to the ability to send DNT requests.

At present, the decision to opt out of tracking must be made affirmatively by the user. The European Union's European Commission has proposed a regulation that would effectively require DNT to be the default setting, with users required to affirmatively opt-in, on a site-by-site basis, if they wish to be tracked. This regulatory position clashes with the U.S. proposal, which would maintain the current default (users are opted-in to tracking by default), but encourages, perhaps even mandates, a broader measure of user-controllable options. While the EU and the U.S. struggled over their divergent positions, Microsoft announced that its new version of Internet Explorer, IE 10, to be released with Windows 8, would have DNT turned on by default. While Microsoft asserted that this was a necessary step in giving users more control over their online lives—control that would build much-needed trust between consumers and e-commerce providers—most of the online marketing industry has objected.

However governments, Microsoft, and other stakeholders resolve or fail to resolve the issue of default opt-in versus default opt-out of tracking, it is crucial for users to recognize just how powerful they themselves are online. Whatever the default, we advise playing offense with your opt-in/opt-out position. If you want to receive targeted ads—information, after all, is power—opt in. If you want to receive targeted ads in some categories but not in others, opt in selectively, on a site-by-site basis. If targeted ads are a low priority for you, or if it bothers you to be tracked online, opt out (at least in those situations where you are given the choice) and clear your third-party cookies (see below) regularly.

Deleting Cookies

The vast majority of websites that track your browsing do so with cookies, small text files that are downloaded from the website. Cookies enable a website to remember your user preferences and settings, track your navigation within the site, and offer such services as automatic logon next time you visit. Some cookies are quite sophisticated, such as those Amazon uses to remind you about past searches and to offer recommendations for additional purchases related to your previous searches and purchases. Some cookies are automatically deleted when you leave the site that uploaded them. Others are "persistent," and remain on your computer potentially forever.

Cookies can enhance your browsing by personalizing your settings and tracking your purchases. They also uniquely identify your browser, thereby enabling an online merchant to track you and build a profile about you. This information may be used by the merchant itself (as in the case of Amazon, for instance) or by third parties that contract with the merchant to place cookies on your browser when you visit that merchant's website. The information collected through cookies may also be sold to third parties, including advertisers and ad networks. When you surf the web, various third parties may track you as you view or click through advertisements, thereby adding to your profile.

All modern web browsers allow you to block cookies, but blocking all cookies is generally not practical. Most browsers allow you to choose whether to block so-called 'first party cookies' and/or so-called 'third party cookies.' Blocking first party cookies will lead to a loss of certain interactive features or even basic site functionality. We do not suggest you do this. Blocking third-party cookies, on the other hand, will rarely affect your experience on a website but will prevent much (but not all) online tracking. If you decide that you do not want to be tracked online and you do not want to receive targeted advertisements, one step you can take to minimize the tracking is to block third-party cookies.

If being tracked is your major concern, another practical measure you can take is to use the DNT controls on your browser or download a DNT add-on, such as that from AVG or Abine. This said, the persistence of cookies on your computer does present some risk to privacy because each cookie contains the name of the website you visited. If you don't want somebody looking into your computer and discovering that you have looked at hothothot.com or were visiting websites devoted to a dread disease or have been job hunting on the website of your current employer's competition, you should go to the appropriate tab in your browser and "delete" or "clear" your browsing history. Going to the help tab on your particular browser will show you how to do this. Be certain that you include "cookies" in your deletion. If you simply want to erase recent history—you've just browsed a "sensitive" website—you may want to delete only browsing records from the last hour or two. If you want to cover all of your tracks, delete everything.

There is a better alternative to after-the-fact clean-up. Don't leave tracks in the first place. Before you surf to any sensitive websites, turn on your browser's "private," "stealth," or "incognito" mode. This option, offered by most current browsers, disables any record of the browsing session (when you end the session by closing the window or quitting the browser), including cookies, temporary Internet files, history, and other data.

BlueCava

As mentioned earlier in the chapter, a company called BlueCava has developed an alternative to cookie-based tracking called device ID technology, which uses a myriad of device characteristics to generate a unique identifier for the device. Using available browser DNT options may or may not affect tracking via device ID technology, and deleting cookies certainly will not, since the technology requires no cookies. If you wish to remove device ID technology tracking from your device (computer, tablet, or smartphone), you will need to visit http://www.bluecava.com/preferences/. After giving due consideration to the company's value proposition—"We help provide you with online advertising that's meaningful while eliminating ads that are meaningless, so everyone wins"— click the link provided and you will be opted out. Do note, however, that "opt out" applies only to the device you are currently using and not to other devices in your office or household. You will have to log on separately to opt out for each of those.

Although easy to do, opting out of BlueCava is not total. "Of course, we don't let you opt out of certain tracking activities that we use to define the reputation status of a device," BlueCava explains. "When a device does good things and bad things we keep a record of it. That makes sense to us." Coming from a company that claims it "wants you to be in control of your experience online," this smacks of Big Brother. The fact is that device ID is not just a tracking device, but a security device that online merchants use to "recognize and block fraudulent devices, or devices behaving badly." Device ID reports this information not only to the merchant interacting with the particular computer, but, creates "a historical record of [a client's] interactions with a particular device" and, through "Reputation Exchange," allows "all of BlueCava's partners to share knowledge of bad devices with other members of the exchange." BlueCava generates a "device snapshot" and sends it to the hosted BlueCava service, which compares it to hundreds of millions of other snapshots to determine if it is unique. If it is, the system generates a device ID that is used to track the device. Because BlueCava places nothing on the consumer's device—no cookies—there is nothing for the user to remove and no way to absolutely prevent the snapshot of your device from being tracked for purposes of fraud detection (or, potentially, for other purposes should Blue Cava decide to put this data to other uses or make it available to a government).

The DNT Nuclear Option

A June 11, 2012 *Poynter* (poynter.org) article quoted the observation of Frédéric Filloux, president of the French ePresse consortium, to the effect that users are becoming so irritated by targeted ads that they deliberately avoid clicking on them: "The more experienced users become, the more cautious they get in order to avoid aggressive tracking. For advertisers, this is the exact opposite of what they meant to achieve." Filloux believes "the trend will accelerate. Marketers have more sense of efficiency than of measure; they were quick to embrace these clever technologies without considering they might end up killing the golden goose. It is happening much earlier than anyone has anticipated" (Myers, June 11, 2012).

Whether or not Filloux's analysis and prediction are accurate, he has clearly identified what might be termed the individual consumer's "nuclear option," the ultimate weapon against OBA. Simply resist clicking on ads that are either self-identified as targeted (by the DAA icon; see Chapter 2) or that you feel have targeted you. Withhold your click and boycott the site, and you declare the ad ineffective. Ultimately, this may prove a more powerful anti-tracking tool than any DNT request or any attempt at industry or government regulation.

There Are Predators—and Then There Are *Predators*

As some people—and governments—see it, all online merchants are predatory stalkers. It's their nature. They just can't help themselves. But there are predators, and then there are predators. Online shopping is a boon for consumers and merchants alike. Everything about it makes it both easier to spend money and to save money. If you have an impulse to buy, you can, for better or worse, gratify it instantly, anywhere and at any time of day. Even better, you can comparison shop for the best merchandise, value, and price just by searching and clicking. Time, distance, parking, and the price of gas cease to exist for you.

Risks?

There are risks. We've already mentioned impulse and instant gratification. You may click before you think. More dangerous, however, is the carelessness and complacency that shopping from home—perhaps reclining on a sofa or even lying in bed—can create and encourage. You may let your guard down.

From the point of view of the merchant, the low cost of entry to doing business online is an extraordinary opportunity. You don't need a brick-and-mortar store with a staff of sales employees. All that is required is a website and some system for warehousing and distribution, a "system" that may be no more elaborate than a spare room in your house. To the outside world, the online "storefront" of the home-based entrepreneur can look just as impressive and imposing as the website of a major, long-established multinational retailer.

But, from the perspective of the consumer, the ability of just about anyone to present themselves as a well-established, impeccably reputable merchant, on a par with the most trusted names in the business, is one of the pitfalls of e-commerce. Don't be taken in by appearances.

To play it safe, you could restrict yourself to dealing only with brand-name merchants. To do so, however, would be to sacrifice one of the key advantages online shopping offers: the opportunity to look beyond the usual and the expected. Fortunately, while the Internet opens the door to scammers and schemers, it is also self-policing to a remarkable degree. Before you do business with a merchant unknown to you, undertake some quick research. Do an online search for feedback concerning Vendor X. People love to share their experiences, good and bad. Assess the vendor's reputation. Don't rely exclusively on reviews you find on the vendor's own website. Look around. It won't take you much time.

The most obvious reason for ensuring that you are about to deal with a reputable, reliable merchant is to avoid getting ripped off—ending up with the wrong product, an inferior product, something less than advertised, or no product at all. But there is an even more important reason to exercise care. To this total stranger, you are about to disclose financial information, most likely including a credit card number, as well as such personal information as your name, home address, email address, and phone number. The cost of these disclosures can be much higher than the price of an unsatisfactory product.

Researching the merchant will help to ensure satisfaction with your purchase. Another step you can take to protect the security of the transaction itself is to shop only on websites that establish a secure connection via the Secure Sockets Layer (SSL) protocol. Once you log onto the portion of the merchant's website where you actually place an order and provide payment information, you should look for the presence of a URL that is preceded by https://. The "s" at the end indicates that the SSL protocol is in force. On many browsers, a padlock icon will also appear in the web bar at the top of the screen or in the bottom "tray." An SSL connection is difficult to hack, and you can be confident that no unauthorized third party is intercepting your payment information.

As for paying, it is a good idea to use a credit card from a bank or financial institution that provides antifraud and satisfaction assurances, including the ability to dispute a transaction, lodge a complaint, and obtain a refund.

Finally, as with any other critical exchange of information over the Internet, be certain that you use a secure network. Airport concourse boredom induced, for example, by waiting for a delayed flight, is a temptation to do some online shopping. Much better, however, to resist the temptation, since you have no control over the security of a public wireless hotspot. It would not be difficult for a hacker to "sniff" your credit card number or other sensitive personal identifying information via a non-secure wireless network.

Put Paranoia in Perspective

Do not dismiss or ignore the risks of shopping online. Take control of the variables you can control, but be aware that, provided you deal with a researched or well-known merchant and make your payment over an SSL connection and via a secure network (not an open public hotspot), doing business online is probably less risky than physically handing over a credit card to a store clerk. And there is absolutely no doubt that you are safer surfing from one online storefront to the next than you are driving from one brick-and-mortar store to another.

CHAPTER EIGHT
Mobile Menace and Miracle

Throughout the twentieth century, American government was slow to grapple with electronic communications technology. The Communications Act of 1934, which created the Federal Communications Commission, regulated "interstate and foreign commerce in communication" until President Bill Clinton signed into law, on February 8, 1996, the Telecommunications Act of 1996. The Clinton-era legislation included the Internet in the broadcasting and spectrum allotment, but did not contemplate the emergence of the smartphone, which had debuted in the form of the IBM Simon Personal Communicator prototype at COMDEX in 1992 and was sold by BellSouth two years later to consumers in 190 U.S. cities. At 9 by 3 by 2 ½ inches and weighing in at a very solid pound, DOS-based Simon featured a predictive on-screen keyboard and combined mobile phone capability with a pager, PDA, and fax. Big, clunky, and costly (the original price was $899), Simon was clearly a business machine, and it did not seem likely to claim a significant share of the broadband spectrum anytime soon.

Advance nineteen years after Simon's debut to 2011: smartphone sales worldwide have overtaken sales of PCs (Taylor, February 3, 2012). In the spring of 2012, Gartner Research predicted that mobile Web access will overtake PC access by 2013 (EngineerLive, April 25, 2012). By 2014, the "personal cloud" will be the means by which most users will access digital information through smartphones and other non-PC devices (Carrasco, March 22, 2012).

Clear and Present Dangers

In 1949, the mathematician and computer scientist John von Neuman laid the theoretical and conceptual groundwork for what came to be called the "computer virus," and the first instance of a virus attack, called "Creeper," was documented in the early 1970s on the ARPANET (Advanced Research Projects Agency Network), the precursor of the Internet. The first widely available antivirus software programs were released in the late 1980s. Today, 80 percent of home-based PCs and 70 percent of business-based PCs are protected by some form of antivirus software (Kaiser, 2009), yet even as smartphones are poised to overtake personal computers as the platform of choice for Internet access, a "majority of mobile devices ... go around without any sort of antivirus protection on them whatsoever," according to the authors of *Mobile Device Security for Dummies* (Campagna et al, 2011. Loc. 4542). The absence of this most basic defense against threats to online security is the proverbial canary in the coal mine. If mobile users aren't taking elementary precautions against dangers familiar to computer users since the dawn of computer networking, how vulnerable have they left themselves to all of the dangers in mobile communication and mobile Internet access?

The most obvious threats include those familiar to all computer users: viruses, Trojan horses, and phishing schemes, all of which are discussed in Chapter 4 of this book. Because relatively few smartphone users protect themselves with antivirus software, the devices tend to be even more vulnerable than desktop and laptop computers.

Trojan Horses

The most common type of malware that infects mobile phones is the Trojan horse, or Trojan. It is estimated that, at any given time, 40 percent of personal computers are infected with some form of malware, often in the form of a Trojan. If we extrapolate from this figure, it is not difficult to assume that the rate of infection among smartphones is also very high, perhaps comparable or even higher.

Like viruses, Trojans are malicious programs that evade whatever security measures may be in place—including the better judgment of the user—by masquerading as something fun (typically a free game, wallpaper, an interactive joke, a greeting card, or even a business card [vCard], and the like). These days, Trojans are most often received as email attachments or Internet links contained in emails, SMS messages, or Twitter tweets. Click on the attachment or go to the link, and your device becomes infected. Your device may also be infected by someone who manually loads the Trojan, typically via the USB port. For this reason alone, you should never let your smartphone out of your physical control (the programs are small, and the download takes seconds), and you should also make use of phone's password access feature. In contrast to viruses, which are programs designed to replicate and spread to other devices, often by commandeering an email program, Trojans invade the target device only.

Trojans infecting mobile devices are generally spyware, the purpose of which is to perform such activities as:

Listening in on your calls
Listening to your voicemail messages
Recording calls using your phone's own memory
Making your phone dial someone
Activating your microphone, so that it is always on, always eavesdropping
Activating your video camera
Copying photographs and other images stored on your device
Remotely stealing your contact lists
Commandeering your text messaging software to send counterfeit messages

as if from you
Sending you counterfeit texts
Remotely downloading lists of your calls and text messages
Remotely downloading a list of the phone numbers you have called and the phone numbers of those who have called you
Remotely downloading lists of the length of particular calls
Alerting a remote eavesdropper whenever you get a call or text
Getting your new phone number after you install a new SIM card
Tracking you with your phone's GPS
Tracking you through cell tower pinging (without GPS)

Jailbreaking and Other Invitations to Invasion
Apple is famous for allowing only Apple-vetted, Apple-approved apps to be installed on iPhones and iPads via the App Store. If this policy makes you feel constrained, you can always log onto   www.jailbreakme.com. Here you can download a piece of software that will allow you to hack into your own iPhone or iPad in order to "free" it from the controls Apple has imposed on the device. There are certainly benefits to jailbreaking your Apple device (despite the name, the Library of Congress has said that jailbreaking your device is legal), but jailbreaking does expose Apple devices to the same vulnerabilities that plague open-source mobile devices that run (for example) on the Android operating system. Most unvetted apps are perfectly useful and safe, but some are malware, including Trojans designed to collect data from your device and transmit it to third parties. This is bad enough, but the fact is that if you can jailbreak your phone, so can a hacker by luring you to visit a website or to download a useful-seeming app or game.

Most users believe the Apple platform is very secure. Jailbreak it, however, and it becomes relatively porous. Leave Apple behind and venture into the open-source platforms, such as Android, Symbian, or MeeGo, and there is no need for a jailbreak. Anyone can create apps for these platforms, honest programmers and nefarious ones alike. Indeed, Black Hat DC 2010, a conference concerning online security, revealed in 2010 that Android users were downloading a series of wallpaper apps that surreptitiously gathered such data as the user's phone number, International Mobile Subscriber Identifier (IMSI), and currently entered voice mail. The apps transmitted this data, unencrypted, to a server. Obtaining the IMSI of a device gives a fraudster great power. By creating an "IMSI catcher," the eavesdropper can impersonate a cell tower from a specific carrier. Phones in the area will connect to this spoofed tower, by which the fraudster can intercept outbound calls. These can be routed to the intended recipient—as the eavesdropper listens and records.

Mobile users have access to hundreds of thousands of apps, some of them malicious. Of these some are doubtless the work of digital criminal prodigies.

Most, however, are not. The BBC, in collaboration with the security firm Veracode, conducted an experiment to see just what was involved in building a crude but effective piece of malware. They created a downloadable game that gathered a mobile user's contacts and text messages, then logged onto the phone's location, and sent everything to a specified email address. The app was made from legal software toolkits using the standard library functions that legitimate programs use. Anyone with basic programming knowledge and a will to mischief could have made the game and offered it as a download to mobile owners of open source devices or to jailbroken iPhone and iPad users.

Open Networks

Another set of portals open to invaders are unsecured, or open, WiFi networks. These are often encountered in public places, including stores, coffee shops, airports, waiting rooms, and the like. Recently, for example, HealthcareIT reported that 85 percent of U.S. hospitals have wireless networks supporting iPads, iPhones, Blackberries, Androids, and other smartphones and personal devices patients may own. Of these hospitals, 58 percent require no password (Mearian, February 24, 2012). Such open networks are very convenient, because they can be joined by any user from any device without the need for a password. "Any user" includes you and, well, any user. Among the latter group may be eavesdroppers who have the networking skill and technology (not much of either is required) to view the devices of other users connected to the open network. It is very easy to spy on unsecured Web browsing (including activity on Facebook, Twitter, Yahoo, and the like). Via open networks, more skilled and determined spies may even be able to gain access to files residing on a device.

Public networks are not the only open networks. Millions of homes and businesses have their own WiFi routers and networks. All routers allow for some form of encryption so that only authorized users can log onto the network. It is, however, up to the person who sets up the router and network to implement the password. Many never do. This has resulted in a lot of wireless networks open to any passerby, neighbor, or "wardriver"—the term for hackers who drive around in search of open wireless networks.

For some, wardriving is a kind of sport, like wearing roller skates and hitching a ride on some passing car's rear bumper. For others, it's a way of getting "free" Internet service at your expense. For others still, it is a means of transacting nasty business on the Internet under cover of your identity. Recently, men in Buffalo and Syracuse, New York, and in Sarasota, Florida, were stunned by FBI or police raids, the officers acting on surveillance that revealed that the wireless networks of these individuals were being used to download child pornography. After considerable anguish, embarrassment, and legal expense, charges against all three were dismissed when it was discovered that neighbors had, in each case, logged onto WiFi networks left wide open without password protection and themselves downloaded child pornography (Cheng, April 25, 2011). In 2012, it was revealed that the search titan Google had captured huge amounts of WiFi data worldwide in a massive wardriving campaign attached to the Google Street View project. Street View cars assigned to photograph ground-level views to go with Google Earth were equipped to capture any unencrypted WiFi data, including usernames and passwords, they happened to encounter. Although Google suffered a PR disaster and was fined for obstructing an FCC investigation of what was revealed to have been a two-year wardriving campaign, the agency found that Google had broken no laws in intercepting the unencrypted data (Schwartz, April 30, 2012).

Defending Against the Clear and Present Dangers
Fortunately, defending yourself against the obvious dangers is fairly straightforward and relies far more on common sense and vigilance than on technical sophistication.

1. Keep physical control of your smartphone. This means, don't loan it (unless you can keep an eye on it the whole time), don't lose it, and don't let it get stolen. Do not let anyone, even a close friend, install any app on it, no matter how cool or how free.

2. Buy your own phone from a trusted source, such as a nationally recognized vendor or carrier. Never accept a phone as a gift.

3. Be careful what you download. Avoid apps, wallpaper, ring tones, games, and other attachments offered in unsolicited emails or text messages. Download only from reliable sources.

4. Install only those apps that are absolutely necessary.

5. Use the most restrictive settings for Internet access and app functionality.

6. Resist the temptation to jailbreak your phone.

7. Lock your phone with a good password. See Chapter 4 for password tips. And, yes, keep your password secret.

8. Be careful with SIM cards. Some mobile security authorities advise that you neither use your old SIM in your new phone, nor put a new SIM in your old phone. Some of the more sophisticated spyware in circulation can detect a SIM card swap, which prompts the spyware to report your new phone number to the eavesdropper.

9. Keep your phone turned off as much as you possibly can.

10. Stay off open networks. Certainly avoid financial transactions and other sensitive data exchanges over public networks.

11. If you use WiFi at work or at home, make sure that access is password protected. Never leave your WiFi network open.

12. Consider using a CDMA phone rather than a GSM phone, since most

spyware is written for GSM phones.

13. Use a separate cheap cell phone or a prepaid phone for important, sensitive, or confidential calls. Reserve your regular smartphone for everyday business.

14. Avoid making financial transactions using your smartphone. For example, do not use it for banking or to make online purchases.

If it seems to you that some of these preventative steps require sacrificing convenience, maybe even fun, for safety, congratulations. You have successfully recognized an essential tradeoff in mobile technology.

Security software for mobile devices is available from the major security software vendors, including AVG Technologies (AVG Mobilation), Symantec, F-Secure, and Kapersky. Android users, who may have the most to fear from rogue apps, also typically benefit from free security suites supplied by carriers.

Warning Signs of Infection

All spyware has one function in common. It causes your smartphone to transmit, even when you are not using it; therefore, look for the following symptoms:

1. Your phone comes to life—lights up—from time to time for no reason apparent to you.

2. Your phone beeps without discernible cause.

3. You hear clicking and other strange background noises when you are on the phone.

4. Your phone gets unusually warm, indicating intensive use.

5. Battery life sharply decreases.

6. Your phone bill contains a volume of text, data, or SMS usage you cannot account for.

7. Your call duration log does not jibe with your actual usage.

8. You get frequent error messages.

9. You receive strange text messages with cryptic numbers and symbols.

10. Callers report that your phone is often busy or their calls go straight to voicemail—yet you know you were not using the phone when these calls came in.

11. Your phone is sluggish, especially in keypad response.

12. Your phone is slow to shut down when you turn it off.

13. You discover the presence of apps you never downloaded.

Cures

If you discover that your smartphone has been infected, the easiest cure is to purchase a new phone. If you do, make sure you really do start from scratch. Use a new SIM card, and do not reinstall your data from a backup file. If you do, you will probably infect the new device.

Depending on whether you are at the beginning or the end of your current carrier contract, buying a new phone can be expensive. The cheapest way to deal with an infection is to reinstall the operating system on the device you already have. Many smartphones, including Blackberry and iPhone, make it easy for you to do this yourself. If you are unsure how to do it, consult your carrier's website or the website of the device manufacturer, or make a phone call. Once you reinstall the operating system software, do not restore any backups. These files should be erased.

Dangers Less Clear, Just as Present

Spyware attacks and exposure to unsecured public networks are obvious dangers. Users of smartphones are also subject to hazards that are less obvious, but just as real.

Social Engineering

As explained in Chapter 6, "social engineering" is the term for methods used to persuade or manipulate people, typically to divulge confidential information (including passwords, account numbers, and the like) or to perform actions that result in the compromise of security. Social engineering may be very low-tech or even no-tech. A fraudster creates a "pretext" sufficiently persuasive to prompt the victim to disclose some piece of valuable information, such as an account number, a Social Security number, date of birth, credit or bank account numbers, or smartphone or online account passwords. Such "pretexting" may involve a fraudster who identifies himself or herself as a police officer, a bank officer, an IRS agent, a credit company officer, or other authority. Frank Ahearn made his living as a skip tracer, a private investigator specializing in tracking down people who don't want to be found. The key to discovering someone's identity, he says, is pretexting. "You don't even have to be good with computers, although it doesn't hurt. People ask me all the time how many computer languages I know. The answer is zero. I know one language: pretext" (Ahearn, loc. 177).

Low- or no-tech pretexting can be done in person, over the phone, by snail mail, or by a simple email. Slightly higher up the technology scale are phishing attacks, in which the fraudster sends an email that appears to be from a legitimate (usually nationally known) business, bank, credit card company, online merchant, or other organization with which you may have business. (The fraudster may have actually discovered you have a business relationship with the company his email impersonates or, far more likely, you are just one of thousands of recipients of the email, and you happen to be one who does indeed bank at Such-and-Such Bank.) The phishing email typically requests "verification" of your account information, warning that if you do not supply the verification (account number, Social Security number, etc., etc.), access to your account will be suspended. The credibility of a phishing attack depends on two things: 1) the fact that the email appears to come from a firm with which you do business and 2) the very legitimate and official look of the email, which is achieved by the fraudster's ability to mimic the HTML code actually used on the firm's legitimate website or email communications.

Another phishing scam to which smartphone users may fall prey is known as baiting. As explained in Chapter 6, a fraudster may plant a CD-ROM or USB thumb drive in a strategic location, such as the men's room of the offices of a corporation he is trying to breach. The item left will be labeled "Executive Salaries," "Confidential Contact List," "Hot, Hot, Hot," or something similarly inviting. The assumption is that, at some point, the curiosity of an individual who stumbles across the item will be piqued. He or she will literally take the "bait," insert it into a computer linked to the corporate network, and thereby infect the machine—and quite possibly the entire network.

The smartphone version of baiting uses an email rather than physical media as bait. The target receives a message that lists him as one of several recipients, some of whom may have recognizable names or titles. The email subject line is similar to one of the labels used in the physical medium version of the scam. It may say "Salary List," "Confidential Contacts," or something else sufficiently provocative to entice the recipient to click on the attachment. Once that is done, the Trojan in unleashed on the phone and, if the phone is connected to the corporate intranet via WiFi, throughout the corporate intranet as well.

Finders Keepers

The least sophisticated means of compromising smartphone security is obtaining physical possession of a smartphone, either by borrowing it, stealing it, or simply finding it. If the phone is not password locked, the borrower, thief, or finder is free to comb through and copy contact lists, account lists, photos, telephone numbers, email messages, text messages, and other records at will—anything that isn't password protected. The fraudster may install spyware on the phone and see that it is returned to you by a good Samaritan. Before returning your phone, the fraudster may even clone it, copying its identity in order to make fraudulent telephone calls that will be both ascribed and billed to you.

Note that even if the phone has a password, a determined fraudster may be able to guess it. Most passwords are quite obvious and simple—making them convenient for the legitimate user as well as the borrower, thief, or finder.

Hacked SMS

Text messaging is the highest-volume service offered by smartphone carriers, and SMS (short message service) is the number one text messaging application. It is widely believed that the GSM encryption employed in SMS is highly secure. In fact, it can be cracked, and the target phone thereby transformed into a surveillance device that captures text messages.

Roaming Hotspot

One of the newer features of such high-end smartphones as the Motorola Droid X, the iPhone 4, 4s, and 5, and the HTC EVO 4G, to name a few examples, is the ability to use the device as a WiFi hotspot, which can be "tethered" to a laptop computer to provide access to the Internet in locations that lack standard WiFi. It's a great feature, but it also means that hundreds of thousands of smartphone users are walking hotspots. If one of them is using the device to log her laptop onto the Internet, it is quite possible for an eavesdropper to come along for the ride. Bad enough for the spy to gain access to some of your private information, but what if you are tethering in order to download critical data from your business or your employer—data meant for your eyes only?

Vulnerable Bluetooth?

Bluetooth is a technology by which Bluetooth-enabled devices can communicate with each other wirelessly over short distances—typically no more than 30 feet, though some applications have a range of as much as 300 feet. When it was first deployed, Bluetooth made devices vulnerable to eavesdroppers (known as bluejackers); however, all of today's smartphone models that include Bluetooth connectivity require authentication before devices are "paired" (that is, allowed to communicate). This significantly reduces your odds of being bluejacked, provided that you exert the small amount of effort required to change and personalize the authentication password of your device or the devices you wish to pair.

Geolocation Hazards

High-end smartphones include GPS transceivers, which track your location to within yards or even feet. This is a useful feature to provide you with directions or with information on local points of interest (the nearest drugstore or bar, for instance). Geolocation also allows advertisers to send ads your way that are geared to your location and often very nearly in real time, so that as you pass XYZ Clothing Store you are alerted to a sale on Madras slacks. All this may be fine with you, but it is also true that someone who has gained covert access to your smartphone can also pinpoint your location. The person carrying out this surveillance may be a cop, your employer, your spouse, or a would-be burglar, waiting for your house to be empty and you far away. In fact, even if your phone lacks GPS capability or you have turned it off, you can still be tracked via the cell tower network. Your device constantly communicates with one cell tower after another, broadcasting to each its unique identifier.

You may or may not care whether or not a record is being created of your whereabouts, but give it some thought. Certainly, you should think very carefully before issuing a GPS-equipped smartphone to your child.

Defending Against the Less Clear but Just as Present Dangers

As with avoiding the clear and present dangers, defending against the less obvious hazards is less an issue of your technological sophistication and more a matter of exercising common sense and vigilance.

Avoid falling victim to social engineering by using your street smarts. Don't divulge any private information to anyone you do not know. No legitimate business, government agency, bank, credit card company, or other organization will phone or email you out of the blue requesting confidential identifying information. They don't need any of this. They already have it.

As for baiting, do not open email attachments from anyone except a trusted source. Also recognize that a fraudster can commandeer the contact list from a trusted source, sending you (and others) an email that appears to be from your friend, acquaintance, or customer. Look at the context. If the email does not seem typical of the sender—say your pastor sends you an email with the message line "Hot, Hot, Hot!"—don't open the attachment. Instead, email, text, or phone the putative sender. Tell him or her what you have received. Chances are his or her email account has been breached.

Guard your smartphone. Don't lend it. Don't leave it unattended. Don't lose it. Do what you can to keep it from being stolen. This said, prepare in advance for the loss. Regularly and frequently backup your data. Make sure you or your carrier can remotely lock down and disable the phone. The safest thing you can do is also to remotely wipe the phone, destroying all data. This will foil the thief and won't cause you undo inconvenience—provided that you have a recent data backup. Promptly report any loss to your carrier and/or your corporate IT manager, whichever is appropriate.

Guard against SMS hacking by installing good anti-malware software, by maintaining physical possession of your phone, by not jailbreaking your phone, by being highly selective about opening email attachments, and by downloading only those apps you absolutely need and that come from a known and reliable source.

If you use your device as a mobile hotspot in public places, password protect the hotspot you have created just as you would password protect your WiFi network at home. If you are using an app to create the hotspot, make sure the app is trusted and will not itself search through your browsing data—research its reputation online and read its privacy policy carefully. Certainly, you should never download or upload sensitive data while tethered in public.

Avoid being "bluejacked"—eavesdropped on via a Bluetooth connection—either by turning off Bluetooth and using a wired connection instead or by ensuring that you are using something other than the default authentication code or password. GPS is another feature to turn off unless you are actively using it to find your way around.

<u>Consequences Personal and Corporate</u>
The consequences of a compromised smartphone include those outlined in the broader context of Chapters 4 and 6, especially including identity theft and outright theft of your funds. For the smartphone user, as opposed to the user of a desktop or laptop computer, the consequences may be magnified because mobile devices are typically poorly protected when compared with PCs, they are used more casually and carelessly, they are exposed to an array of open networks, they are exposed to an array of potential miscreants, and, because they have become for most of us quite intimate objects, they are overly trusted. Carried anywhere and everywhere and often consulted or played with out of boredom—whether waiting for a plane or a physician—they invite impulsiveness, including the temptation to open email attachments without thinking twice.

It is bad enough if your personal and financial data is compromised, and it can be a costly nightmare for you and your family if your identity is stolen. But consider this: you and everyone else working for your employer or for your company who has company data on their smartphone or accesses company data files via their smartphone is a potential portal into your organization—a window left open, a gate left swinging wide. If you own, manage, lead, or participate in an enterprise, you should be most concerned about these four hazards:

1. Loss and theft of mobile devices: Smartphones aren't cheap, but the most valuable thing lost is the data, not the device.

2. Malware and spyware: Smartphones are as vulnerable as PCs, yet typically aren't nearly as well protected.

3. Data leakage: If users combine personal and enterprise applications, such as email, on their phones, accidental transmission of corporate data outside of the organization is a very real possibility.

4. Open network exposure: Employees can readily and thoughtlessly connect to open, unsecured networks, exposing corporate data.

And you should consider taking the following security measures:

1. Limit employee access to data on a need-to-know-basis. The data-access needs of the sales rep on the road differ markedly from those of your financial controller, your corporate counsel, or your accountant.

2. Create a well-crafted mobile device security policy for the enterprise. Security measures certainly must cover company-owned as well as

employee-owned computers, laptops, and mobile devices. A company security policy should spell out what, if any, corporate data may be moved to an employee's personally owned computer or mobile device and what steps employees must take to protect confidential business information when they remotely access it. Moreover, it is probably also necessary to remove any legal expectation of privacy by telecommuting employees, who should be required to sign an acknowledgement that they understand that certain aspects of their employment will be monitored, including computer files and documents prepared or used in business.

3. Institute a mobile device management (MDM) solution that allows central control of the configuration of employee devices. This will help to ensure that all devices comply with corporate security policies.

4. Protect against malware and other threats with good antimalware software.

5. Use a secure VPN (Virtual Private Network) to secure mobile device traffic.

6. Deploy a sophisticated digital authentication scheme instead of static usernames and passwords.

So, Who Will Regulate?

The threats in the mobile space are real, and the stakes are high. No wonder we find ourselves in the midst of a frenzy of debate over regulation. Just in time for the transition from the dominance of the PC to the reign of the mobile device, the EU European Commission's Directorate-General for Justice (DG JUST) presented on January 25, 2012, its proposal (EC Justice, January 25, 2012), and a month later, the U.S. White House released its "Framework" and Consumer Bill of Rights (White House, February 2012).

Internet stakeholders—who more and more are using mobile devices for web access—have reason to be concerned, for different reasons in each instance, about the European Commission's government-driven default opt-out approach, the U.S. White House's proposed hybrid FTC-enforced self-regulation, and the impending conflict of global interoperability between the EU and U.S. approaches. (As European Commission representative Françoise Le Bail ominously warned, the United States "cannot escape" the EU privacy rules [Szabo, March 26, 2012]).

The regulatory outlook is further complicated by proposed U.S. privacy legislation directed exclusively at mobile technology. On January 30, 2012, U.S. Representative Ed Markey (D-MA) released a "discussion draft" of The Mobile

Device Privacy Act (Markey. House Bill, January 30, 2012). Proposed in response to the recent Carrier IQ controversy over the installation of monitoring software that transmitted personal information, including who is called and what is typed in text messages, to third parties, the Markey bill requires, among other things, the detailed disclosure of any mobile telephone monitoring software present on a phone, as well as consumer consent before the monitoring software begins collecting and transmitting information (Markey. Press Release, January 30, 2012; Wikipedia, "Carrier IQ"; "Android Security Test"; Holly, November 15, 2011).

It is important and instructive to note three significant points about Representative Markey's bill, the last three of which are typical of regulatory and legislative attempts to "protect" online privacy.

First there is the bill's focus on mobile privacy, which underscores the ascendency of the smartphone as it begins to eclipse the PC as the Internet device of choice (EngineerLive, April 25, 2012).

Second, without identifying it by name, the target issue addressed by the Markey bill is "big data," which is best described by Craig and Ludloff as the "digital footprint" created by everything people do, deliberately or not, online: "We work online, we socialize online, we follow news and our favorite shows online, we file taxes online, we bank online, we may even gamble or pursue sexual interests online" (Craig and Ludloff, 2011. Loc. 276). As these authors observe, "Our smart phones and other devices are more effective collectors of individual information than the KGB or Stasi, the most feared security agencies of the Cold War era" (Craig and Ludloff, 2011. loc. 1453). Again, without using the phrase, the Markey bill identifies mobile devices as the great collectors and aggregators of "big data," which can be sold to third parties, used by authorities of all kind (from the police to the local bank officer), and exploited commercially, criminally, or in some combination of the two.

Third, without debating the significant merits of the proposed legislation, the Markey bill, like most proposed digital regulation by governments, is more the product of fear than of vision. While laws are often framed as prohibitive and punitive sanctions rather than enabling and liberating mandates, the great pity, in the case of Representative Markey's proposed legislation, is that a bill whose very existence acknowledges the vast potential of mobile technology is being offered as a protection of "privacy" instead of for what it more significantly is. As we have suggested earlier, the truly powerful issue in mobile technology is not, in fact, privacy. It is the user's control of personal data, and this is actually the most compelling issue the legislation would address by requiring consumer consent before monitoring software installed on mobile phones can collect and transmit information.

About to become the primary means of connecting the individual to the entire digital universe (EngineerLive, April 25, 2012), the smartphone is also the most personal and intimate of digital devices. People fondle the device, stare at it, and clothe it in silicone skins. When nature has called, 75 percent of us have, at one point or another, taken it into the bathroom with us (Mello, January 31, 2012). We routinely use the smartphone to post family photographs and reveal details of our daily lives on Facebook and other social sites. As Craig and Ludloff point out, "70 percent of the digital universe is actually generated by all of us through email, Facebook, Twitter, LinkedIn, Flickr, YouTube" (Craig and Ludloff, 2011. loc 298), a growing proportion of it using mobile devices. We conduct innumerable financial and other confidential transactions with it. Online ad spending reached $8.4 billion in the first quarter of 2012 (IAB, June 11, 2012) and is projected to reach $50 billion for the year 2015 (Craig and Ludloff, 2011. Loc. 1558).

The evidence is incontrovertible. Day after day, hour after hour, we voluntarily choose to relinquish solitude—our "privacy"—to share aspects of ourselves and take in the offerings of others online. In this context then it is not privacy we covet, but rather, the right to decide for ourselves and by ourselves what is strictly private and what is not. Consider this: The objective of a miser is to keep a tight fist around his money and let none of it go. In contrast, the objective of a prudent spender is to choose investments thoughtfully, exchanging value for value. Most of us are not privacy misers, but instead endeavor to invest our privacy prudently, relinquishing a portion of it only in exchange for some desired value.

The EU regulation would put government in control of privacy. The Markey bill looks away from the big picture, and the major thrust of the other U.S. proposed legislation would leave issues of privacy to a largely self-regulated industry. Neither the EU nor the U.S. approach will satisfy both the privacy miser and the prudent privacy investor when it comes to digital access that is increasingly mobile. In addressing issues of mobile privacy and security, nowhere is our "third approach" more appropriate.

Whereas the EU and U.S. propose sharply different measures to protect privacy, the third approach empowers individual users to control their personal data by equipping and enabling them to choose when, where, how, and in what to invest their own privacy. Users, each individually as well as in their aggregate billions, have the greatest stake in the control of privacy: greater than that of governments or of industry. What is more, privacy is by commonsense definition private; therefore, control of privacy should be a product of individual decision making. Privacy is not just a word or an abstract concept; rather, it is the product of a series of decisions and the actions and consequences that flow from them.

"What Is Most Personal Is Most Universal"
To be sure, laws prohibiting and criminalizing illicit and malicious assaults on mobile security and privacy are necessary. Nevertheless, it is clear that individual users are ultimately positioned on the frontline and therefore have the best vantage from which to defend themselves against these threats.

We also believe that individuals are in the best position to make decisions about commercial demands on their privacy and that, in addition, the third approach benefits all stakeholders. It relieves government of the Sisyphean labor of attempting to impose one-size-fits-all regulation on millions of individuals in billions of cases. Additionally, it benefits e-commerce. Giving consumers full knowledge of their online data and complete control over how this data is used, shared, or withheld enhances the effectiveness of online behavioral advertising (OBA) because consumers choose how, when, where, and by whom to be tracked, thereby signaling to e-commerce providers their interest in this or that product or service and their lack of interest in certain others. Consumers, of course, benefit by attracting the information they need and want, without the annoyance and distraction of ads they don't want.

Empowered to make privacy decisions, the individual consumer/user is not only positioned to defend against attack and intrusion, but, even more important, to play offense in his or her own digital life. The Internet is a window and a portal of unprecedented possibility. Mobile devices are the most intimate and personal means of access to that window and that portal. It is the very personal nature of these devices that is rapidly making them the preferred means of access. Years before the advent of the personal computer, the smartphone, and the Internet, the great American psychologist Carl R. Rogers wrote, "What is most personal is most universal." The ascendency of mobile devices is not proof of this assertion—the proof requires no technology—but rather an amplification and intensification of it.

Mobile technology is at the core of emerging mobile-centric platforms under development by funf (funf.org), SwiftRiver (swiftly.org), Ushahidi (ushahidi.com), PAX (paxreports.org), and others that promise benefits to individual, regional, and even global welfare, wellbeing, and progress. All of these organizations are developing ways to harness the capabilities of mobile devices to capture, record, process, visualize, map, disseminate, and analyze big data, including, for example, social network posts, video and photo posts, cell signals and call detail records, geolocation data, and e-commerce data. For an individual, this may simply mean tracking diet, exercise, and personal health. For a region, this may mean learning to understand trends in local development in order to improve the life, health, and wealth of the community. For a nation, this technology may enable beneficial changes in government and administration. Ushahidi, for instance, began as a website to map reports of violence in Kenya after the elections of 2008 (Ushahidi. "About Us."). For the world, mobile-centric big data projects may provide (as PAX aspires to create) "a global digital system to give early warning of wars and genocide" (PAX. paxreports.org). And for providers of e-commerce, the new mobile-centric big data technology may identify new markets while simultaneously providing the precise guidance needed to serve those markets efficiently and profitably.

The intimate technology we carry in our hands, pockets, and purses, to which we may commit personal data foolishly or prudently, with which we expose ourselves to a world of threat and possibility, transforms each of us into a node on the universal net. With mobile on the cusp of digital dominance, and governments and companies debating—sometimes clashing over—issues of "privacy," the moment is prime to put control of data in the right hands, the very hands that hold the smartphone. To do otherwise, no matter from what laudable motives, threatens not only privacy, but the boundless benefits of current and emerging mobile technology.

CHAPTER NINE
One Nation, Under Surveillance ...

Thirty years ago, when very few people owned cell phones (which were not only costly, but brick-like in both heft and dimension) and before there was a viable Internet, it was common to encounter crazy people walking along any big-city street. You knew they were crazy because they either talked to themselves incessantly and with emphatic gestures even as they strode along earnestly, or they wore a homemade hat of aluminum foil to shield their thoughts from corporate and government eavesdropping, or they did both. These days, it's much more difficult to separate the truly deranged from the mildly paranoid and even the perfectly rational. To begin with, we all stride earnestly down the street, conversing incessantly and emphatically, not to a proximate human but into Bluetooth earpiece-microphones, our smartphones small enough to hide in purse or pocket. And while few of us sport aluminum-foil headgear, many of us talk, even in polite and conventional company, of government or corporate surveillance conducted 24/7, routinely, without our knowledge let alone permission.

Thirty years ago, privacy was pretty much the baseline assumption of normality: the way things were. Those who believed reality was otherwise were either very important people—important enough to merit attention from corporate entities, government authorities, the media, or perhaps a presidential enemies list—or they were just nuts. Today, the baseline has moved. To assume that you exist in a high level of privacy is now the delusion. However, it is still no easy matter to decide just where to pin the new normality and just how to feel about being a citizen of a nation—any nation—pretty much always under surveillance.

Matters of Record
Again, back up thirty years. We all left paper trails, beginning with a birth certificate and ending with a death certificate. In between were tax returns, records of litigation, military service records, employment documents, marriage licenses, divorce papers, maybe the occasional newspaper clipping, and perhaps a bundle or two of personal letters. Much of the paperwork was public, at least theoretically, but actual access to it required finding the appropriate repository, making a trip to it, and filling out forms. Access was possible, but it was a hassle littered with logistical, legal, and bureaucratic obstacles. As for tracking down the

other pieces of paper—personal letters, for instance—this often required genuine scholarship or even detective work and a hands-and-knees crawl through any number of dusty attics.

Record keeping is hardly new. The continuity, speed, and thoroughness with which records are kept, along with the sheer volume of data on each of us, is today unprecedented. What is more, access by third parties—including government agencies, police departments, lenders, creditors, lawyers, disgruntled employees, curious employers, vengeful spouses—has never been easier. No one wears out shoe leather or scrapes their knees when sitting at a computer keyboard.

So just what is the current "normal" state of unprivacy?

<u>Types of Personal Data Routinely Collected</u>
Somewhere, someone has collected or is collecting data on:

- Your credit history
- Your health history
- Your educational history
- Your employment history, including how much you earn
- What you eat
- What you do in your spare time
- What magazines and books you read
- What calls you make
- What you buy (credit card and check)
- Where you shop
- Your insurance companies and coverage
- Your friends, associates, and family
- What websites you visit
- Your sexual preference(s)
- Your political activities and affiliations
- Your professional and social affiliations

And this is hardly exhaustive.

Top General Issues in Privacy
It is difficult to enumerate the top issues in privacy, since different people and various organizations have their own priorities, but the Electronic Frontier Foundation (EFF), founded in 1990 and long the highest-visibility public interest organization devoted to issues of electronic privacy, identifies the following areas of greatest interest and concern (Electronic Frontier Foundation, "Privacy"):

1. Biometrics systems.   These systems identify or verify identity by using

intrinsic physical or behavioral characteristics, such as fingerprints; iris, face and palm prints; walking gait; voice prints; and DNA. Law-enforcement agencies see biometric databases as tools to combat terrorism, enforce border security, and identify criminals. Commercial interests are developing biometrics to allow quick and secure access to accounts, products, services, and entertainment venues. Arguably, well-designed biometric systems can increase personal security and reduce fraud for all of us; however, government and other organizations can combine face-recognition (and other biometric) software with video surveillance and readily track individuals at will and without warrants. Because biometric data is readily digitized, it can be combined with other digitized personal data, such as an individual's name, address, and Social Security number, as well as geolocation technology, to identify and track individuals at will, anywhere, and with little or no judicial authorization. Moreover, such aggregated biometric databases, if stolen or compromised, could create a large-scale risk to privacy and security.

2. CALEA and Internet Wiretapping. The Communications Assistance for Law Enforcement Act (CALEA), passed in 1994, was expanded by the FCC in 2004 and 2005 to make Voice-Over-IP (VoIP) telephone communications over the Internet easy for law enforcement to wiretap. (As of 2010, VoIP subscribers numbered 20 million in the United States, according to arstechnica.com.) Privacy advocates believe this expansion, if upheld, will open the door to "wiretapping" the Internet generally, including text and email communications, not just telephone calls.

3. Cell tracking. At issue in a number of courtroom cases is whether the government can use cell phone records to track a subject's physical location without obtaining a warrant. The question has yet to be resolved definitively.

4. CISPA and other cyber bills. The Cyber Intelligence Sharing and Protection Act (CISPA, HR3523) was recently passed in the House of Representatives. CISPA would remove many legal and procedural barriers to allowing the federal government and businesses to share information, including users' private communications. In July 2012, the Senate filibustered cybersecurity legislation, known as the Cybersecurity Act of 2012, which would have provided measures to protect "critical infrastructure" networks (such as the power grid) in the United States and also would have removed many legal barriers to data sharing between the government and the private sector. Privacy and civil liberties advocates objected to the bill on the grounds that it would have overridden current privacy laws and would have posed serious threats to individual privacy.

Critics also objected to data sharing extending to the military, thereby blurring barriers between military intelligence and intelligence gathering by civil law enforcement. Perhaps most problematic was a provision of CISPA that allowed shared information to be used for any criminal investigations, including investigations that have nothing to do with cybersecurity, provided that the information "appears to relate to a crime which has been, is being, or is about to be committed." This was widely seen as a violation of Fourth Amendment guarantee against unreasonable searches and seizures.

5. International Privacy Standards. Privacy advocates worry that failure to establish universal international privacy standards will effectively render futile any national or regional attempts to establish such standards, given the borderless reach of the Internet.

6. Locational Privacy. Mobile communication and other Internet-based communication that incorporate GPS or other locational technologies are widely seen as threats to privacy, especially if, without warrant, government and law-enforcement officials are permitted to track individuals.

7. Mandatory Data Retention. Many government and law enforcement agencies are pushing for laws to require Internet Service Providers (ISPs) and telecommunications providers to collect and store records of the online activities of customers. These records would be available to law enforcement officials. Critics claim that retention laws threaten both the right to privacy and the right to free expression. Moreover, the records are subject to hacking or other theft, posing a severe security danger to millions of Internet users, especially since these laws stipulate that the responsibility for the security of the records is solely that of the ISP or telecom.

8. Mass surveillance technologies. U.S., Canadian, and various European companies are producing technologies that certain authoritarian regimes have been using to filter and block online content and monitor or spy on citizens. Technologies supplied include systems for eavesdropping on cell phone calls, systems employing voice recognition to scan mobile networks, systems to read emails and text messages, systems to alter email messages, systems to censor web pages, and systems to track physical movement with GPS devices. It was recently revealed that the California-based Boeing subsidiary Narus sold surveillance technology to the Mubarak regime in Egypt, and BlueCoat Systems, Inc., another California company, has sold software to the violently repressive regime of Syria's Hafiz al-Asad. U.S.-based Cisco Systems is facing litigation related to its sales of surveillance equipment to the Chinese, equipment that may have been used to track,

monitor and otherwise facilitate the arrest, detention, or disappearance of human rights activists and religious minorities.

9. NSA domestic activities. EFF has revealed that the National Security Agency (NSA) secured the cooperation of AT&T to create and carry out a massive program of illegal "dragnet surveillance" of "ordinary Americans since at least 2001."

10. PATRIOT Act. As discussed below, the PATRIOT Act, passed in the wake of the terrorist attacks of September 11, 2001, expanded law enforcement's powers of surveillance and investigation in ways that seriously challenge civil liberties in general and privacy in particular.

11. Printers. The U.S. government has persuaded some manufacturers of color laser printers to encode each printed page with identifying information. Ostensibly, the purpose of this is to catch counterfeiters, who use color printers, but there is nothing to prevent the use of the technology to identify the origin of non-currency documents.

12. RFID. Radio Frequency Identification tags pinpoint the physical location of whatever they are attached to. Privacy advocates are concerned that this technology could be used to track people without the need for a warrant.

13. Search engines. Search engines such as Google, Yahoo, Bing, and others record search queries and maintain massive query databases of your "private" searches. Much of this information may be sensitive, embarrassing, or even compromising. Because this personal information is stored with a third party, it is weakly protected by the Fourth Amendment and is vulnerable to subpoena by government prosecutors or private litigants. It may also be especially vulnerable to theft by hackers.

14. Search incident to arrest. Arresting police officers are generally limited in the extent to which they can conduct searches without an additional search warrant; however, they are always permitted to search the person of the arrestee (to prevent harm to themselves from concealed weapons and the like) and to search other adjacent objects, such as nearby drawers or containers, which might conceal weapons. Such a limited search is known as a "search incident to arrest." Recently, attempts have made to extend "search incident to arrest" to the digital-file contents of cell phones and computers, which privacy and civil rights advocates deem a dangerous and illegal extension of the warrantless search.

15. Travel screening. Any digital device you carry across the U.S. border is subject to seizure and its contents subject to copying for investigation and analysis. Privacy advocates believe this is a clear violation of the Fourth Amendment.

9/11

The attacks of September 11, 2001, against the World Trade Center and the Pentagon, along with the failed (but still deadly) attack on Washington, D.C., killed 2,996 and injured more than twice that number. The assault was so horrific and the immediate cost so high that lawmakers panicked, misinterpreted a terrorist assault as an existential threat against the nation, and rushed through Congress the USA PATRIOT Act, which the ACLU has accurately characterized as "an overnight revision of the nation's surveillance laws that vastly expanded the government's authority to spy on its own citizens, while simultaneously reducing checks and balances on those powers like judicial oversight, public accountability, and the ability to challenge government searches in court" (ACLU, "Surveillance under the USA PATRIOT Act").

The product of high anxiety and a political atmosphere in which legislators were made to feel that any attempt to study, let alone object to, the law would make them culpable for any subsequent attacks, the USA PATRIOT Act greatly expanded government surveillance authority in four areas:

1. Section 213 expanded law enforcement's authority to search private property without notice to the owner. The PATRIOT Act has given law enforcement broad "sneak and peek" power, allowing searches without first notifying the subjects of the search.

2. Section 214 allowed so-called "trap and trace" searches, expanding a type of search that the Supreme Court has held does not require a warrant by the Fourth Amendment. Trap and trace searches permit the collection of "addressing" information, and Section 214 expands this class of information to include significant parts of the content of email and text messages.

3. Section 215 broadened the government's access to records on an individual's activity that are held by third parties.

4. Section 218 greatly expanded a type of narrowly-defined warrantless search that was originally created by the 1978 Foreign Intelligence Surveillance Act (FISA) and had been interpreted to live outside the Fourth Amendment. FISA permitted the government to conduct a wiretap or search without meeting normal standards of probable cause if the purpose of the investigation was to gather foreign intelligence. The PATRIOT Act expanded

the exception to cover wiretaps and searches that do collect evidence for regular domestic criminal cases when "a significant purpose" is also intelligence. This opens the door to wholesale circumvention of the Fourth Amendment even in the course of domestic law enforcement.

All of the measures to broaden surveillance authority have direct application to digital communication, data, and record keeping. Enacted in a climate of intense fear, the law has not gone away in the intervening years but has been substantially reauthorized three times, in 2005, 2006, and 2010. Thus, the terrorist attacks that Presidents George W. Bush and Barack Obama have repeatedly characterized as "attacks on our freedom" have engendered laws that privacy and civil liberties advocates likewise characterize as such attacks.

Cyberwar

It requires no great insight to observe that the stock in trade of the terrorist is terror. The bloody, flaming terror of human and economic loss on 9/11/2001 was sufficient to persuade a majority of Americans to sacrifice individual liberty for security or the possibility of security or even the sense of security. A dozen years after the attacks, it is not very difficult for a majority of us to question the ongoing sacrifice of these liberties and, perhaps, even to cite the oft-mangled quotation from Benjamin Franklin: "They who can give up essential liberty to obtain a little temporary safety deserve neither liberty nor safety."

But consider the essay William J. Lynn III, at the time U.S. Deputy Secretary of Defense, published in the distinguished journal *Foreign Affairs* in the autumn of 2010, a decade after 9/11. Titled "Defending a New Domain: The Pentagon's Cyberstrategy," it begins with a frank admission of Defense Department vulnerability:

> In 2008, the U.S. Department of Defense suffered a significant compromise of its classified military computer networks. It began when an infected flash drive was inserted into a U.S. military laptop at a base in the Middle East. The flash drive's malicious computer code, placed there by a foreign intelligence agency, uploaded itself onto a network run by the U.S. Central Command. That code spread undetected on both classified and unclassified systems, establishing what amounted to a digital beachhead, from which data could be transferred to servers under foreign control. It was a network administrator's worst fear: a rogue program operating silently, poised to deliver operational plans into the hands of an unknown adversary (Lynn, 2010).

"This previously classified incident," Lynn wrote, "was the most significant breach of U.S. military computers ever, and it served as an important wake-up call." In fact, it was only one attack in what Lynn characterized as a relentless assault against "U.S. military and civilian networks," which "every day ... are probed thousands of times and scanned millions of times." Writing late in 2010, Lynn reported that "Over the past ten years, the frequency and sophistication of intrusions into U.S. military networks have increased exponentially." The 2008 intrusion prompted the military launch Operation Buckshot Yankee, resulting in the creation of the United States Cyber Command (USCYBERCOM), which "is responsible for planning, coordinating, integrating, synchronizing, and directing activities to operate and defend the Department of Defense information networks and when directed, conducts full-spectrum military cyberspace operations (in accordance with all applicable laws and regulations) in order to ensure U.S. and allied freedom of action in cyberspace, while denying the same to our adversaries" (U.S. Strategic Command, "U.S. Cyber Command"). Some interpret this as meaning that the U.S. military now considers cyberspace a battlefield, on a strategic par with the land, the sea, and the air.

It is, according to Lynn, a most active battlefield: "Adversaries have acquired thousands of files from U.S. networks and from the networks of U.S. allies and industry partners, including weapons blueprints, operational plans, and surveillance data" (Lynn, September/October 2010). In a 2011 *Foreign Affairs* follow-up to his earlier essay, Lynn elaborated: "Alarmingly, foreign intruders have already extracted terabytes of data from defense industry networks in recent years. In a single intrusion in March [2011], 24,000 files were taken. Some of the data stolen during this and other attacks is mundane, but a great deal concerns the United States' most sensitive systems, including aircraft avionics, surveillance technologies, satellite communications systems, and network security protocols." He added: "Current countermeasures have not stopped this outflow of sensitive information." (Lynn, 2011).

Like terrorists, those who wage war against U.S. cyber interests enjoy the benefits of "asymmetric" warfare. As Lynn observes, the "low cost of computing devices means that U.S. adversaries do not have to build expensive weapons, such as stealth fighters or aircraft carriers, to pose a significant threat to U.S. military capabilities. A dozen determined computer programmers can, if they find a vulnerability to exploit, threaten the United States' global logistics network, steal its operational plans, blind its intelligence capabilities, or hinder its ability to deliver weapons on target.... Some governments already have the capacity to disrupt elements of the U.S. information infrastructure" (Lynn, 2010). Sabotage poses a significant threat as malware known as "logic bombs" can be inserted into software as it is being developed and later cause sudden malfunctions. Remotely operated "kill switches" and "backdoors" can also be written into code, allowing outsiders to remotely manipulate systems.

The discovery in June 2010 of the Stuxnet computer worm targeting Siemens industrial software and equipment, specifically uranium enrichment infrastructure in Iran, revealed an actual cyberwarfare attack—against Iran, not the United States—and a June 1, 2012 *New York Times* article reported that Stuxnet was the product of a joint U.S.-Israeli operation (Sanger, June 1, 2012). Another malware program, Flame, reported in 2012, infected computers in the Middle East, again, mostly in Iran. The program (also known as Flamer, SKyWIper, and Skywiper), which has been called by software engineers the most sophisticated malware thus far detected, is capable of recording audio, making screenshots, logging keyboard activity, and monitoring network traffic. On June 19, 2012, the Washington Post reported that Flame was jointly developed by the U.S. National Security Agency (NSA), the CIA, and the Israeli military, and that it is closely related to Stuxnet (Nakashima, June 19, 2012).

The risks go beyond theft of military and state secrets. Lynn wrote that "Hackers and foreign governments are increasingly able to launch sophisticated intrusions into the networks that control critical civilian infrastructure. Computer-induced failures of U.S. power grids, transportation networks, or financial systems could cause massive physical damage and economic disruption." Industrial espionage and the theft of commercial information are also grave risks. Lynn cited a 2010 attack against Google, which "lost intellectual property as a result of a sophisticated operation perpetrated against its corporate infrastructure, an operation that also targeted dozens of other companies." Lynn observed that, "Every year, an amount of intellectual property many times larger than all the intellectual property contained in the Library of Congress is stolen from networks maintained by U.S. businesses, universities, and government agencies. As military strength ultimately depends on economic vitality, sustained intellectual property losses could erode both the United States' military effectiveness and its competitiveness in the global economy" (Lynn, 2010).

Military-Industrial Complex

Former Deputy Secretary Lynn has reported that U.S. cyberwarfare defense involves "a public-private partnership called the Enduring Security Framework," in which "the chief executive officers and chief technology officers of major information technology and defense companies now meet regularly with top officials from the Department of Homeland Security, the Office of the Director of National Intelligence, and the Department of Defense" (Lynn, 2010). Indeed, the demands of cybersecurity have brought the military and civilian sectors of government into close cooperation with private industry, since the entire digital infrastructure must be regarded as a target of military interest. Beyond this relationship is the burgeoning partnership between the military and civilian software companies, which are creating the digital arsenal of Cyber Command. Such partnerships between the military and its civilian armaments suppliers have long made many Americans uncomfortable, including, most famously, President Dwight D. Eisenhower, the former World War II supreme Allied commander in

Europe who, in his January 17, 1961 farewell address as U.S. president warned his fellow countrymen to beware the "military-industrial complex."

Whatever unease relations between the Pentagon and the digital industry may stir, disturbing stories have surfaced in the press concerning the role firms based in the U.S. and Europe have played in supplying privacy-penetrating software and hardware systems to a variety of authoritarian and typically brutal regimes. Rebecca MacKinnon recently wrote in *Foreign Affairs* that Egyptian protesters who stormed the country's national security headquarters after the fall of Hosni Mubarak "uncovered files focusing on friends and colleagues. There were wiretap transcripts, reams of printouts of intercepted emails, and mobile messages, communications once thought to be private." MacKinnon reported that "American-made technology had helped Mubarak and his security state collect, compile, and parse vast amounts of data about everyday citizens." In particular, the Egyptian government used so-called "deep packet inspection" technology purchased from Narus called NarusInsight. Ostensibly designed to help "network and security operators obtain real-time situational awareness of the traffic traversing their networks," NarusInsight can also be used (according to MacKinnon) to "help governments patrol their citizens' online activities." In addition to Egypt, Palestine, Saudi Arabia, Libya, and other foreign powers, Narus's principal clients included in 2005 the U.S. Department of Homeland Security and the NSA (MacKinnon, April 26, 2012).

Author MacKinnon found it ironic that she was reporting on Narus even "as the White House announced new sanctions against Iran and Syria on Monday, aimed at technology that Tehran and Damascus are using to target their own citizens. On Monday [April 23, 2012], President Barack Obama said of the Internet and mobile technologies that they, 'should be in place to empower citizens, not suppress them'":

Yet, even as the White House clamps down in Iran and Syria, other parts of the U.S. government are driving the development of policies, regulatory norms, and business practices that make a mockery of Washington's well-meaning efforts to expand Internet freedom abroad. Put another way, although the State Department funnels millions of dollars to nonprofits fighting censorship and surveillance beyond U.S. borders, repressive digital surveillance around the world continues to expand in scope and sophistication (MacKinnon, April 26, 2012).

Secretary of State Hillary Clinton has justly received praise for promoting a U.S. "global Internet freedom" agenda, and "the State Department has spent more than $70 million promoting Internet access around the world. The money has funded projects that produce circumvention software— for example, Tor, Psiphon, Ultrasurf, and Freegate—that has helped millions of people in China,

Iran, and other countries access censored websites. Other initiatives have provided Internet security training for activists and bloggers. State Department-funded groups now publish technical training manuals in more than a dozen languages." Nevertheless, "path breaking as Clinton's global Internet agenda may be, it is dwarfed by a multi-billion dollar global censorship and surveillance technology industry" (MacKinnon, April 26, 2012).

Sari Horwitz of the *Washington Post* reported in 2011 on an annual surveillance technology trade show held near Washington, D.C. and known informally as the "wiretappers' ball." In 2011, thirty-five federal agencies, as well as many representatives from state and local law enforcement, joined representatives of forty-three foreign countries to shop the wares purveyed by Narus and other high-tech surveillance firms that belong to an industry that sells some $5 billion in equipment and software annually (Horwitz, December 1, 2011).

The wiretappers' ball is closed to the public and journalists, and no agency of the U.S. government will discuss what types of technology it purchases. Alluding to "revelations over the past several years," MacKinnon concluded "that these technologies are deployed in illegal and unconstitutional contexts," including in the pursuit of cell-phone tracking by "police departments around the United States ... in non-emergency situations—without court orders or warrants." She also mentioned a 2004 whistleblower revelation that the NSA had "built a secret room inside an AT&T facility in San Francisco, into which all phone and e-mail traffic passing through the facility was copied. The software used to inspect the data and transmit anything of interest back to the NSA came from Narus, and national security expert James Bamford believes that "secret NSA rooms using Narus technology are still operating at AT&T facilities around the country." (MacKinnon, April 26, 2012).

Can We Restore Balance?
Defending our democracy has always required establishing a balance between surveillance and privacy. The events of September 11, 2001 prompted a radical shift in that balance, which the rapidly evolving threats and countermeasures of digital technology have made, it seems, increasingly difficult to reset and restore. Yet this same evolution has made it increasingly difficult for governments all over the world, including the United States, to avoid at least a small degree of transparency.

Just as the genie of digital liberty—as manifested in the kind of global connections the Internet enabled in the still-roiling "Arab Spring" overthrow of repressive regimes in the Middle East—cannot be put back into the bottle, so, perhaps, no government will be able to renounce the full potential of digital surveillance. One thing is certain, if citizens acquiesce in the role of clueless and feckless "subjects" of surveillance, the activity will only increase and grow increasingly intrusive and even outrageous. Becoming informed and politically active is one way to refuse acquiescence. Another is to practice the same level of savvy prudence with personal data when it comes to dealing with governments as we advise in Chapter 5 that you employ in using the social web and, as we advise in Chapter 7, that you observe when transacting e-commerce. Play offense with your data. Regard it as an asset you invest only as absolutely necessary to receive a benefit of significant value in return. Because governments (and some companies) can often peer into the metaphorical "pipes" that facilitate the transmission of data, the more you reveal, even to a trusted source, the more risk you create.

In the Private Sector
It is easy to forget that surveillance not only poses risks, but also actually yields positive benefits. The preamble to our Constitution mandates that the government "provide for the common defense," and surveillance, as Deputy Secretary Lynn suggested, does promote that mission and therefore promotes our collective security. In the private sector, surveillance can also enhance security, safety, and productivity. Employers have certain rights to protect their property and other assets and to monitor a range of activities that take place within the context of their business. Indeed, principles of due diligence require business owners to audit and monitor activities that emanate from their organizations. Whether you are an employer, an employee, or both, you have a responsibility to understand the legal rights and legal limitations of surveillance and the use of other digital technologies in a business context. Again, in the arena of employment specifically and business generally, the best strategy is to play offense with personal as well as corporate data. Guard it, understand it, never simply spend it or automatically surrender it. Always endeavor to invest it as you would any other valuable asset: only on the reasonable expectation of gaining greater value in return.

CHAPTER TEN
Wide Open Privacy

In recent years, the fiction and philosophy of Ayn Rand, popular with many Americans during the Cold War era, have reemerged among those who would lead a new charge in the name of "Objectivism," Rand's philosophical belief that objective knowledge can be obtained by each person alone and directly through individual perception and the application of inductive logic. The moral corollary of this epistemology is "rational self-interest," the doctrine that the purpose of human life is the pursuit and fulfillment of one's own happiness and that the role of society and culture is to get out of the way. Today's often extreme political climate has shone so bright a spotlight on this point of view that we may fail to see the line-up of distinguished social scientists and social thinkers who oppose Objectivism—and do so not for political or moral reasons, but on evolutionary grounds.

Jeremy Rifkin (*The Empathic Civilization: The Race to Global Consciousness in a World in Crisis*, 2009), Roy F. Baumeister (*The Cultural Animal: Human Nature, Meaning, and Social Life*, 2005), and Robert Wright (*Nonzero: The Logic of Human Destiny*, 2000) all argue some version of Nicholas Christakis and James Fowler's assertion, discussed in Chapter 5, that evolution has transformed Homo sapiens into Homo dictyous, "network man," and that social networks are, in effect, "a kind of human superorganism" (Christakis and Fowler, 2009, xvi). Their contention is that humanity has become increasingly connected as a species of cultural animals and that the Internet is a technological expression of a biocultural evolution. This is not only the way things are, they argue, but a very good thing indeed.

The Internet and Its Discontents

Then why are so many of us so often so stressed out about life online?

You may already know that the Internet had its origin in something called ARPANET (Advanced Research Projects Agency Network), a project funded by an agency of the U.S. Department of Defense, DARPA (Defense Advanced Research Projects Agency) to link universities and research labs that were working on Deparment of Defense (DoD) projects. From this kernel—and by way of NSFNET (National Science Foundation Network)—the Internet as we know it began to emerge in the late 1980s. Instead of a tightly closed, centrally controlled place, the Internet was a vast, exuberantly decentralized network, open, collaborative,

125

free, and even joyous. And that is how many of us came to embrace the Internet. These days, however, with its litany of threats, invasions of privacy, too-often predatory commercial practitioners, too-often intrusive government operatives, and its haunting by outright criminals, the Internet can seem a hostile and degraded place, a techno-Eden no more.

As we saw in Chapter 2, a majority of Internet users are very concerned about privacy. Understandable though this is, the concern may well be self-defeating. Proposed legislation to allow government and business to share information had for a while garnered rare bipartisan support in Congress, but, in a recent United Technologies/National Journal Congressional Connection Poll reported on July 10-11, 2012, 63 percent of respondents voiced their objection to government and businesses sharing information "because it would hurt privacy and civil liberties." Twenty-nine percent, however, believed the "information should be allowed to better protect computer networks" (Smith, July 10-11, 2012). That is, some two-thirds of Internet users favor protecting "privacy," even at the expense of protecting the security of the Internet itself. More than anything, perhaps, this response suggests the complexities of talking about "privacy" online. The question is less *Privacy: good or bad?*, than it is *Privacy from whom?*, *Privacy with respect to what types of data?*, *Privacy in what context?*

In the UK, skepticism over data collection may run even deeper than it does in the United States. A *Wall Street Journal* blog has reported on a 2012 Deloitte survey that found that while 82 percent of UK respondents "are aware that their data is collected by organizations, only 29% are confident companies will not sell or share their data with other groups without their knowledge" (Rooney, July 9, 2012).

By any quantitative measure, a majority of Internet users are concerned about the privacy of their personal data. Looked at qualitatively, however, one can detect an emerging minority backlash against this concern. In a recent opinion piece for *The Street*, Atlanta-based tech reporter Dana Blankenhorn commented on Google's latest privacy policy (last modified on March 1, 2012), describing it as a straightforward bargain: "Give me your data and I will help it serve you. Or don't." If you allow Google to link to your personal data, "the search engine delivers results that are more personal, more likely what you are trying to find." Blankenhorn acknowledges the objection of privacy advocates, that Google "may also be sharing this knowledge with people who want to sell you stuff," but, unlike those advocates, he finds "this Google bargain perfectly acceptable," noting that if "search engines are to become 'find' engines they must know us and adapt to us" (Blankenhorn, May 31, 2012).

Some have gone even further than Blankenhorn. In 1999, Scott McNealy, at the time CEO of Sun Microsystems, famously pronounced consumer privacy issues a "red herring," telling reporters, "You have zero privacy anyway. Get over it" (Sprenger, January 26, 1999).   Much more recently, privacy author Don Tapscott has observed that "a growing number of people argue that the notion of having a private life in which we carefully restrict what information we share with others may not be a good idea. Instead, sharing our intimate, personal information with others would benefit us individually and as a society." Tapscott cites "some of the smartest and most influential thinkers and practitioners of the digital revolution," including Jeff Jarvis, author of *Public Parts*, who "argues that because privacy has its advocates, so should 'publicness.'" Tapscott goes on to cite David Kirkpatrick's explanation in *The Facebook Effect* that Facebook's founders believe that "more visibility makes us better people. Some claim, for example, that because of Facebook, young people today have a harder time cheating on their boyfriends or girlfriends. They also say that more transparency should make for a more tolerant society in which people eventually accept that everybody sometimes does bad or embarrassing things." There is even a name for this point of view: "radical transparency." (Tapscott, May 11, 2012).

Tapscott does not himself advocate these radical positions on "publicness," but he does suggest that, perhaps, "our fundamental ideas about identity and privacy, the strategies that we have collectively pursued and the technologies that we have adopted must change and adapt in a rapidly evolving world of connectivity, networking, participation, sharing and collaboration." He identifies "a real upside to participating in communities, seeing photos, hearing stories or knowing the location of friends and family" and points out that "Sharing also helps companies deliver personalized products and services. It can improve advertising, as we are targeted for products and services that correspond to our interests." Moreover, by revealing "personal information we can help society too. Every time a gay person comes out or someone with depression opens up about his condition, it helps break down stigma and prejudice." He also concedes a dangerous downside to renouncing privacy: "massive commercial and government interests, as well as malevolent individuals, that have a lot to gain from each of us revealing highly granular personal information, much of it in the public domain by default and in real time as we travel through life." Nevertheless, on balance, the potential benefits of information sharing seem to outweigh the liabilities—though Tapscott emphasizes the need for "each of us" to develop "a personal privacy strategy governing what information we release and to whom."

Put another way, provided we have transparency into how our data is collected and used, and real, meaningful control over our data—as long as we have the tools we need to strategically share our data and manage our identities online—we stand to reap incredible rewards for engaging the "network man" in each of us. Tapscott suggests that developing a personal privacy strategy is especially critical now that we may be on the verge of seeing the introduction of software that could digitize, catalog, and retrieve "every conceivable scrap of information about your own life that you could want, such as photos, rock-concert tickets and wedding invitations," software that has the potential, for better or worse, to act "as a surrogate memory." The software is MyLifeBits (http://research.microsoft.com/en-us/projects/mylifebits/), a research project under way at Microsoft. And Google, Tapscott notes, has a similar project in the works (Tapscott, May 11, 2012).

Technological Solutions

At present, in part because of the lack of real transparency and control offered by companies and governments alike, there is no single technological means of implementing a "personal privacy strategy," though there are some high-tech partial solutions to consider.

Reputation Management

A number of online services have emerged recently offering online reputation management (ORM), which is (as reputation.com puts it) "the practice of making people and businesses look their best on the Internet." The core of these services, which include reputation.com, Reputation Hawk (reputationhawk.com), Brand Yourself (brandyourself.com), Safe Shepherd (safeshepherd.com), Secure Me (secure.me), Metal Rabbit Media (metalrabbitmedia.com), and others, is controlling Internet search results—the information that is returned when someone searches on your name or the name of your business. ORMs search for your personal data online, automatically generate and transmit removal requests to companies exposing your data, and monitor the Web to detect and remove reposting of previously removed data.

In a 2011 *New York Times* story, "The Growing Business of Online Reputation Management," reporter Nick Bilton cited Bryce Tom, founder of Metal Rabbit Media, who equated online reputation to the modern day credit report, pointing out that Americans have had to learn to manage their credit cards and bills to maintain a good credit score. The Web, he said, contains the modern day version of inaccurate credit reports, and reputation managers will be the equivalent of companies that monitor or fix people's credit (Bilton, April 4, 2011). This is a telling comparison. While credit monitoring is important to managing your credit score, no one thinks it alone is sufficient to building and maintaining good credit. Savvy financial management and prudent spending are also required. Much the same is true of managing your reputation online. Monitoring personal data and cleaning up what you can are important, but not in themselves sufficient to create a strong and productive personal brand online.

Onion Routing

Tor, at www.torproject.org, is a civilian iteration of the onion routing project developed by the U.S. Naval Research Laboratory, a system "for low-latency

Internet-based connections that resist traffic analysis, eavesdropping, and other attacks both by outsiders (e.g., Internet routers) and insiders (Onion Routing servers themselves)." Onion Routing (OR) works by preventing "the transport medium from knowing who is communicating with whom—the network knows only that communication is taking place. In addition, the content of the communication is hidden from eavesdroppers up to the point where the traffic leaves the OR network" (http://www.onion-router.net/). While OR was originally designed by the Navy to protect government communications, the makers of Tor claim that it is currently "used every day for a wide variety of purposes by normal people, the military, journalists, law enforcement officers, activists, and many others" (https://www.torproject.org/about/overview.html.en#thesolution).

A network of virtual tunnels, Tor defeats traffic analysis, a common form of Internet surveillance that can be used to infer who is communicating with whom over a public network. If the source and destination of your Internet traffic are known, a third party can track your behavior and your interests. Tor points out that such tracking "can impact your checkbook if, for example, an e-commerce site uses price discrimination based on your country or institution of origin." In some instances, it might "even threaten your job and physical safety by revealing who and where you are" (https://www.torproject.org/about/overview.html.en#thesolution).

Tor can be used by individuals to prevent websites from tracking them and their family members. Tor allows users to publish websites without revealing the location of the site. It can be used for "socially sensitive communication: chat rooms and web forums for rape and abuse survivors, or people with illnesses." Journalists might use it "to communicate more safely with whistleblowers and dissidents" (https://www.torproject.org/about/overview.html.en#thesolution). If you are interested in exploring Tor, it can be downloaded at https://www.torproject.org/index.html.en. Using Tor is one of the best ways to control your data—to protect your privacy, if you prefer that moniker—online.

Personal Data Store

Another technological approach to a personal privacy strategy is something called a "personal data store" (PDS), "personal data service," "personal data locker," or "personal data vault." PDS is a cloud service for storing anything created or done online. Unlike an ordinary cloud storage service, however, a PDS is very much like a personal bank account. You control it. No third party—including the PDS provider—can access the stored data without your permission. The data that you choose to share, known as volunteered personal information (VPI), is shared only with PDS-enabled individuals, merchants, or organizations. The individual user decides what VPI to share with what other PDS-enabled individuals and entities, when to share it, under what conditions to share it, and for what purposes to share it. When dealing with businesses, the consumer manages the vendor to the same degree that the vendor manages the consumer.

PDS and the VPI concept are already available in the UK. According to Alan Mitchell, strategy director for Ctrl-Shift, a UK-based PDS provider, "a dozen" new PDS services will have launched by the end of 2012, and within five years "they could be hosting 100 million data sets for individuals in the UK alone" (Mitchell, May 30, 2012).

PDS requires very widespread adoption by Internet stakeholders—consumers as well as providers of goods and services. Mitchell predicts that "Within the next few years, every customer-facing organization will need to develop its own VPI strategy" (Mitchell, May 30, 2012). At this point in time, there is no telling whether and to what extent PDS will take root as the privacy solution of choice. It is worthwhile, however, immediately to take note of the rationale on which the PDS VPI concept is based. Mitchell argues "that privacy is a personal setting and that it makes sense for individuals rather than organisations to look after their own personal data." He believes that "privacy cannot be set by a policy decided on by an organization" because only "I know what information I feel comfortable sharing with who, for what purposes, in what contexts." Mitchell further argues that "it's been an accident of history that has led organisations to collect and manage data about their customers. The effect of this accident is to disperse information about me across hundreds of separate, isolated data silos, each one run by a different organisation. This," he says, "is crazy." Although all organizations that collect user data make heroic efforts to "create 'a single view,' none of these organisations can see me in the round because they only have access to a very thin sliver of data about me." Should they "try to join the dots by bringing different sets of data together they risk becoming highly intrusive." Ultimately, it is "only natural that the individual should be the place where data about 'my money,' 'my health,' 'my behaviours,' and so on should converge" (Mitchell, May 30, 2012).

The benefits of PDS to consumers are self-evident, but, Mitchell argues, e-commerce providers and businesses of all kinds also stand to benefit. When consumers feel in control of their information—when it is truly volunteered personal information—they become increasingly willing "to volunteer additional information ... that only they know and only they can contribute: information about their plans and intentions, their current priorities and interests, their changing context and circumstances, their changing preferences ..." (Mitchell, May 30, 2012). Bear this in mind, as we continue to the next two sections of this chapter.

A Wide Open Privacy Strategy

Alan Mitchell's optimistic view that personal data storage systems will proliferate rapidly and become widespread if not universal is understandable—his company creates PDS/VPI solutions—and not unreasonable. Yet, as of fall 2012, PDS, despite being an idea that has been kicked around for years if not a decade, has yet to receive a great deal of attention outside of the UK and among Silicon Valley insiders. There is no way to predict whether the technology will become widely adapted. Nevertheless, as just mentioned, the key policy assumptions on which PDS is based are relevant right now as the basis for a rational and productive personal data policy:

1. Privacy policies are best decided by the individual user, not by governments, e-commerce providers, or other organizations.
2. Only the individual user knows what information he or she wants to share, with whom, for what purposes, and in what contexts.
3. An individual's personal data is currently collected by many entities and is dispersed across the Internet. Put the data in the hands of each individual, and it will be consolidated for greater security as well as higher informational value.
4. If individual users feel they control their own data and have trust in those they choose to share data with, they will be likely to share more data and data of higher quality, thereby enhancing the effectiveness of e-commerce and other VPI-intensive online activities.

With the tools currently available, the most effective privacy strategy an individual user can create should embody as many of these four principles as possible. The defensive steps have already been outlined in the chapters of Part II. Beyond these steps, play offense with your personal digital data by talking these additional steps:

1. Stop thinking (and stressing) about "privacy" in the abstract. Start thinking in terms of data—personal information—and the data footprint you create with everything you do online.
2. Many privacy advocates, especially those in Europe, are adamantly opposed to the concept of personal data as property. Yet the truth is that "privacy," once committed to the digital environment, becomes data, a quantifiable commodity. The only meaningful, let alone effective, way to manage and protect this data is to treat it as we do most items of private property. They are owned. They can be legally shared, traded, or sold. They must be protected against theft. Think of your personal data as your private property, a portfolio of assets, and treat it accordingly. (Note, however, that data does not have all the legal protections that property, commonly understood, has.)
3. Understand that an e-commerce provider may argue that the data he

collects from you—from your interactions with him—is *his* property. This does not mean you have to think of it this way.

4. To the extent you have control, give careful thought as to how you invest your VPI assets. You may decide that some companies give you little or no value in return for it, whereas others offer products or services of interest to you and about which you want to hear more on an ongoing basis. Accordingly, click through online ads selectively, and manage do-not-track options closely. But keep in mind that just to get online, you end up sharing your VPI—all of your browsing data—with your ISP or mobile carrier, many of the websites you visit and all of the ad networks they partner with (even if you don't click on ads), and possibly even your government.

5. Give thought to how you manage privacy controls on social websites. Always remain mindful of the digital footprint you create and add to every day.

Another aspect of the PDS discussion we can benefit from right now is the idea of putting consumers and producers on an equal footing. E-commerce providers are accustomed to "managing" their customers and the data they collect from them. PDS promises to give consumers the power to manage their vendors. Even without PDS, we can all do some of that managing right now. Decide which of your vendors you want to fully engage with. Accept emails, newsletters, and the like from them. You may want to engage with them on Facebook or wherever else they have a social presence. Decide this on the basis of a fair exchange of values. If what the vendor offers is valuable to you, it may be worth volunteering more of your personal data to create fuller engagement. With other vendors, you may decide to be as stingy with your personal data as possible (recognizing that as things stand right now, there is only so much you can control). Do provide feedback to vendors whose "consumer engagement" practices you really like as well as to those whose policies are objectionable. Let them know how you feel. Many e-commerce providers are very responsive.

The other dimension of your online presence you can manage, even without special technology, is your online brand. We have spoken of personal online branding in Chapter 3 and will return to it in Chapter 12. Applied to individual users online, personal branding means projecting a presence intended to create the impression you want to make and the emotional response you want to elicit. Once you decide who you are—or who you want to be online—everything you post online, everything you say online, everything you do online should contribute to the personal brand you mean to project.

Personal branding is especially important professionally of course, but it applies to any individual presence online. It is an opportunity to present yourself productively, confidently, and securely to the world. Every successful enterprise understands that if it fails to brand itself effectively—if it does not project to the world a productive identity, the identity it wants—others will force a brand or identity on it and will rarely do so to the firm's advantage. The same is true in the case of any individual who wants to develop a strong online presence.

Before you randomly engage on the social web, tweet on Twitter, start a blog, post material in a forum, decide how you want to be known. What qualities do you want others to associate with you?

Make a list. Put the list away. After a day or two, return to the list. Examine it, grouping similar qualities together, editing out what you don't like. Distill the list to two to four major qualities. If you are satisfied with these, make these the basis of your personal brand, the identity you project online. If you find yourself stuck, just think about what excites you and what you are most passionate about. Build your brand around these passions.

Promote yourself online, but never confuse promoting yourself with boasting. If you regularly update followers on Twitter or share with friends on Facebook, use these occasions to describe and promote your latest achievements; don't boast about how much you paid for your new watch. If you are moved to announce something of which you are proud or about which you are excited—or if you want to share a thought, an insight, a product recommendation—do so with complete confidence that you are engaging in productive self-promotion of your brand. If, however, your motive is to make others drool with envy, you are not promoting your brand. You are bragging, a move that will contribute nothing to your brand and possibly damage it.

Offer information to others. Tweet or blog about events you know others will be interested in. Discuss your experience with products and services of interest to others. On the forums you regularly visit, strive to make yourself useful and helpful to others. However you may specifically brand yourself, you can never go wrong by being identified as the guy who solves problems or is always ready with a worthwhile suggestion. Tell others what you think they should know—what you believe will benefit them. If you can put your offerings in the form of stories, so much the better, so long as the stories are not blatantly self-centered or self-serving, but, on the contrary, provide information and/or entertainment of interest and use to others.

The Island Paradox Revisited

These exercises in self-branding will ultimately enable you to create circles of relationships online. The value of networking has long been recognized in business. Marketers know that no form of promotion is more powerful than word-of-mouth. Transform the Internet from a field of anonymous contacts to a network of productive personal and professional engagements. Ultimately, the purpose of your brand is to create productive networks. To the degree that you can replace anonymity with trust, you will increase your security online. The process of this replacement is a function of active networking and, by allowing you to better control how you are perceived, will create privacy within the vastness of the Internet, a privacy not founded on secrecy or aloofness, but a wide open privacy, one created by selective transparency, openness, and sharing.

We believe wide open privacy is the most productive and rewarding, yet most genuinely secure approach to full individual engagement with the Internet. It is also the most achievable, especially with the technology currently available and in the current, albeit changeable, state of government and industry management of digital privacy. Recall the "Privacy Paradoxes" of Chapter 1. The last of these, the "Island Paradox," describes the ambivalence many Internet users feel of being simultaneously isolated in a vast ocean of connectedness yet also exposed and helpless among connections wanted and connections unwanted. Many users feel so uncomfortable online that they endeavor to make themselves islands, "safely" isolated from the dangers of the Internet, whether apparent, imagined, exaggerated, or actual. To the degree that a user cuts himself off from connectedness, however, he misses out on the liberating and enlightening—some authorities would say the downright evolutionary—benefits of digital technology.

The Island Paradox can be resolved far more effectively by envisioning your "island" not as isolated from the rest of the world, but as connected to it whenever, wherever, however, under what circumstances, and for whatever span of time you wish it to be. Think about your presence on the Internet, shape it, manage it, curate it, be an active steward of it, and you become within it not an island backwater—cut off until someone decides to attack—but an island nexus, a source of selective, productive, generous, and rewarding connections. Under your active control, and if you have the right tools in hand, your privacy will be wide open, yet also as private as you choose for it to be.

.03

[*The Future of Privacy*]

CHAPTER ELEVEN
Find the Cybergaps

Futurists and technologists as well as legal, political, and policy pundits have speculated and will continue to speculate on the "future of privacy" in our digitally networked world. The more privacy continues to figure as a topic of intense and intelligent discussion, the better. Nevertheless, such discussions, no matter how deeply they may interest us, leave us out—or, rather, put us in the position of mere spectators to the rapid evolution of technology, law, politics, and policy. These, after all, are the province of specialists, of computer scientists, jurists, politicians, and bureaucrats, not "the rest of us."

And yet "the rest of us" are by any measure the majority stakeholders in the future of privacy. Fortunately, the majority of this majority possesses not only the most urgent stake in the future, but has access to the most direct means of contributing to the shape of it. By what is very nearly a tautological definition, the most potent force that will determine the future of privacy is the rising generation of digital users and online consumers. It is our children, and this chapter as well as the next is devoted to strategies for influencing and guiding them in creating secure, productive, and ethical lives in a future that, whatever else it may be, will certainly be increasingly networked. The first step we must take is to identify the intellectual, cultural, developmental, and even physiological gaps that tend to make our children's online experience different from our own. The second step is to begin to bridge these gaps.

The phrase *generation gap* first appeared in print in 1967 (*Online Etymology Dictionary*) to express something centuries of parents and children have probably felt, but that the culture began to pick up sometime in the 1950s (think of 1955's *Rebel Without a Cause*) and seriously started stressing about in the mid-1960s. The stress faded somewhat by the mid-1970s, but the phrase remains a fixture of the English language (and now in other languages as well) to describe the chasm that seems inevitably to separate parents' perceptions, values, and understanding from those of their children. The phrase endures, but does so only as a cliché so well worn that we believe it inadequate to describe the widely reported generational divide that has developed at the end of the twentieth century and beginning of the twenty-first with the rise and dominance of the Internet and all other digital intermediation of "real life."

Let's call this new divide the cybergap.

Although the word is not currently in use to describe a digitally defined incarnation of the generation gap, we can easily identify its most dire

137

interpretation. It was expressed most succinctly in a headline from *The Guardian* (UK) that appeared on January 18, 2009 (Curtis, January 18, 2009):

"Internet generation leave parents behind"

The article cites an unspecified "study of five- to 16-year-olds" showing that "online activity is building barriers between parents and children ... with a third of young people insisting they cannot live without their computer." We are told that, from "the age of seven children are building multimedia hubs in their rooms, with games consoles, internet access and MP3 players, which they wake up to in the morning and fall asleep to at night." Experts quoted assert that digital media is producing "toxic childhoods" and creating a "digital divide" between parents, teachers, and other adults on the one hand and children and teens on the other. Rather less panic-stricken among the authorities cited is Rosemary Duff, director of a Norwich (UK)-based market research agency called ChildWise. She comments that it is "hard for the older generation to understand what's going on with their children because they communicate in a completely different way" (Curtis, January 18, 2009).

Natives vs. Immigrants

In 2001, an American writer on learning and education, Marc Prensky, coined the terms *Digital Natives* and *Digital Immigrants*. Digital Natives, he explained, are people of Gen X and younger, born with "digital DNA" in the digital era, and sometimes even called the "iGeneration." Digital Immigrants, in contrast, are those born into the pre-PC/Mac/Internet world (Prensky, October 2001). While Prensky doesn't mention a precise before-and-after date for the divide between Natives and Immigrants, some sources peg it to the mid to late 1960s, but most imply a somewhat more recent vintage. In any event, Prensky's terms are now sufficiently pervasive in discussions of digital culture to have provoked subsequent elaboration and refinement. Psychologists Ofer Zur and Azzia Zur now distinguish three major varieties of the Digital Immigrant:

1. The avoiders. These are people who strongly resist digital technology. They hang onto their landline rather than carry a cell phone, and they watch television and listen to the radio rather than surf the web. They still send letters via snail mail instead of using email or SMS. The avoiders have the least in common with Digital Natives.

2. The reluctant adopters. These Digital Immigrants probably have a computer in the house and use one at work, but they nevertheless prefer landline telephones to cell phones. They do own a cell, but it's a basic model

—not a smartphone (and they may often forget to turn it on!). Like the avoiders, the reluctant adopters prefer to send letters through the post office rather than rely on email, and they almost never turn to their computer for entertainment.

3. The enthusiastic or eager adopters. These are Digital Immigrants who enjoy digital technology and use it extensively. They have a good deal in common with Digital Natives (Zur and Zur, 2010).

As Prensky originally presented the Immigrant/Native dichotomy, the separation between the two generations was conceived as profound: the proverbial chasm. Although the Zurs elaborated a range of technological acceptance and savvy among the pre-digital generation, even they suggested that the most enthusiastic Digital Immigrant adopter tends not to deal with digital culture as naturally as the most enthusiastic Digital Native. He or she is quite fluent in digital, but nevertheless speaks it with a noticeable accent. The Zurs thus preserve the terms of the metaphor. Immigrants may become well assimilated into their adopted land, but they will never be natives, and thus the cybergap is deep, wide, and destined to endure at least until the last of the Digital Immigrant generation shuffles off this mortal coil.

From Chasm to Common Ground

The Hans Bredow Institute was founded by the Nordwestdeutscher Rundfunk broadcasting organization and the University of Hamburg in 1950 to conduct research on "mediated public communication." In 1950, that meant radio and television. Today, it's the Internet, and German journalist Manfred Dworschak recently drew on Bredow research to offer a more moderate—and dare we say more hopeful—view of the cybergap. He concludes that in place of a yawning chasm defining the digital divide, there is actually considerable common ground between Digital Natives and Digital Immigrants (Bredow, 2009; Dworschak, June 8, 2010).

Teens do spend a significant amount of time online, Dworschak concedes, quoting a study by the Stuttgart-based media research group MPFS, which reported that 98 percent of twelve- to nineteen-year-olds in Germany had access to the Internet in 2010 and "by their own estimates ... are online for an average of 134 minutes a day—just three minutes less than they spend in front of the television." Dworschak goes on to point out that "the raw figures say little about what these supposed digital natives actually do online." While many Digital Immigrants assume that their Digital Native children travel to strange new worlds on the web, wandering among myriad wonders from which parents are barred and which they could not begin to comprehend in any case, it turns out that "the kids of today are very similar to previous generations of young people:

They are mainly interested in communicating with their peers. Today's young people spend almost half of their time interacting socially online. E-mail, instant messaging and social networking together accounts for the bulk of their Internet time." Dworschak notes that blogging and tweeting—specialized online activities addressed to people beyond one's real-life social circle—are actually down among teens. "Only 3 percent of young people keep their own blog, and no more than 2 percent regularly contribute to Wikipedia or other comparable open source projects." The journalist concludes that these Digital Natives, "the first generation that cannot imagine life without the Internet," do not "actually consider the medium particularly important." While online activities are important, they are not—as many parents assume—all-consuming (Bredow, 2009; Dworschak, June 8, 2010).

Could it be that what we call the cybergap—and picture as an ultimately unbridgeable quasi-genetic, epoch-making techno-cultural phenomenon—is mostly hype?

Well, Dworschak does point out that those who write of the radically revolutionary nature of the Internet—who claim, in effect, that it has created a generation of teenage cyborgs built on "digital DNA"—are almost all in their middle age or older. The theorists of the digital divide are themselves Digital Immigrants who are chronologically quite far removed from the iGeneration. Marc Prensky, for example, was sixty-four when Dworschak wrote his article in 2010, and Prensky's Canadian colleague Don Tapscott, author of the provocative *Grown Up Digital: How the Net Generation Is Changing Your World*, was sixty-two (Tapscott, 2009). The implication is that these Digital Immigrants do what immigrants everywhere have always done. They stand in far greater awe of their adopted country than natives do.

No wonder, then, that the older commentators on digital life are more impressed with it than the youngsters who actually live that life. Talk to the Natives themselves, as the Bredow Institute researchers did, and you will discover that "young people primarily use the Internet to interact with friends. They go on social networking sites like Facebook ... to chat, mess around and show off—just like they do in real life" (Bredow, 2009; Dworschak, June 8, 2010).

If you are a Digital Immigrant and are surprised to learn that Digital Natives are not radically different from you in how they use the Internet—that they don't see it as a brave new world so much as a flexible and convenient means of interacting with the same old world they share with you—you may be even more shocked to discover (as the Bredow research concludes) that the majority of Digital Natives are not even particularly adept at "getting the most out of the Internet" (Bredow, 2009).

We are accustomed to film and television portrayals of super-savvy hacker youths—from the hero that Matthew Broderick played in John Badham's 1983 *WarGames* to Jesse Eisenberg's 2010 rendition of Mark Zuckerberg in David

Fincher's *The Social Network*—but the mundane reality is that the Internet generation is neither universally adept at navigating and manipulating the digital world nor uniformly enthusiastic about it. As Ofer Zur and Azzia Zur argue, the range of interest and involvement in things digital among Digital Natives actually mirrors that of Digital Immigrants, occupying a spectrum that runs from outright avoidance to avid enthusiasm. The Zurs concede that "Enthusiastic participants make up most of the digital natives." These are young people who "enjoy and thrive on technology and gadgets. They interact on Facebook all day long, many of them Tweet, all of them are online in some capacity (YouTube, watching TV shows or movies online, Facebook, surfing, etc.) all day long or as much as possible" (Zur and Zur, 2011).

The Bredow data suggests that "all day long" is actually an exaggeration. Less than two and a half hours a day is a more realistic estimate. Nevertheless, as the Zurs point out, when enthusiastic Digital Natives "want to know something—such as a language translation, directions to a party, how to spell a word—the first thing they do is turn to Google." Yet, the two psychologists contend, the ranks of the Digital Natives include, in addition to the "enthusiasts," both "avoiders" and "minimalists."

> Avoiders. These are young people, born digital, who nevertheless feel no "affinity for digital technologies and, unlike most of their peers ... are not enamored by Facebook, texting or mobile technologies."

> Minimalists. These Digital Natives "realize that technology is a part of today's world," but "try to engage with it minimally and only when they perceive it is necessary. They Google for information if they have to and purchase online only if they cannot do so in a local store. While they may have a Facebook account, they may check it only once a day or every couple of days. They will ask for directions to a friend's house instead of simply getting the address and looking it up on Google maps. If absolutely necessary, they will use Skype or a GPS system, but they are not eager to do so" (Zur and Zur, 2011).

It is evident that a digital divide does separate those who came of age before the era of digital dominance and those who were born into that age; however, this psycho-cultural space is both less absolute and more complex than the now-familiar terms "Digital Immigrant" and "Digital Native" imply. The cybergap does not appear to be as profound or as difficult to bridge as the "generation gap" of the 1960s. The reason is that, in the case of the cybergap, there is at least as much common ground as gap between the generations. The proposition to the contrary, that the Children of the Machine are born of digital DNA and therefore constitute virtually a new species, appears to be chiefly a perception conceived and projected by the older generations—the Digital Immigrants—and is not believed, let alone embraced, by the Digital Natives themselves. Contrast this with the 1960s generation gap, in which the most enthusiastic Baby Boomers proclaimed themselves Flower Children, professed a counterculture, and vowed to trust no one over thirty. The post-thirty generation was given no say in the matter at all.

The discovery of common ground is reason for hope that Digital Natives and Digital Immigrants may not only come to peacefully coexist, but can actually help each other and generally enrich one another's lives. Not only can parents and teachers perform their traditional roles as nurturers, protectors, mentors, and guides, they can also learn from their children and students, and the intellectual and cultural benefits of new technology can be passed up from the younger generation to the older. This said, there is still our other discovery to contend with—that the digital divide is more complex than commentators have hitherto acknowledged.

Cybergap x 4

Both real and significant, the cybergap is neither as absolute nor as monolithically simple as it is typically portrayed to be. In fact, the digital divide is exactly four times more complex because there is really not a single cybergap, but four:

1. The generational cybergap. Call this one the gap between Digital Natives and Digital Immigrants—those born into the digital age and those born before.

2. The intra-generational cybergap. This is the divide separating the majority of the Digital Natives, who are enthusiastic about their digital pedigree, from the minority, who are (in the Zurs' terminology) either "minimalists" or "avoiders," either unengaged adopters or downright resistant to technology.

3. The developmental cybergap. The one immutable difference between Digital Natives and Digital Immigrants is that most of the Natives are children or teens and all of the Immigrants are adults. Many (maybe most) of today's children and teens may be Internet- and tech-savvy by right of birth, but they are nevertheless by biological fact immature, which means they have yet to acquire an adult capacity to effectively handle all of the challenges of real life. There is a gap between the young Digital Native's tech savvy and his or her real-world faculties of judgment and perception as well as coping and reasoning skills. This is not an invidious value judgment made from the perspective of Digital Immigrant middle age, but a well-studied issue of neural development (Palfrey and Gasser, 2008:165). As Doctors

Daniel R. Weinberger, Brita Elvevag, and Jay N. Giedd explain in *The Adolescent Brain: A Work in Progress*, "Contrary to long-held ideas that the brain was mostly grown-up—'fully cooked'—by the end of childhood, it is now clear that adolescence is a time of profound brain growth and change. In fact, the brain of an early adolescent in comparison to that of a late adolescent differs measurably in anatomy, biochemistry, and physiology." In particular, "new research suggests that the PFC [prefrontal cortex] is one of the last areas of the brain to fully mature." The prefrontal cortex "is often referred to as the 'CEO' or executive of the brain and is responsible for such skills as setting priorities, organizing plans and ideas, forming strategies, controlling impulses, and allocating attention." Adolescent thought processes are immature in large part because the adolescent brain is anatomically and functionally immature. What is more, children and teens congregating online effectively tend to reinforce each other's immature thought processes (Weinberger, et al., June 2005).

4. The cybergap between cause and effect online. Despite evidence that most Digital Natives regard life online as an extension of "real life" and not as a life lived in some parallel digital universe, the online experience is significantly different from experience in real life, especially for a child or teen. The online environment engenders a feeling of anonymity or invisibility: *You can't see me. Nobody can.* It is conducive to a sense of omnipotence coupled with an absence of rules. It is an environment that facilitates ready rationalization, even of highly questionable or downright foolish or reckless actions. Often, the online environment provides the ability and the occasion to act through an online persona, perhaps more than one. The environment online often feels like a game, especially since so many actual games are played in it. Children and teens may therefore find it difficult to think in terms of real-world consequences of acts committed online. The digital environment is made even more conducive to impulsive behavior because, despite sensations of privacy and even invisibility, it is a crowded universe in which an "everybody does it" ethos readily applies.

Perils of the Cybergaps

None of us has to look very hard to find thoroughly alarming statistics on the dangers our kids may encounter on the Internet. The Enough-Is-Enough "Internet Safety 101" site (http://www.internetsafety101.org) is as good a place as any to locate these (Enough-Is-Enough):

Pornography

• Every second 28,258 Internet viewers are viewing pornography.

- One out of three youths report viewing pornography intentionally.
- Seven out of ten youths report having viewed online pornography unintentionally.
- Nearly 80 percent of exposure to pornography takes place at home.

Predators

- Eighteen percent of youth use chat rooms; the majority of Internet-initiated sex crimes against children are initiated in chat rooms.
- Thirty-seven percent of sexual solicitations of youth occur in chat rooms; 40 percent via instant messaging; 21 percent via other digital means, such as online gaming.
- Sixty-five percent of online sex offenders used the victim's social networking site to gain home and school information about the victim.
- One in seven children has received a sexual solicitation online.

Social networking dangers

- Sixty-nine percent of social media-using teens believe peers are mostly kind to each other on social networking sites, but 88 percent report having seen someone be "mean or cruel to another person on a social networking site."
- Seventy-two percent of teens have a social networking profile.
- Forty-seven percent of teens have a social networking profile viewable by anyone.
- Forty-one percent of social media-using teens have experienced "at least one negative outcome as a result of using the social networking site."
- Twenty-nine percent of Internet sex crime relationships were initiated on a social networking site.
- In 26 percent of online sex crimes against minors, "offenders disseminated information and/or pictures of the victim through the victim's personal social networking site."
- Teens also use social media to "hook up," arranging casual sexual involvements without any commitment. Some believe that this behavior mimics adult matchmaking sites. A mobile location-based "flirting app" called Skout, which was created for adults, initiated a "community" for thirteen- to seventeen-year-olds. Whether this resulted in teen hook-ups is not known; however, three reports of sexual assaults in which men allegedly posed as teenagers prompted the voluntary suspension of the site on June 12, 2012 (Tam, June 12, 2012)
- Sexual harassment—unwanted sexual communications—is also a hazard of social networking for some younger users.

Cyberbullying

- One in six parents know their child has been bullied via a social networking site.
- One million children were harassed, threatened, or subjected to other forms of cyberbullying on Facebook in 2011.
- Forty-three percent of teens (aged 13 to 17) report having experienced some sort of cyberbullying in 2011.

Unsafe online communities

- Vulnerable young people may seek companionship in online communities of other at-risk children, including those who engage in self-harm activities ranging from cutting, to anorexia, to suicide.
- Also problematic on the Web are communities of hate groups and even street gangs.
- Another troublesome online community consists of hackers and hacker tribes—young people who conduct disruptive (and illegal) attacks on other computer users, including eavesdropping and infecting computers with viruses.

Mobile dangers

- Twenty-four percent of teens (ages 14-17) report involvement in "some type of naked sexting" by cell phone or on the Internet.
- Forty-four percent of teens say it is common for sexually suggestive text messages to get shared with people other than the intended recipient.
- Thirty-nine percent of teens report having sent or posted sexually suggestive emails or text messages.

Online gaming

- Dangers most frequently reported and feared include the effects of violence (particularly interactive violence) and sexual content, Internet addiction, and use of online gaming by predators.
- Gambling is widely available on the Web, and it is not difficult for underage users to pass themselves off as adults.

Piracy and plagiarism

- Piracy, the illegal downloading and sharing of copyrighted material—

mostly songs, videos, and motion pictures—is common among young people on the Web. It also can subject those who engage in the activity to criminal prosecution and civil suits, which may well put parents on the hook.

• Related to piracy (copyright infringement) is plagiarism: presenting work created by someone else as your own. The problem is widespread among young Internet users preparing reports and term papers for classroom use. Indeed, a thriving industry exists through which students may purchase finished papers. Plagiarism is not illegal, but it is immoral, impedes learning, and may have severe and long-lasting consequences, including suspension or expulsion from school, high school, or college. (In fact, many educators now scan student papers through specialized software that checks for evidence of plagiarism.) The incident may well become part of the student's permanent record. In the case of college students, loss of scholarships and the like is a real possibility.

Identity theft

• A study released in 2011 by ID Analytics, a California-based consumer Risk-management firm, found that about 140,000 identity frauds against minors occur each year. In fact, according to Carnegie Mellon researchers, children are actually more likely than adults to be targeted for identity theft. The researchers examined the records of 42,000 children and discovered that more than 10 percent of the records showed signs of identity theft.

• Identity thieves apply for credit and secure loans using data stolen from minors. Credit agencies have no ready and reliable way of determining the age of applicants, even based on Social Security numbers.

• Very often, the results of the identity theft do not show up for years—typically when the "child," now a young adult, applies for credit herself. See Chapter 6.

Without dismissing or minimizing the dangers of online activity for children and teens, many recent authorities, including John Palfrey and Urs Gasser in *Born Digital: Understanding the First Generation of Digital Natives*, point out that "reports [of Internet hazards] are often long on hyperbole but short on data" and are not unique to the digital age but have an "offline context that predates the Internet" (Palfrey and Gasser, 2008: 83-84).

Clearly, the Internet surely did not spawn the dangers of childhood, and it can even be a source of support for troubled teens, as psychologists Meyran Boniel-Nissim and Azy Barak note (Boniel-Nissim and Barak, December 12, 2011) and Erica Newland discusses in a Center for Democracy and Technology blog (Newland, April 5, 2012). Nevertheless, the medium's potential for intensifying dangers is undeniable. The Internet contributes an abundance of convenience to our lives and to those of our children, but, as Palfrey and Gasser observe, "too often, the decisions that we make in favor of convenience mean giving up control that, at some point in the future, we may wish we had retained" (Palfrey and Gasser, 2008: 81). Each of the four cybergaps plays a role in exacerbating this intensification effect:

1. The generational cybergap leads to non-communication and miscommunication between children and teens on the one hand and adults, including parents, teachers, and (in some cases) employers, on the other.

For example, parents and teachers may be concerned that Digital Natives are not reading newspapers and magazines but instead rely on browsing websites. The Immigrants assume, therefore, that the digital generation doesn't care about what's going on in the world (the real world) and that "their understanding of current events is superficial." Adults may worry that what information their children and students do acquire comes "from biased websites, rather than authoritative organizations like the *New York Times* or the big television networks."

Palfrey and Gasser believe that this concern is mostly the product of the Digital Immigrant's failure to appreciate "the depth of knowledge that Digital Natives are obtaining from the Web" as well as "how Digital Natives experience news: interacting with information in constructive ways." They graze, scanning the web for what interests them, then they select an area or two into which they "deep dive." Often, this is followed by entry into a feedback loop: a digital conversation with peers and others online (Palfrey and Gasser, 2008: 239-240, 242-242). Arguably, this method of acquiring information is an even more meaningful and "authoritative" learning style than that familiar to the worried parents and teachers—who may, in fact, have something valuable to learn from their children and students. Of course, the Digital Natives can in turn benefit from guidance by the more experienced Digital Immigrants, who are familiar with the value of multiple sources and the proven quality of some sources versus others. Communication and understanding, flowing both ways, is the key.

Another common breakdown in understanding is the Digital Immigrant's tendency to diagnose the Digital Native's preference for multitasking over single or limited tasking as a symptom of flawed concentration skills or even attention deficit disorder. In fact, the difference is one of learning style. The formative experience of Digital Immigrants tends to make them prefer undertaking one task or experiencing one pleasure at a time, whereas Digital Natives have become comfortable engaging in several tasks or activities at once or, more accurately, hopping rapidly from one task or activity to another. For instance, they frequently watch television while simultaneously studying and even socializing. The Zurs point out that although it would intuitively seem "that those who intensely multitask or 'hop' [from task to task] are not likely to comprehend, digest and remember well the important information they read or hear while multitasking," the "research on the effects of multitasking on retention and comprehension is still in its infancy, and we do not yet have conclusive results on the issue."

At present, "some research supports the assertion that multi-tasking/ hopping interferes with retention and comprehension" even as other "equally well-constructed research shows that retention and comprehension of essential and most important information is not affected by such diverse attention." The Zurs believe that the "brains of [Digital] natives born these days are even more adept at hopping than the teenagers we observe now. Toddlers are growing up playing with iPads and smartphones. Being able to navigate online amongst different applications and functions seamlessly is completely normal to them. And importantly—this has relevance for education—having control over the exploration of material seems normal to them" (Zur and Zur, 2011). (Some of the very latest data suggests that multitasking has a more negative than positive impact on learning and on productivity. See, for example, Laura E. Levine et al, "Mobile Media Use, Multitasking and Distractibility" [Levine, Waite, and Bowman, 2012]).

2. The intra-generational cybergap. Generations of parents and educators have understood that children with more access to sources of information and more developed reading, research, and study skills have great educational and vocational advantages over children who lack these things. Today's parents and teachers need to recognize the similar advantage that "enthusiastic" Digital Natives (those more engaged with the Internet and skilled in exploiting its benefits) enjoy over Digital Natives who are either "minimalists" or "avoiders." Moreover, the less engaged Digital Natives may be at greater risk when they do use the Internet, since they typically lack the enthusiasts' awareness of the dangers of privacy exposure as well as cyberbullying, predators, and scammers.

3. The developmental cybergap. Matthew S. Eastin, among other writers, has discussed the effect of the teenager's immature prefrontal cortex (PFC) on focus, judgment, and the assessment of the credibility of information (Eastin, 2008). There is a gap between the abundance—what Palfrey and Gasser call the "overload"—of information available on the Internet and the teenager's cognitive and neural capacity and competence to evaluate it constructively " (Palfrey and Gasser, 2008: 185ff). Parents and educators need to recognize this developmental cybergap and provide appropriate guidance. Beyond the hazards of poor judgment, Internet overload can lead to issues of Internet addiction or addictive behavior (Stanford, October 17,

148

2006; Young, 2007; Young, "Addiction to MMORPGs") and what Palfrey and Gasser call "technostress" (Palfrey and Gasser, 2008: 190).

4. The cybergap between cause and effect online. As already discussed, the online environment tends to engender a feeling of anonymity or invisibility, which can be especially compelling for children and teens, making it difficult for them to think in terms of real-world consequences of acts committed online. Digital Immigrants need to understand that this is a structural effect of the online environment, not a defect in the morality of their children. They should therefore be ready to guide Digital Natives to an awareness of the real life consequences of online actions.

Building Bridges

Because it is multiplied by four, the cybergap is more complex than the phrase "generational digital divide" implies, yet the gaps are not so wide as to be unbridgeable. That they must be bridged seems to us self-evident for at least two equally self-evident reasons. First, the benefits of the Internet to Digital Natives and Digital Immigrants alike far outweigh the risks. Second, the proverbial genie is not going back into the bottle. Not ever. The Internet and other modes of digital life are not only here to stay, they are certain only to become more powerful and more pervasive. We must, therefore, devise effective ways to bridge the cybergaps.

This enterprise is not simple, but neither is it as novel or as arcane as Digital Immigrants may imagine and fear. To be sure, bridging the cybergaps requires a willingness to understand the distinctive, perhaps seemingly alien, reality of the Digital Native. And this, in turn, requires an openness to technologies that may be unfamiliar and to which some Digital Immigrants may be resistant. But the Digital Immigrant generation already possesses the principal bridge-building materials. They are the willingness, experience, and mature common sense to provide good parenting. As Palfrey and Gasser write, "In shaping solutions ... we need not think in radically new paradigms. Often, the old-fashioned solutions that have solved similar problems in the past will work in the digital age, too. Those solutions are engaged parenting, a good education, and common sense" (Palfrey and Gasser, 2008: 9). Having found and explored the four cybergaps in this chapter, we will in the next chapter apply real-world parenting, leavened with a generous dash of technological savvy, to bridge them all.

CHAPTER TWELVE
Bridge the Cybergaps

As we saw in Chapter 11, the cybergaps are real, and they are significant. There really are differences between parents and children, Digital Immigrants and Digital Natives, when it comes to living life online. We also saw, however, that these differences are often exaggerated by the media, by psychologists and sociologists, and by parents and teachers themselves. That is, while the gaps are real, they are also bridgeable.

Big Brother, Mother, and Father

Parenting is a real-world skill, usable both offline and on, yet the catalogue of online threats is admittedly daunting: pornography, predators, social networking hazards, cyberbullying, unsafe online communities, pitfalls of mobile phone and smartphone use, problems with online gaming and gambling, temptations to piracy and plagiarism, and the often overlooked risks children face from identity thieves. Many parents feel so overwhelmed that they turn to digital technology itself for help in conquering, if not actually bridging, the cybergaps.

Parental blocking software, which mainly functions to filter or block children's access to inappropriate websites, was introduced years ago. As we will see, this and other parental controls and "parental empowerment" software packages and online services remain useful tools, especially where younger children have access to the family computer or even have one of their own. A recent *New York Times* article notes that current software goes far beyond mere blocking: "today's technologies promise to embed Mom and Dad—and occasionally Grandma—inside every device that children are using, and gather intelligence on them wherever they go." There is an online service that "helps parents keep tabs on every chat, post and photo that floats across their children's Facebook pages" and another service that "scans the Web in case a child decides to try a new social network that the grown-ups have not even heard of yet." In the mobile realm, there is "a smartphone application [that] alerts Dad if his son is texting while driving" (Sengupta, June 25, 2012, "Big Brother").

Some parents—and grandparents—really dive in. Sixty-two-year-old Mary Cofield, for instance, bought her fifteen-year-old granddaughter an Android phone with full Internet access on condition that she be permitted to monitor the girl online. Ms. Cofield's rationale was that you couldn't keep the technology out of kids' hands; therefore, you, the adult, had "to be in the game to help [your children] know what's wrong and what's right. . . . You can either be out there with them in the game—or they'll be out there without you." The grandmother used an online monitoring service called uKnowKids (www.uknowkids.com), which "combs the granddaughter's Facebook page and text messages." It sends her "alerts about inappropriate language" and includes "dashboard of the child's digital activities, including what she says on Twitter, whom she texts and what photos she is tagged in on Facebook." uKnowKids even "translates teenage slang into plain English she can understand" (Sengupta, June 25, 2012, "Big Brother").

Jeana Lee Tahnk, a mother and technology blogger, offers a selected list of what reporter Somini Sengupta describes as other solutions "to measure and filter how your children use technology, from potty training to prom" (Sengupta, June 25, 2012, "Tools,").

- BubCap is a simple cover for the "home" button of smartphones and tablets—the equivalent of a childproof bottle top to keep toddlers from leaving whatever application has been approved by parents. Apple's iOS 6 mobile operating system includes a built-in tool to keep children locked into a particular application.
- Parental controls intended to filter out and block age-inappropriate content are offered by all major Web browsers and by vendors of standard security suites. Some of these also permit parents to track every site their child visits. The problem with many parental control solutions, however, is that the filtering is so literal that it blocks the good along with the bad, putting useful and appropriate sites off limits because of the random occurrence of a suspicious or objectionable word or two.
- Mobiflock and SecuraFone are designed variously to turn off mobile devices when children are supposed to be sleeping, to disable the phone's camera, and to prevent the downloading of "questionable applications."
- Safely is one of a class of mobile apps that prevent texting while driving, using the phone's motion sensor to trigger blocking of texting capabilities when the phone is in a moving car. The limitation of this and similar apps is that it cannot distinguish between a driver and a passenger.
- Secure.me monitors a child's activity on social networks, even if he or she logs on from someone else's computer. The service watches who has befriended the child on Facebook and tracks where pictures of a child show up on the site.
- MinorMonitor (like uKnowKids) offers tools to do in-depth monitoring. These services include menus of keywords associated with sex, drugs, and hate speech, among other unsavory things.

Although surveys (including one conducted by the much-trusted Pew Research Center) indicate that approximately two-thirds of parents periodically check on their children's "digital footprint" and 40 percent actively follow their offspring on such social sites as Twitter and Facebook. Such monitoring is not entirely harmonious; it frequently triggers arguments between parents and children. What is more, kids don't just object to monitoring by protesting it. "Sometimes children deactivate their Facebook accounts except at night, when they know their parents are not likely to be logging on. They roll over to new sites, often using pseudonyms. Very often they speak in code designed to stump parents" (Sengupta, June 25, 2012, "Big Brother"). A 2012 study by the security firm McAfee found that 70 percent of teenagers, ages thirteen to seventeen, hide their online behavior from parents.   Forty-three percent "access simulated violence on the Web, while 32 percent view nude content or pornography." In addition, "15 percent of teens have hacked a social network account, and nearly 31 percent have pirated movies or music. About 9 percent of kids have hacked into another person's e-mail account." The McAfee study suggested that at least half of the parents surveyed were blissfully confident that "Their teens tell them everything they're doing online" (Reisinger, June 25, 2012).

The Limits of Technology

Parents need to know about the filtering, blocking, and monitoring tools available to them. Clearly, this technology has a role to play in both guiding and protecting children online. Just as clearly, however, the technology is limited. Not only can it be circumvented in many cases, reliance on such technological solutions tends to breed distrust, resentment, and cynicism in relations between parents and children.

Anybody who uses a computer for just about any task cannot fail to be impressed by the benefits of the digital technology. Nevertheless, it does not take extensive experience with computers to understand that they are tools to aid human intellect, not substitutes for it. The same is true when using technology to help protect and guide children online. The available tools can be useful aids to parenting, but none substitute for it.

Real-World Parenting Strategies

The online universe can seem a bewildering place, and the thought of one's children recklessly wandering through it can be both daunting and frightening. In the end, however, the parenting mission online is the same as that offline. It is to assist and guide children to make safe and responsible choices.

Many parents wish the Internet had never happened. Doubtless, these are the same kinds of parents who also seek to shelter their children from the world at large, not just the online portion of it. Children do, of course, sometimes need sheltering. We all know that a toddler cannot simply be turned loose to play in traffic. For infants, we set up enclosures, even sealing off forbidden rooms with gates. When children are a little older, we let them play in fenced yards. As they mature, perhaps the driveway and sidewalk in front of the house come to be regarded as safe areas of play. Soon, the permitted territory may be extended to the entire block—and so on. For untold generations, parents have introduced their children to the world, controlled sector by controlled sector, as it were, shielding and monitoring them but always with an eye toward progressively exposing them to more and more of what lies "out there."

Even as we allow our growing children more space, greater scope of action, and more freedom, we continue to monitor them—usually in a friendly way, asking them questions: "Where are you going?" "Who are you playing with this afternoon?" "Whose house will you be at?" "How long will you be gone?" And we set limits: "Dinner is at five, sharp." "I don't want you crossing Madison Street." "You can play with Tommy and his friends, but not with Nate."

Throughout this process of growth, we also work to instill our values in our children, in the hope that they will learn to apply these values to their young lives. We may talk about being kind to others, about treating your friends with respect, and about behaving toward others as you would want them to behave toward you. We may talk about honesty and telling the truth. We may talk about loyalty. We try to equip our children to be safe, telling them not to talk to strangers, not to accept rides or gifts from people they don't know, not to share certain private information with others. We impart values and rules of all kinds.

All of these aspects of the parenting mission—centuries old, at least—are fully translatable to life online. It's just that some of us get lost in the translation. We may be insufficiently informed about the digital world. We know our neighborhood. We know our city. But the Internet, for some of us, is a foreign country. What is more, whereas parents are usually quite comfortable in their physical environment—know how to drive and know what roads to take and what roads to avoid, know where it's safe to walk and where it's not, understand how to use mass transit and where the A, B, C, and D rapid transit lines go as well as what stations are local and what stations are express only—they may be fearful of all or parts of the Internet. Their children, in contrast, who can't drive, don't really know "safe" neighborhoods from "dangerous" ones, and aren't accustomed to using mass transit alone, are Digital Natives who have grown up with the Internet and its associated technologies. Fearless and comfortable online, they want to explore.

Our task as parents is to do our best to apply real-world, offline parenting principles to the digital environment. We have to do this despite our own fears and limitations. The differences between being online and being offline are significant—we saw that in Chapter 11, and we see it in everyday experience—but, ultimately, the similarities far outweigh the differences, especially when it comes to parenting.

Parenting Styles

In the generation of our grandparents or perhaps our parents, there was much debate over whether "permissive" parenting was better or worse than "traditional"—"authoritarian"—parenting. Today, these polarizing terms are heard less often, but the debate continues nevertheless, and the intensified demands of parenting in a world that includes an Internet merit a revival of those earlier terms. They describe the ways many parents approach their children's experience online.

In *Cyber-Safe Kids, Cyber-Savvy Teens: Helping Young People Learn to Use the Internet Safely and Responsibly*, author Nancy E. Willard cites classic research by the developmental psychologist Diana Baumrind into the effectiveness of "authoritarian" versus "permissive" parenting styles. In fact, Baumrind proposed an alternative to both poles, what she called the "authoritative" style. Whereas Baumrind described in Goldilocks fashion the "authoritarian" approach as "too hard" and the "permissive" approach as "too soft," the "authoritative" style seemed to her "just right" (Willard, 2007; Baumrind, 1966).

Authoritarian Parenting

Baumrind explains: "The authoritarian parent attempts to shape, control, and evaluate the behavior and attitudes of the child in accordance with a set standard of conduct, usually an absolute standard, theologically motivated and formulated by a higher authority. She [the parent] values obedience as a virtue and favors punitive, forceful measures to curb self-will at points where the child's actions or beliefs conflict with what she thinks is right conduct. She believes in keeping the child in his place, in restricting his autonomy, and in assigning household responsibilities in order to inculcate respect for work. She regards the preservation of order and traditional structure as a highly valued end in itself. She does not encourage verbal give and take, believing that the child should accept her word for what is right" (Baumrind, 1966, p. 890).

Permissive Parenting

"The permissive parent attempts to behave in a nonpunitive, acceptant and affirmative manner towards the child's impulses, desires, and actions," Baumrind writes. "She [the parent] consults with him [the child] about policy decisions and gives explanations for family rules. She makes few demands for household responsibility and orderly behavior. She presents herself to the child as a resource for him to use as he wishes, not as an ideal for him to emulate, nor as an active agent responsible for shaping or altering his ongoing or future behavior. She allows the child to regulate his own activities as much as possible, avoids the exercise of control, and does not encourage him to obey externally defined standards. She attempts to use reason and manipulation, but not overt power to accomplish her ends" (Baumrind, 1966, p. 889).

<u>Authoritative Parenting</u>
"The authoritative parent attempts to direct the child's activities but in a rational, issue-oriented manner. She [the parent] encourages verbal give and take, shares with the child the reasoning behind her policy, and solicits his objections when he refuses to conform. Both autonomous self-will and disciplined conformity are valued.... Therefore she exerts firm control at points of parent-child divergence, but does not hem the child in with restrictions. She enforces her own perspective as an adult, but recognizes the child's individual interests and special ways. The authoritative parent affirms the child's present qualities, but also sets standards for future conduct. She uses reason, power, and shaping by regime and reinforcement to achieve her objectives, and does not base her decisions on group consensus or the individual child's desires." (Baumrind, 1966, p. 891).

<u>Parenting Styles Online</u>
Nancy Willard believes that authoritarian parents tend either to forbid their children from going online altogether or rely on "parental empowerment tools, including child safe portals or filtering software" when they do permit it. This reliance produces "false security" and creates an atmosphere of distrust and resentment. Even worse, "Children of authoritarian parents are unlikely to gain the knowledge and skills necessary to independently make safe and responsible choices online" (Willard, 2007, loc. 335-343).

Children of permissive parents, Willard believes, are left to fend for themselves and, for that reason, also fail to make safe and responsible choices online (Willard, 2007, loc. 351).

"The only approach to parenting that will effectively empower children and teens to make safe and responsible choices online," Willard suggests, "is the authoritative approach" (Willard, 2007, loc. 351-355), which Baumrind characterizes as a parental attempt to "direct the child's activities ... in a rational, issue-oriented manner." This is engaged parenting, founded on what Baumrind calls "verbal give and take" (Baumrind, 1966, p. 891). Whereas the authoritarian approach is dictatorial and the permissive approach essentially an abandonment, the authoritative style is above all a commitment to reason and explanation. Like all good Internet policy—from government regulation to the practices of e-commerce providers—authoritative parenting online is transparent. It is an appeal to practicality and reason.

Authoritative and Age Appropriate
It seems clear that the "authoritative" parenting style holds the most promise as a successful approach to productively guiding and effectively protecting your children online. Parenting is in large part a task of leadership and management,

and nowhere is this more the case than in helping your kids online. Like most other managers, parents too often make the mistake of trying to "fix" people rather than addressing the issues and problems that affect them. Things—issues and problems—can be fixed; people cannot be. The authoritative style does not try to mold, remold, control, or alter personality. Instead it addresses issues in a reasoned and transparent manner.

There are some very important basic issues that are quite easy to resolve. Up to age sixteen or seventeen, it is crucial to keep computers out of the kid's bedroom and in a relatively public area of the house. Recall from Chapter 11 that the online experience may create its own reality. This is true of adults, but it can be especially intense in the case of children. Integrating the computer—the means of accessing the Internet—into the mainstream of your household will help to reduce the isolating, "alternative-reality" impact of online activity. Perhaps more to the point, it will provide you with the opportunity to "shoulder surf" your child's activity—from time to time, to look over her shoulder, casually, to check on what she's doing. Of course, you could also do this if the computer were in the child's room, but then you would have to "intrude" into that room and make a point of checking up. That would be likely to create the kind of friction, resentment, and distrust that provide a motive for evasion and deception. Better to avoid coming on like a cross between a spy and a cop, and to keep the atmosphere light and matter-of-fact.

In addition to planting the computer strategically, establish set hours for computer use. This is where some of that "parental empowering" software can be a really big help. Most parental suites include a time-management module, which will make the computer available to your child only at the times you prescribe and unavailable at all other times.

Insert yourself into your child's online world. Make time to engage in computer activities together. Explore the Internet with your child. Play games. Guide your child to the websites and online activities you consider worthwhile. This should not be done at the expense of visiting websites your son or daughter enjoys, but in addition to them.

Perhaps the most powerful and effective way to make yourself part of your child's online experience is to get into the habit of communicating with him or her digitally. Send emails, instant messages, and texts. Keep these positive and informational. If you have something of more stern "correctional" nature to say, better say it in person.

Finally, review the chapters in Part II to be certain that you have a realistic understanding of online security issues and risks. These not only affect your children directly, they have an impact on all household computers and devices that are networked with the child's.

Stage 1: Children under Eight

No parenting style, including the favored "authoritative" style, can be applied in boiler-plate fashion to every child of every age. Remember, the most effective overall strategy is to replicate online what good parents have done offline since parenting began. They guide their children through an ever-expanding view of and interaction with the world, beginning with the safety of the indoor enclosure and fenced-in yard, then progressively moving out from there.

Many parents naturally turn to software solutions that create "child-safe portals" designed to confine the youngster to age-appropriate websites while filtering out and blocking those intended for older children or adults. This class of software can be quite useful, but bear in mind that these products are not created by cadres of altruistic child psychologists. They are commercial products that are certainly intended to shield kids from dangers, but not necessarily from the online marketing and advertising of toys, clothing, and other merchandise intended to appeal to children. You may believe there is nothing wrong with this. To an extent, there certainly is not. We live, after all, in a consumer society, and children, even very young children, start swimming in it very early. Nevertheless, we suggest that parents play offense with the online experience of their youngest children. Instead of relying on a commercial, corporate view of what is appropriate for your kids, surf the Web yourself to identify the websites you actually want your young children to experience. These websites should reflect your family's values—your personal online brand. You don't need elaborate software to confine your kids to these sites. Just bookmark them, and make two rules for your child's surfing:

1. He or she can visit only the special bookmarked sites.
2. If he or she wants to visit a new site, one that isn't bookmarked, they have to visit it first with you. If you find it acceptable, you can add it to the bookmarked collection.

Depending on your child's level of interest and your own feelings in the matter, it is appropriate to set up an email account even for a child of six, seven, or eight. You need to establish firm rules specifying who is permitted to send messages into the child's account. Use the settings on your email client (such as Outlook) to exclude all messages from other sources. Explain to your child that if he wants to add another correspondent, the two of you need to add that correspondent together. Of course, you must have complete access to the account, which you should audit on a daily basis.

In addition to restricting the young child to bookmarked websites only, help your child create a username and instruct her to use only this username online. Explain that her real name, phone number, and address are for family use only and are never to be typed on the computer unless the two of you do so together.

Even though your child may agree to visit nothing but bookmarked websites and despite the age-appropriate filtering and blocking software you may install, it is almost inevitable that something inappropriate will pop up from time to time. Don't make a big deal of it when it does, and don't punish your child. Instead, encourage him or her to turn off the screen (show your child how to do this) and then come and get you. When he or she does this, offer enthusiastic congratulations on a job well done.

Stage 2: Pre-Tweens
At about eight years old and through age ten, your child should be encouraged to expand her collection of bookmarked "favorite" websites. Even as you encourage this exploration, continue to make clear that you will look at the websites as well. Share with your child the rationale for this approach. Explain basic safe searching practices. Set as an absolute rule that your child must never register on any website without getting your permission. Do not grant this permission without personally examining the website. Although you should, at this stage, supervise any registration you approve, explain just what it is you are doing and why. Emphasize the importance of not disclosing personal information.

Do not yield to the temptation to become an accomplice in violating the rules of websites that bar registration by children under age thirteen. You will be cajoled by your child's pleas that "everybody's parents let their kids sign up." Although the "everybody's" is an exaggeration, a word like "many" or even "most" would be quite accurate. Many, perhaps most, parents are complicit in registering their underage children on social websites. This doesn't make it a good idea. There is no benefit in teaching your child to lie, and there is even less good in giving him the message that it is okay to lie if he really, really wants something. If you expect your kid to abide by your rules, demonstrate your willingness to respect the rules of the website.

In addition to teaching your child how to close inappropriate pop-ups and the like as well as how to exit a "bad" website, be firm and explicit about never, ever clicking on a link without thinking first. Emphasize to your child that she must know exactly where the link will take her before she clicks on it. Lay down absolute rules putting the following kinds of links strictly off limits:

> links in email messages
> links in pop-up ads
> links in banner ads

Explain the consequences of thoughtless clicking, with emphasis on infection by malware. If your child's computer is networked with other devices in the household, such an infection can cause serious problems. Assign your kid some real responsibility by asking her to "Help keep us all safe from viruses and identity thieves." She's old enough to understand and to appreciate her assigned role in helping to protect her family.

Stage 3: Tweens

The age group from eleven to twelve has been getting a lot of attention lately because these years witness a sudden expansion in the interest of children in celebrity, music, fashion, and media. Kids this age have one foot in childhood proper and the other, however tentatively, in full-on adolescence. Tweens tend to do a lot of testing of limits and rules, a tendency that is counterbalanced by some profound ambivalence over venturing out into the world versus remaining cocooned in the security of home. These attitudes and feelings are reinforced in many places by the transition from elementary to "grown up" middle school. The connection to the world provided by the Internet raises the pitch of emotion even higher.

Most tweens put a premium on websites designed to appeal to teens, including social networking sites. Most of these websites, however, set thirteen as the minimum age for registering. Your child may ask your permission to lie about her age. More likely, feeling pressure from peers, she will do the lying all on her own. Even worse, she will justify her lying with the line (actually more true than false) that "everyone's parents let their kids sign up."

You will have to decide whether or not keeping your tween off the popular teen websites is worth a showdown. Certainly, it is worth a discussion, which may lead to a mutually agreed on solution. Perhaps, however, the best approach is the one Nancy Willard proposes. It is to take the proactive and preemptive step of forming "a partnership with the parents of your child's best friends," not only to enforce the rules, but to "foster electronic communication within this safe group of friends—and no further" (Willard, 2007, loc. 255). This is an ambitious, perhaps even quixotic, goal, but it may be worth trying. At the very least, efforts to create such a partnership will foster cooperation and communication among parents and may well serve to populate your child's online social network mostly with neighborhood, school, and community kids you already know.

Stage 4: Early Adolescence

Entry into adolescence at age thirteen makes youngsters eligible for "legitimate" registration on most social networking sites. Look on this as a positive step, since it removes one source of parent-child friction and one reason to lie (whether to mom and dad, to the website, or to both), but it also signals entry into a highly charged online social world at a time when hormones are beginning to surge. The early teen years are a period of anxiety for many parents, and the opportunities and challenges offered by increased online access to the world tend to increase that anxiety.

Recognize that the ages from thirteen to fifteen are a time when teens are deeply engaged in figuring out who they are, who they want to be, and how they want to present themselves to the world. This enterprise can be facilitated by the Internet, which introduces the teen to a variety of possible roles and invites her to experiment with any number of online self-identities. For parents, it is an opportunity to speak to your teen about the self-branding concept, the idea of projecting an identity that embodies admirable and effective values, that develops a reputation for integrity, intelligence, and good judgment. It is an opportunity to speak with your teen about the record-keeping capacity of the Internet: how impulsive behavior or reckless postings can linger for years, cropping up when college admissions officers and potential employers perform a deep online background search or even just Google your name. In short, it is a time to talk— not to lecture, but to reason and to weigh the enormous opportunities the Internet offers against the pitfalls. Each of these conversations should end not with a warning, but with a statement of empowerment and responsibility. To make the most of the opportunities while minimizing the risks does not require good luck. It calls for good choices, and those, parents should emphasize, are well within the young person's power. Express confidence in your child.

This doesn't mean you should not provide help in the form of continued monitoring. Keep that computer out of the teen's bedroom, no matter how much he wants it put there. Keep glancing over your young surfer's shoulder from time to time. Talk to her about her activities online—what she does, who her friends are. Do what you can to reinforce online friendships with kids she knows "in real life," at school or elsewhere in the community. The less anonymous the Internet can be made to appear to the early teen, the more sensitively and responsibly he or she will tend to act while on it. Boost this sense by continuing to communicate with you kid online, via email and IM.

And do take advantage of the privacy features of the social websites your teen uses. These features should be set for the maximum of privacy. Discuss with your teen the advantages of carefully controlling who can access her information. Ideally, at this stage in a teen's development, the social web should be an online extension of his or her offline network. Everyone needs to see and appreciate that, online or off, life is all "real life" with real impacts, feelings, and consequences.

Make your access to your teen's pages and accounts a condition of his use of the social web. Tell (don't warn!) your kid that you'll be looking in from time to time. Follow the links on his profile. See who his friends are. Talk to him about anyone unfamiliar—and talk to him in exactly the same way and in the same tone as you would discuss any of his friends and acquaintances at school.

There are clear and present dangers for young teens online. The most obvious are the threats of impulsive sexual activity via hookups, impulsive sharing of sexual information online—including photographs—and the possibility of being victimized by adult online predators. In addition, young males in particular may be attracted to online pornography. Recognize the risks but bite your tongue when you find yourself on the verge of embarking on a lecture. Look upon the dangers as subjects for discussion about creating an online self-brand that embodies your family's values and that projects an image of intelligence and integrity. Discuss impulse and its consequences. Talk to your teen about the "digital footprint" he is creating with every step he takes across the Web.

Stage 5: Later Adolescence

By the time their child turns sixteen, it begins to dawn on most parents that their "baby" is getting ready to leave home within a couple of years. Ready or not, the older teen will have to accept full responsibility for the choices he makes online—and, for that matter, offline as well. You can help develop your teen's readiness for this level of responsibility by turning the tables on him or her. Instead of giving them guidance and advice for getting the most out of the social web and other aspects of the Internet, seek their advice on some of these issues. Demonstrate your confident expectation that your teen can and will make good choices.

Keep talking values. Resist the urge to wall off your teen's online world as something apart from "real life." It is, in fact, contiguous with offline existence and produces the same real results, impacts, and consequences. Have the same conversations about your child's online friends as you do about her offline friends. Bring them all into your line of sight. Ask questions—friendly, conversational questions—about what your teen does online and who she communicates with. Extend these questions to requests for advice, opinions, and recommendations: "What movie review site do you use? Your mother and I are always stuck when it comes to deciding what movie's worth going to."

At about sixteen or seventeen, if you feel your teen's behavior warrants it, you should consider finally allowing your child to put the computer in her room. After all, you are probably also beginning to trust her, however ambivalently, behind the wheel of a car. The idea of at long last moving the computer into the teen's private room is to give him or her the experience of full online responsibility—while you are still around to give counsel, direction, supervision, and correction (much like you are introducing your teen to the freedom and responsibilities that come with driving while you are still around to offer guidance). For this reason, continue to maintain communication, especially electronically. Keep asking about your child's online life. Talk about websites. Talk about friends.

Values and Brand

Your family's values should guide you and your child throughout all five stages of his or her engagement with life online, but it is in stages 4 and 5, the teen years, that you can most productively explain the value of those values by using the analogy of a brand. The brand concept is one with which your teen has much experience and one that he understands intuitively. He understands that some brands of a product are more highly valued and sought after than others. He understands that a brand represents the value and integrity a product. Build on this understanding by suggesting that all of us have a brand, whether we realize it or not. We continually communicate our reputation, our approach, our values, and our integrity in everything we say and do. Online, this communication may be both broader and longer—it may reach more people at any one time, and traces of it may linger across the Internet for years. Just as a company nurtures, develops, and protects its brand—the expression of its reputation for quality, integrity, and value—all of us should nurture, develop, and protect our own brands.

Your teenager understands what it means to want to be valued and trusted. She readily grasps the idea of getting her brand known and respected and valued. She should also understand the consequences of a brand that becomes damaged by some breakdown in quality, in value, in integrity. If a company works hard and quickly, it may repair and recover its damaged brand. Then again, it may not. We all know that acting in a mean, petty, irresponsible, or dishonest manner can damage a person's reputation, the perceived value of his brand. And teens are all too aware that one nasty rumor can also damage a person's reputation (or brand) pretty permanently. The message parents need to convey to their teenagers—to children on the verge of adulthood and soon to experience their first large dose of independence—is that the Internet is a real-life platform that instantly amplifies and magnifies every word, image, and deed. After echoing and re-echoing them, the Internet records them, filing them away for name-searchable access, perhaps for years and possibly for longer.

These properties of the Internet can be invaluable assets in building a strong, useful, and enduring personal brand. Make the wrong choices, however—lie, break the rules, act without thought, act upon the impulse of the moment, associate yourself with irresponsible and unthinking people—and these same online properties will conspire to tear down a personal brand, tarnishing it, battering it, perhaps even destroying it, thereby rendering it incapable of conveying and promoting your identity as a person worthy of being trusted, of being supported, of being befriended, of being put on the team: a person worthy of employing for the summer, of gaining admission to a top-choice college, even of embarking on a career long thought and dreamed about.

Before your son or daughter turns eighteen and takes that computer from the bedroom to the dorm room, this is the conversation you need to have.

CHAPTER THIRTEEN
Engage

There is a moment in the 2010 David Fincher film *The Social Network* in which the newly invented Facebook is really taking off at Harvard, and Eduardo Saverin (played by Andrew Garfield) urges his business partner Mark Zuckerberg (Jesse Eisenberg) to begin "monetizing" the website by selling ads. Zuckerberg curtly rejects the suggestion. "We don't even know what it is yet," he says.

We Don't Even Know What It Is Yet
The public Internet became operational by the 1980s, but what Eisenberg's Zuckerberg said of Facebook, circa 2004, in *The Social Network* may still be applied to the entire Internet today. "We don't even know what it is yet," and yet "we"—our governments in the United States, Europe, and elsewhere—struggle to write policy and law to govern activity on the Internet. In many respects, it is policy for the wilderness and law for terra incognita. Little wonder that there is much debate, much confusion, and much tension over threats to collective security versus threats to human rights, threats to privacy, threats to commerce, and threats to technological progress. In the early nineties, the Internet seemed to promise a new and benign globalism, a limitless expansion of knowledge and the sharing of same, a linking of humanity worldwide that called to mind the "Ode to Joy" at end of Beethoven's *Ninth*.

In 2012, the Internet has produced terabytes of legislation and proposed legislation, litigation, industry promises, and privacy policies. Internet security and Internet privacy have become multi-billion-dollar industries. Offered an ecstasy of interconnectedness, many people—citizens, lawmakers, corporate interests—shrink back in fear and trembling. As the great Net renders borders moot, national sovereignty looms larger than ever. As global commerce is conducted by the click of a mouse, the loss of privacy and the specter of commercial predation become subjects of heated argument. Privacy, once protectable by the concept of private property, has itself become property—or, at least, a commodity: private data, a collection of zeros and ones, traded, purchased, shared, borrowed, and stolen online every second of every hour of every day.

We don't even know what it is yet. Or, for that matter, what it will become.

On the simplest level, technology is outrunning political, administrative, and legal policy. On a more significant, complex level, technology is remaking society and culture so that society and culture themselves are outrunning political, administrative, and legal policy. Some of modern humanity's most basic concepts —the nation-state, borders, taxes, duties, import, export, property, privacy—are suddenly in flux or under challenge. No wonder it is so tempting to look at the current welter of legislative, bureaucratic, and diplomatic attempts to "regulate" aspects of behavior on the Internet and simply shake our heads in something between bemusement, confusion, and fear.

The idea of attempting to legislate regulation of the Internet is like the notion of carrying water in sieve. The Internet? We don't even know what it is yet. Is it merely an instrumentality, a technology and system of communication and commerce? Or is it the next step beyond the nation-state, if not a nation itself? This idea was suggested as early as March 1999 in a paper Christoph Engel presented to the German Society for Public International Law (Engel, March 1999) and seems to have been given some substance (at least according to Lori B. Andrews, author of the 2012 *I Know Who You Are and I Saw What You Did*) when David Cameron, upon becoming prime minister of Britain, "made an appointment to talk to another head of state—Mark Zuckerberg" at 10 Downing Street. Zuckerberg and the prime minister "discussed ways in which social networks could take over certain government duties and inform policymaking." A month later, Cameron sought Zuckerberg's advice on a possible role for Facebook in helping the UK out of its financial woes. "Is it odd to think of Mark Zuckerberg as a head of state?" Andrews asks. "Perhaps. But Facebook has the power and reach of a nation." She points out that its membership—750 million in January 2012, when her book was published; some one billion as of October 2012—would make it the planet's third largest nation. "It has citizens, an economy, its own currency"—that is, prior to June 20, 2012, when the Facebook credits system was replaced by local currency—"systems for resolving disputes, and relations with other nations and institutions."

Moreover, Andrews insightfully observes, "People are drawn to Facebook, as early settlers are drawn to any new nation, by the search for freedom" (Andrews, 2012, p. 1). Her characterization of the "new" Facebook nation is strikingly reminiscent of the United States, at least when it, too, was a new nation. She explains that "Social networks expand people's opportunities," so that an "ordinary individual can be a reporter ... Or an investigator" or a filmmaker, or a musician, and so on (Andrews, 2012, p. 2). Back in the day, parents told their children that, in America, "you can be anything you want to be." (Maybe this is still heard today, over the prevailing groans of disappointment with the "American dream.")

Even those who would protest that to equate Facebook with a nation is to engage in extreme hyperbole or just plain hype must concede some parallels. Facebook has a population, contains communities within that population, and hosts varied social interactions. There is a lively commerce, there is often intense personal identification with being part of Facebook, and members frequently complain about the Facebook "government," which, fearful of rebellion, at least endeavors to be responsive to their complaints.

To the degree that Facebook (and, by extension, the Internet) is nation-like, how, then, should it be governed, how can it be governed, and by whose authority should it be governed?

This is the class of questions the leaders of the world's more conventionally established nation-states are currently struggling with, even as the digital newcomer in their midst remains in large part an evolving entity, the nature of which is as yet not fully known to us. When will it be known? We take for granted that the political governance of the planet—at least the "developed" portion of the planet—is based on the concept of the nation state. Yet that concept, a state that derives its political legitimacy from functioning as a sovereign entity for a nation, may be no older than some three and a half centuries, dating (many political historians believe) to the 1648 Peace of Westphalia. That series of treaties ended the Thirty Years' War by recognizing the independence from Spain of the Dutch Republic and, in the process, inaugurating a new political order in central Europe based on what we now call the nation state concept: a sovereign state governed by a sovereign and (at least in principle) therefore immune to interference in its affairs by other sovereign nation states and barred from meddling in the affairs of those other nation states. Today, we accept the nation state concept without really thinking about it, even though the history of the last 364 years or so has revealed many lapses—often turbulent, tragic, and bloody—between the concept and its practical application. Despite these, the concept itself seems so culturally normative that we are hardly even conscious of it, except, perhaps, when we encounter "failed states," such as Somalia, where sovereignty itself has collapsed, and we are therefore prompted to recoil (or marvel) at its chaotic condition compared to that of the "rest of us."

Framework versus Regulation

The nation state has been with us for at least three and a half centuries, and, while we accept it—automatically and thoughtlessly—we still don't know how to govern it without frequent descents into abuse, hardship, injustice, oppression, economic catastrophe, and outright war. It is therefore reasonable to assume that the journey toward a modus vivendi—a way of living—in a digitally networked world will be at the very least bumpy, even hazardous, and often bewildering. This is why we, in this book, have argued for government and industry policies that put the maximum of control in the hands of the individual user, and why we have advised the individual user to become sufficiently techno-savvy to play effective offense with his or her identity online. For at this point, the attempt to impose one-size-fits-all regulation on an as-yet-to-be-fully-known Internet strikes us as impractical, ineffective, and quite possibly counterproductive to continued innovation. For this reason, we favor the intent and spirit of the word the White House has used in presenting its proposals governing the Internet —"framework"—over what the European Commission calls its legislation: a "regulation" (White House, February 2012; EU-U.S., March 19, 2012). What is needed, at this point in our evolving understanding of the Internet, is support for the individual user: a "framework" of general principles, instead of a detailed regulatory catalogue, most of which promises to become obsolescent even as it is enacted.

Some of those who have proposed thinking of the Internet as a nation have likewise suggested creating the documents appropriate to nationhood. Back in 1996, John Perry Barlow wrote "A Declaration of the Independence of Cyberspace," which spurned the "Governments of the Industrial World" as "weary giants of flesh and steel," asking them, the creatures "of the past," to "Leave us alone. You are not welcome among us. You have no sovereignty where we gather" (Andrews, 2012, p. 187). In 2010, those who attended the 21st Annual Computers, Freedom, and Privacy Conference declared it time "for a Social Network User's Bill of Rights," and in 2012, the Obama administration promulgated a "Privacy Bill of Rights" for users of the Internet. In 2012, Lori Andrews actually published a "Social Network Constitution," at least some of which might well serve as a suitable "framework" of principles to support the individual user-navigator not just of the social web, but of the Internet at large. We believe that workable legislation and industry standards can be formulated to protect the user rights outlined in Article 3 of Andrews's constitution:

> The right to privacy in one's social networking profiles, accounts, related activities, and data derived therefrom shall not be abridged. The right to privacy includes the right to security of information and security of place. Regardless of active security settings or an individual's efforts to guard his or her digital self, social networks are private places. (Andrews, 2012, p. 189)

From Article 8:

> ... No information shall be collected or analyzed without advance notification of the individual. That notification shall include an explanation of the specific use and purpose of the collection and analysis of that information. There shall be a warning about possible repercussions of giving consent for the collection of that particular information ... An individual shall have the right to know what entities are in possession of or are using that individual's information and he or she shall have a right to gain access to and obtain a copy of all the information regarding him or her. (Andrews, 2012, pp. 190-191)

And from Article 10: "People shall have ... the right to keep their [online] associations private." (Andrews, 2012, p. 192)

We would add to this "constitution" the absolute right of Internet users to be free from the political agendas of particular nations, at least online. We strongly believe that proposals made at the 2012 World Conference on International Telecommunications pose a profound threat to that right, and we applaud the Concurrent Resolution introduced in the U.S. House of Representatives on May 30, 2012, opposing "the proposals, in . . . the United Nations General Assembly, the United Nations Commission on Science and Technology for Development, and the International Telecommunication Union, [that] would justify under international law increased government control over the Internet . . ." (H.Con.Res. 127, May 30, 2012).

The Preamble to the Charter of the United Nations establishes the world body not on the authority of the governments of the world but in the name of "we the peoples of the United Nations," and it announces among the UN's purposes the employment of "international machinery for the promotion of the economic and social advancement of all peoples" (UN Charter Preamble). Among the UN's many agencies, one, the International Telecommunications Union (ITU), founded as the International Telegraph Union in 1865 and incorporated into the UN in 1947, is responsible for the coordination, standardization, and promotion of international communication technologies (ICT), including the global Internet. Its mandate is clearly technical in nature, chiefly to ensure global interoperability and to "bridge the digital divide" by "expanding access to ICTs globally," which, according to the ITU website, "is in everybody's interest" (ITU website). The Preamble to the ITU Constitution of the ITU "fully recognize[es] the sovereign right of each State to regulate its telecommunication" while also seeking to foster "international cooperation among peoples and economic and social development by means of efficient telecommunication services" (ITU Constitution Preamble).

Clearly, the United Nations, chiefly through the ITU, claims a legitimate role in global ICT development, including that of the Internet. Just as clearly, that role is primarily technical (the Internet is part of the "international machinery for ... the advancement of all peoples") with the added mission of expanding access. The current proposals under UN discussion would, contrary to the UN Charter and the ITU Constitution, make the international community complicit with governments and regimes that may want to, in effect, "rewire" the Internet, cutting off their citizens' access to data and communication, patrolling content and communication, censoring information, suppressing bottom-up Internet constituents and political and cultural institutions, and imposing taxes and other restrictive charges on international communication.

No wonder Congress is sufficiently alarmed to protest. Exacerbating that alarm is the utter absence of transparency that has so far characterized discussions of the issue within the UN. Most of what we know of these discussions has surfaced through the work of George Mason University researchers Jerry Brito and Eli Dourado, who in June 2012 created a website called WCITLeaks.org, inviting anyone with access to the emerging but unreleased documents to post them. It is both supremely ironic and dramatically telling that the freedom of the Internet is being used so effectively to expose potential threats to that freedom.

While U.S. and EU lawmakers continue to struggle over important differences in how to regulate the Internet and promote, protect, and support individual digital privacy, it is clear that neither the U.S. nor the EU nations want to give any government the authority to manipulate or censor the flow or the content of data across the global Internet. Even less do they relish the prospect of the United Nations being used as an instrument to sanction such control. Certainly, the future of digital democracy should not be debated, let alone decided, behind closed doors.

Full Engagement

To play offense with your own "brand" on the Internet is to take control at the medium's micro level. But what can you—what can any of us—do at the macro level to manage our collective fate online? Researchers Brito and Dourado have done a great deal to shape the powerful opposition to proposed UN regulation of the Internet, but technological expertise and affiliation with a great university, both of which they enjoy, are not prerequisites to activism in the field of Internet policy.

Membership in—or even awareness of—the major Internet advocacy organizations is the most effective way to get informed on the issues and to have a voice in legislative and industry initiatives. The Internet Defense League, founded in 2012, is the latest in organized efforts to "mobilize the planet to defend the internet from bad laws & monopolies" (http://internetdefenseleague.org/). Its efforts have already received bipartisan applause from members of the U.S. House of Representatives and the Senate (Seidman, July 19, 2012), as well as enthusiastic support from other Internet advocacy organizations, most notably Fight for the Future (www.fightforthefuture.org). Also prominent are the well-established Electronic Frontier Foundation (www.eff.org) and the Center for Democracy and Technology (www.cdt.org). We suggest that you visit the web pages of each of these organizations and choose what most thoroughly engages you. At the very least, you will find these websites to be sources of the latest and most reliable information about privacy, security, and freedom online. We especially recommend that you follow at least a selection of these groups on Twitter and that you also peruse their blogs. Whatever challenges the Internet presents, it is supremely self-reflexive and offers absolutely no excuses for failing to access timely insider information relating to itself.

The United States can lay claim to having "invented" the Internet, at least insofar as the Internet owes its existence to DARPA's ARPANET project. We advocate pushing this claim even further back in time. After all, the American Revolution was a product of the internet—or at least what "internet" the technology of the late eighteenth century allowed. British governing authorities, who looked upon the colonies below Canada as a collection of thirteen disparate settlement units, were stunned and confounded by the degree of communication and coordination among them. This extraordinary interconnectedness was the product of covert organizations in every major American community variously called Committees of Correspondence, Committees of Public Safety, or Sons of Liberty. They were groups of revolutionary leaders who met individually yet were in close communication with one another through relays of couriers—among whom Paul Revere was the best known. They forged the independence movement, they grew it, they maintained it, and they advanced it from concepts, ideas, and expression into action.

The impulse behind the Internet—the "right of the people peaceably to assemble"—existed in America long before the silicon chip, and it found expression in the technology then available. The political movements of the Arab Spring and other recent instances of national, regional, and global activism hint at how effective an electronic Internet, instead of one that relied on pen, paper, print, shoe leather, and horseflesh, would have been in America during 1775-1776. Part of American history, the internet, is now planetary, and we each owe to ourselves and to one another active, thoughtful, informed, principled, and courageous stewardship of the wide open privacy this revolutionary technology offers.

SOURCE NOTES

Chapter 1

Craig, T. and Ludloff, M. (2011). *Privacy and Big Data*. Sebastopol, CA: O'Reilly.

McDonald, A. and Cranor, L. (2008). "The Cost of Reading Privacy Policies. I/S/: *A Journal of Law and Policy for the Information Society*. Retrieved from http://lorrie.cranor.org/pubs/readingPolicyCost-authorDraft.pdf.

Mehrabian, Albert (1971). *Silent Messages* (1st ed.). Belmont, CA: Wadsworth.

Mozilla. Collusion 0.16.3. Retrieved from https://addons.mozilla.org/en-US/ firefox/addon/collusion/.

Riesman, D., et al. (1953) *The Lonely Crowd: A Study of the Changing American Character*. Garden City, NY: Doubleday.

Suler, J. (2004). "The Online Disinhibition Effect." *The Psychology of Cyberspace*. Retrieved from http://users.rider.edu/~suler/psycyber/ disinhibit.html.

White House (February 2012). *Consumer Data Privacy in a Networked World: A Framework for Protecting Privacy and Promoting Innovation in the Global Digital Economy*. Retrieved at http://www.whitehouse.gov/sites/ default/files/privacy-final.pdf.

Chapter 2

Angwin, J. (July 30, 2010). "The web's new gold mine: your secrets." *Wall Street Journal* on-line. Retrieved from http://online.wsj.com/article/ SB10001424052748703940904575395073512989404.html.

Center for Digital Democracy (April 4, 2012)."Massive Scale '30 billion audience data' archive linked to real-time targeting of consumers." Retrieved from http://www.democraticmedia.org/massive-scale-30-billion-audience-data- archive-linked-real-time-targeting-consumers.

Consumer Reports (June 28, 2011). "CU Poll: Consumers want government to protect Internet Privacy." Retrieved from http://news.consumerreports.org/ electronics/2011/06/cu-poll-consumers-want-government-to-protect- internet-privacy.html.

ConsumersUnion (April 7, 2012). "Consumers Concerned About Their Online Privacy." ConsumersUnion. Retrieved from http:// www.consumersunion.org/pub/core_financial_services/018390.html.

DAA. "The Self-Regulatory Program for Online Behavioral Advertising." Retrieved from http://www.aboutads.info/.

Davis, W. (July 12, 2011). "Ad Networks Continue Tracking Users Who Opt Out. *Online Media Daily*. Retrieved from http://www.mediapost.com/ publications/article/153976/.

EU-U.S. (March 19, 2012). "Joint Statement on Data Protection by European

Commission Vice-President Viviane Reding and U.S. Secretary of Commerce John Bryson." PRNewswire via COMTEX.

Melik, J. (March 25, 2012). "Internet privacy: Genuine concerns or paranoia?" *BBC News Business*. Retrieved from http://www.bbc.co.uk/news/business-17369659.

TRUSTe (July 25, 2011). "2011 Consumer Research Results: Privacy and Online Behavioral Advertising." Retrieved from http://www.truste.com/ad-privacy/TRUSTe-2011-Consumer-Behavioral-Advertising-Survey-Results.pdf.

Ur, B., Leon, P., Cranor, L., Shay, R., and Wang, Y. (April 2, 2012). "Smart, Useful, Scary, Creepy: Perceptions of Online Behavioral Advertising." CMU-CyLab-12-007. Retrieved from http://www.cylab.cmu.edu/files/pdfs/tech_reports/CMUCyLab12007.pdf.

White House (February 2012). *Consumer Data Privacy in a Networked World: A Framework for Protecting Privacy and Promoting Innovation in the Global Digital Economy*. Retrieved at http://www.whitehouse.gov/sites/default/files/privacy-final.pdf.

Yan, J., Liu, N., Wang, G., Zhang, W., Yun J., and Chen, Z. (2009). "How much can behavioral targeting help online advertising?" *Proceedings of the 18 International Conference on World Wide Web* (Madrid, Spain 2009). ACM, 261-270.

Chapter 3

Allan, D. (March 24, 2012). "Facebook to Digest Feedback over Controversial Privacy Policy Update." ITProPortal. Retrieved from http://www.itproportal.com/2012/03/24/facebook-to-digest-feedback-over-controversial-privacy-policy-update/.

Associated Press (March 23, 2012). "Facebook Addresses More Privacy Concerns; User Doubts Are Still Biggest Threat to Growth," *Washington Post* with *Bloomberg Business*. Retrieved from http://www.washingtonpost.com/business/technology/facebook-addresses-more-privacy-concerns-user-doubts-are-still-biggest-threat-to-growth/2012/03/23/gIQAjDBfWS_story.html?tid=pm_business_pop.

Bamford, J. (March 15, 2012). "The NSA Is Building the Country's Biggest Spy Center (Watch What You Say)." Wired.com. Retrieved from http://www.wired.com/threatlevel/2012/03/ff_nsadatacenter/.

Boniel-Nissim, M. and Barak, A. (2011) "The Therapeutic Value of Adolescents' Blogging about Social-Emotional Difficulties." Psychological Services. Retrieved from http://www.apa.org/pubs/journals/releases/ser-ofp-boniel-nissim.pdf.

Brian, M. (March 23, 2012). "Facebook Says It May Launch Legal Action against Employers Who Ask for User Passwords." *The Next Web*. Retrieved from http://thenextweb.com/socialmedia/2012/03/23/facebook-says-it-may-launch-legal-action-against-employers-who-ask-for-user-passwords/.

Egan, E. (March 23, 2012). "Protecting Your Passwords and Your Privacy." *Facebook and Privacy*. Retrieved from http://www.facebook.com/notes/ facebook-and-privacy/protecting-your-passwords-and-your-privacy/ 326598317390057.

EU-U.S. (March 19, 2012). "Joint Statement on Data Protection by European Commission Vice-President Viviane Reding and U.S. Secretary of Commerce John Bryson." PRNewswire via COMTEX.

funf.org. Website at www.funf.media.mit.edu.

Hill+Knowlton Strategies (February 2012). "Proposed Reform to the European Data Protection Network: An Analysis of Key Aspects and Suggestions for an AVG Technologies Position Paper." Privately commissioned by AVG Technologies USA, Inc.

Madrigal, A. (March 19, 2012), "How Much Is Your Data Worth? Mmm, Somewhere Between Half a Cent and $1,200." *The Atlantic*. Retrieved from http://www.theatlantic.com/technology/archive/12/03/how-much-is-your-data-worth-mmm-somewhere-between-half-a-cent-and-1200/254730/

Magid, L. (February 22, 2010). "Many Ways to Activate Webcams sans Spy Software." CNET News, February 22, 2010. Retrieved from http:// news.cnet.com/8301-19518_3-10457737-238.html.

McCullagh, D., and A. Broache (December 1, 2006). "FBI Taps Cell Phone Mic as Eavesdropping Tool." CNET News, December 1, 2006. Retrieved from http://news.cnet.com/2100-1029_3-6140191.html.

Solove, D. (2007). *The Future of Reputation: Gossip, Rumor, and Privacy on the Internet*. New Haven and London: Yale University Press.

Szabo, C. (March 26, 2012). "On Privacy EU Says to US, 'You Cannot Escape.'" NetChoice. Retrieved from http://www.netchoice.org/on-privacy-eu-says-to-us-you-cannot-escape/.

VentureBeat (February 2012). "Wrestling Online Privacy." Retrieved from http:// venturebeat.files.wordpress.com/2012/02/120202onlineprivacy.jpg.

White House (February 2012). *Consumer Data Privacy in a Networked World: A Framework for Protecting Privacy and Promoting Innovation in the Global Digital Economy*. Retrieved at http://www.whitehouse.gov/sites/ default/files/privacy-final.pdf.

Wikipedia. "Anthony Weiner sexting scandal." Retrieved from http:// en.wikipedia.org/wiki/Anthony_Weiner_sexting_scandal.

Chapter 4

Note: The material in this chapter is drawn from AVG Technologies security expertise. Additional specific references are—

Apple. "Safety. Built right in." Retrieved from http://www.apple.com/osx/what-is/.

Microsoft Safety Scanner. Download at http://www.microsoft.com/security/ scanner/en-us/default.aspx.

Sherr, I. (April 6, 2012). "Malware Targets Apple Computers, Fix Released," The Wall Street Journal. Retrieved from http://blogs.wsj.com/digits/ 2012/04/06/malware-targets-apple-computers-fix-released/.

Sophos (April 24, 2012). "One in Every Five Mac Computers Harbors Malware, Sophos Research Reveals." Sophos press release. Retrieved from http:// www.sophos.com/en-us/press-office/press-releases/2012/04/one-in-every-five-mac-computers-harbors-malware.aspx.

TrueCrypt. Download at www.truecrypt.org.

We also recommend consulting the following security resources:

AVG Threat Labs Site Reports. Log onto http://www.avgthreatlabs.com/ sitereports/.

Bailey, M. (2011). *Complete Guide to Internet Privacy, Anonymity & Security*. Nerel Online.

Miller, Michael. (2008). *Is It Safe? Protecting Your Computer, Your Business, and Yourself Online*. Que.

Notenboom, L. (2011). *Internet Safety: Keeping Your Computer Safe on the Internet*. Puget Sound Software.

Chapter 5

Bailey, M. (2011). *Complete Guide to Internet Privacy, Anonymity and Security*. Nerel Online.

Boyd, D., and Ellison, N. (2007) "Social Network Sites: Definition, History, and Scholarship." *Journal of Computer-Mediated Communication* 13 (1), article 11. Retrieved from www. jcmc.indiana.edu/vol13/issue1/boyd.ellison.html.

Christakis, N., and Fowler, J. (2009). *Connected: How Your Friends' Friends' Friends Affect Everything You Feel, Think, and Do*. Boston: Little, Brown.

FTC (June 12, 2012). "Spokeo to Pay $800,000 to Settle FTC Charges Company Allegedly Marketed Information to Employers and Recruiters in Violation of FCRA" (FTC press release).

Garber, M. (April 26, 2012). "On Facebook, Your Privacy Is Your Friends' Privacy." *The Atlantic*. Retrieved from http://www.theatlantic.com/ technology/archive/2012/04/on-facebook-your-privacy-is-your-friends-privacy/256407/.

National Crime Prevention Council. "Cyberbullying." Retrieved from http:// www.ncpc.org/cyberbullying/.

Saikin, G. (June 6, 2012). "FBI issues new warning on social networking risks."

Retrieved from http://www.lexology.com/library/detail.aspx?g=668d7b91-
e8c1-4612-979b-fa778aded589&utm_source=Lexology+Daily
+Newsfeed&utm_medium=HTML+email+-+Body+-+Federal
+section&utm_campaign=Lexology+subscriber+daily
+feed&utm_content=Lexology+Daily+Newsfeed+2012-06-12&utm_term=.

Sandage, T. (1998). The Victorian Internet: The Remarkable Story of the
Telegraph and the Nineteenth Century's On-Line Pioneers. New York:
Walker & Co.

Chapter 6

Ahearn, F. (2010). *How to Disappear: Erase Your Digital Footprint, Leave False
Trails, and Vanish without a Trace.* Guilford, CT: Lyon's Press.

Brown, M. (2000). "Verbal Testimony before the U.S. Senate Committee Hearing
on the Judiciary Subcommittee on Technology, Terrorism and Government
Information." Retrieved from http://www.privacyrights.org/cases/
victim9.htm.

Javelin (2011). Javelin Strategy and Research. *2011 Identity Fraud Survey
Report.* Retrieved from https://www.javelinstrategy.com/research/
Brochure-209.

Symantec. *In Defense of Data.* Retrieved from http://www.indefenseofdata.com/
data-breach-trends-stats/.

Verizon (2012). *Data Breach Investigations Report.* Retrieved from http://
www.verizonbusiness.com/resources/reports/rp_data-breach-
investigations-report-2012_en_xg.pdf.

Chapter 7

AP (June 26, 2012). "Facebook draws user ire with quiet switcheroo in email
contact listing." *The Washington Post.* Retrieved from http://
www.washingtonpost.com/business/technology/facebook-draws-user-ire-
with-quiet-switcheroo-in-email-contact-listing/2012/06/26/
gJQADh6F3V_story.html.

Duhigg, C. (February 16, 2012) "How Companies Learn Your Secrets.' *New York
Times.* Retrieved from http://www.nytimes.com/2012/02/19/magazine/
shopping-habits.html?_r=1&pagewanted=all.

Lifehacker (February 22, 2011). "What 'Do Not Track' Is and Why It's Important."
Retrieved from http://lifehacker.com/5767080/what-do-not-track-is-and-
why-its-important.

Maass, P. "Your FTC Privacy Watchdogs: Low-Tech, Defensive, Toothless."
Wired. Retrieved from http://www.wired.com/threatlevel/2012/06/ftc-fail/
all/.

Myers, S. "'Do Not Track' controversy could limit news sites' dependence on
targeted ads." *Poynter.* Retrieved from http://www.poynter.org/latest-

news/mediawire/176769/do-not-track-controversy-could-limit-news-sites-dependence-on-targeted-ads/.

Rockefeller, J. (June 28, 2012). "Rockefeller Remarks on Insdutry Self-Regulation and Privacy Protections." Retrieved from http://commerce.senate.gov/public/index.cfm?p=PressReleases&ContentRecord_id=83a7523d-30dc-4366-8bcf-0198d6f8ab67.

Samson, T. (June 28, 2012). "Top sites are covertly cramming cookies down users' throats." *InfoWorld*. Retrieved from https://www.infoworld.com/t/internet-privacy/top-sites-are-covertly-cramming-cookies-down-users-throats-196594?source=fssr.

Scism, L. and Maremont, M. (November 18, 2010). "Insurers Test Data Profiles to Identify Risky Clients." *Wall Street Journal*. Retrieved from http://online.wsj.com/article/SB10001424052748704648604575620750998072986.html.

Singer, N. (June 23, 2012). "E-Tailer Customization: Convenient or Creepy?" *New York Times*. Retrieved from http://www.nytimes.com/2012/06/24/technology/e-tailer-customization-whats-convenient-and-whats-just-plain-creepy.html?_r=4&pagewanted=1&ref=technology.

Sullivan, M. (June 28, 2012). "Data snatchers! The booming market for your online identity." *InfoWorld*. Retrieved from http://www.infoworld.com/d/security/data-snatchers-the-booming-market-your-online-identity-196427?page=0,0.

Violet Blue (June 27, 2012). "Berkeley Law's first Web Privacy Census is out and it's troubling." CNET. Retrieved from http://news.cnet.com/8301-1009_3-57461462-83/berkeley-laws-first-web-privacy-census-is-out-and-its-troubling/?tag=mncol;txt.

Chapter 8

Ahearn, F. (2010). *How to Disappear: Erase Your Digital Footprint, Leave False Trails, and Vanish without a Trace*. Guilford, CT: Lyons Press.

Android Security Test. Retrieved from http://androidsecuritytest.com/.

Campagna, R., et al. (2011). *Mobile Device Security for Dummies*. Indianapolis: John Wiley.

Carrasco, K. (March 22, 2012). "Personal Cloud Will Overtake PCs by 2014, Gartner Predicts." Enterprise Systems. Retrieved from http://esj.com/articles/2012/03/22/personal-cloud-2014.aspx.

Cheng, J. (April 25, 2011). "FBI child porn raid a strong argument for locking down WIFi networks." *ArsTechnica*. Retirenved from http://arstechnica.com/tech-policy/2011/04/fbi-child-porn-raid-a-strong-argument-for-locking-down-wifi-networks/.

Craig, T., and Ludloff, M. (2011). *Privacy and Big Data*. Sebastopol, CA: O'Reilly

Media.

EC Justice (January 25, 2012). "Commission proposes a comprehensive reform of the data protection rules" (includes "legislative texts" of the proposal and related material). Retrieved from http://ec.europa.eu/justice/newsroom/data-protection/news/120125_en.htm.

EngineerLive (April 25, 2012). "i-Pad and smartphones to overtake PCs for web access." *EngineerLive*. Retrieved from http://www.engineerlive.com/Design-Engineer/Time_Compression/i-Pad_and_smartphones_to_overtake_PCs_for_web_access/22818/.

Holly, R. (November 15, 2011). "How much of your phone is yours?" Geek.com. Retrieved from http://www.geek.com/articles/mobile/how-much-of-your-phone-is-yours-20111115/.

IAB. June 11, 2012. "Internet Advertising Revenues Set First Quarter Record at $8.4 Billion." IAB. Retrieved from http://www.iab.net/about_the_iab/recent_press_releases/press_release_archive/press_release/pr-061112?preview=1&psid=1&ph=80e4)

Kaiser, Michael (April 17, 2009). "Small and Medium Size Businesses are Vulnerable." National Cyber Security Alliance. Retrieved June 6, 2012.

Markey, E. House Bill (January 30, 2012). "Mobile Device Privacy Act." Retrieved from http://markey.house.gov/document/2012/mobile-device-privacy-act.

Markey, E. Press Release (January 30, 2012). "Markey Releases discussion Draft of Mobile Device privacy Act in Wake of Carrier IQ Software Concerns." Retrieved from http://markey.house.gov/press-release/markey-releases-discussion-draft-mobile-device-privacy-act-wake-carrier-iq-software.

Mearian, L. (February 24, 2012). "85% of hospitals embracing BYOD, survey shows." *HealthcareIT*. Retrieved from http://www.computerworld.com/s/article/9224595/85_of_hospitals_embracing_BYOD_survey_shows.

Mello, J. (January 31, 2012). "Smartphone Owners Prone to Using Their Devices in the Bathroom." *PCWorld*. Retrieved from http://www.pcworld.com/article/249022/smartphone_owners_prone_to_using_their_devices_in_the_bathroom.html.

PAX. paxreports.org. Retrieved from http://www.paxreports.org/index.php.

Schwartz, M. (April 30, 2012). "Google Street View Pursued Wardriving by Design." *InformationWeek*. Retrieved from http://www.informationweek.com/news/security/privacy/232901164.

Szabo, C. (March 26, 2012). "On Privacy EU Says to US, 'You Cannot Escape.'" *NetChoice*. Retrieved from http://www.netchoice.org/on-privacy-eu-says-to-us-you-cannot-escape/.

Taylor, C. (February 3, 2012). "Smartphone Sales Overtake PCs for the First Time. *Mashable Tech*. Retrieved from http://mashable.com/2012/02/03/

smartphone-sales-overtake-pcs/.

Ushahidi. "About Us." Retrieved from http://ushahidi.com/about-us.

White House (February 2012). *Consumer Data Privacy in a Networked World: A Framework for Protecting Privacy and Promoting Innovation in the Global Digital Economy.* Retrieved at http://www.whitehouse.gov/sites/default/files/privacy-final.pdf.

Wikipedia. "Carrier IQ." Retrieved from http://en.wikipedia.org/wiki/Carrier_IQ.

Chapter 9

ACLU. "Surveillance under the USA PATRIOT Act." Retrieved from http://www.aclu.org/national-security/surveillance-under-usa-patriot-act.

Electronic Frontier Foundation. "Privacy." Retrieved from www.eff.org/issues/privacy/.

Horwitz, S. (December 1, 2011). "Trade in surveillance technology raises worries." *Washington Post.* Retrieved from http://www.washingtonpost.com/world/national-security/trade-in-surveillance-technology-raises-worries/2011/11/22/gIQAFFZOGO_story.html.

Lynn, W. (2010). "Defending a New Domain: The Pentagon's Cyberstrategy." Foreign Affairs. September/October 2010. Retrieved from http://www.foreignaffairs.com/articles/66552/william-j-lynn-iii/defending-a-new-domain?page=show.

Lynn, W. (2011). "The Pentagon's Cyberstrategy, One Year Later." *Foreign Affairs.* September 28, 2011. Retrieved from http://www.foreignaffairs.com/articles/68305/william-j-lynn-iii/the-pentagons-cyberstrategy-one-year-later?page=show.

MacKinnon, R. (April 26, 2012). "A Clunky Cyberstrategy: Washington Preaches Interent Freedom But Practices Surveillance." *Foreign Affairs.* Retrieved from http://www.foreignaffairs.com/articles/137607/rebecca-mackinnon/a-clunky-cyberstrategy?page=show.

Nakashima, E. (June 19, 2012). "U.S., Israel developed Flame computer virus to slow Iranian nuclear efforts, officials say." *Washington Post.* Retrieved from http://www.washingtonpost.com/world/national-security/us-israel-developed-computer-virus-to-slow-iranian-nuclear-efforts-officials-say/2012/06/19/gJQA6xBPoV_story.html.

Sanger, D. (June 1, 2012). "Obama Order Sped Up Wave of Cyberattacks Against Iran." *New York Times.* Retrieved from http://www.nytimes.com/2012/06/01/world/middleeast/obama-ordered-wave-of-cyberattacks-against-iran.html?pagewanted=all.

U.S. Strategic Command. "U.S. Cyber Command" factsheet. Retrieved from http://www.stratcom.mil/factsheets/Cyber_Command/.

Chapter 10

Baumeister, R. (2005). *The Cultural Animal: Human Nature, Meaning, and Social Life*. New York: Oxford University Press.

Bilton, N. (April 4, 2011). "The Growing Business of Online Reputation Management." *New York Times*. Retrieved from http://bits.blogs.nytimes.com/2011/04/04/the-growing-business-of-online-reputation-management/.

Blankenhorn, D. (May 31, 2912). "Google and the Privacy Bargain." *The Street*. Retrieved from http://www.thestreet.com/story/11562095/1/google-and-the-privacy-bargain.html?cm_ven=RSSFeed.

Christakis, N., and Fowler, J. (2009). *Connected: The Surprising Power of Our Social Networks and How They Shape Our Lives—How Your Friends' Friends' Friends Affect Everything You Feel, Think, and Do*. Boston: Little, Brown.

Mitchell, A. (May 30, 2012). "Personal data stores will liberate us from a toxic privacy battleground." Wired.co.uk. Retrieved from http://www.wired.co.uk/news/archive/2012-05/30/ideas-bank-personal-data-stores.

Onion Routing. Retrieved from http://www.onion-router.net/.

Rifkin, J. (2009). *The Empathic Civilization: The Race to Global Consciousness in a World in Crisis*. New York: Tarcher/Penguin.

Rooney, B. "U.K. Consumers Deeply Skeptical Over Data Collection." TechEurope. Retrieved from http://blogs.wsj.com/tech-europe/2012/07/09/u-k-consumers-deeply-skeptical-over-data-collection/.

Smith, J. (July 10-11, 2012). "Privacy Trumps Cybersecurity, Poll Shows." National Journal. Retrieved from http://www.nationaljournal.com/daily/privacy-trumps-cybersecurity-poll-shows-20120710.

Sprenger, P. "Sun on Privacy: 'Get Over It.'" Wired. Retrieved from http://www.wired.com/politics/law/news/1999/01/17538.

Tapscott, D. (May 11, 2012). "Should We Ditch the Idea of Privacy?" The Great Debate. Reuters. Retrieved from http://blogs.reuters.com/great-debate/2012/05/11/should-we-ditch-the-idea-of-privacy/.

Tor. Retrieved from https://www.torproject.org/ and https://www.torproject.org/about/overview.html.en#thesolution.

Wright, R. (2000). *Nonzero: The Logic of Human Destiny*. New York: Vintage.

Chapter 11

Boniel-Nissim, M. and Barak, A. (December 12, 2011). "The Therapeutic Value of Adolescents' Blogging about Social-Emotional Difficulties." *Psychological Services*. Retrieved from http://www.apa.org/pubs/journals/releases/ser-ofp-boniel-nissim.pdf.

Bredow (2009), Hans Bredow Institut für Medienforschung an der Universität

Hamburg. "'Growing up with the Social Web': Presentation of Research Results." Retrieved from http://www.hans-bredow-institut.de/en/node/2496.

Curtis, P. (January 18, 2009). "Internet generation leave parents behind." *The Guardian*. Retrieved from http://www.guardian.co.uk/media/2009/jan/19/internet-generation-parents/print#history-link-box.

Dworschak, M. (June 8, 2010). "The Internet Generation Prefers the Real World." Retrieved from http://www.spiegel.de/international/zeitgeist/0,1518,710139,00.html.

Eastin, M. (2008). "Toward a Cognitive Developmental Approach to Youth Perceptions of Credibility." Metzger, M., and Flanagin, A., eds. *Digital Media, Youth, and Credibility*. Cambridge: MIT Press, 2008): 29-47.

Enough-Is-Enough. Web site: http://www.internetsafety101.org. For the organization's library of statistics, see http://www.enough.org/inside.php?id=3K03RC4L00.

Levine, L., Waite, B., and Bowman, L. "Mobile Media Use, Multitasking and Distractibility." *International Journal of Cyber Behavior, Psychology and Learning* 2:3. Retrieved from http://www.igi-global.com/article/content/70087.

Newland, E. (April 5, 2012). "Contrary to Rhetoric, Study Shows Teens Benefit from Use of Pseudonyms." Center for Democracy and Technology. Retrieved from https://www.cdt.org/blogs/erica-newland/0504contrary-rhetoric-study-shows-teens-benefit-pseudonyms.

Online Etymology. "generation." *Online Etymology Dictionary*. Retrieved at http://www.etymonline.com/index.php?search=Generation+gap.

Palfrey, J., and Gasser, U. (2008). *Born Digital: Understanding the First Generation of Digital Natives*. New York: Basic Books.

Pappas, S. (February 6, 2012). "Facebook with Care: Social Networking Site Can hurt Self-Esteem." *LiveScience*. Retrieved from http://www.livescience.com/18324-facebook-depression-social-comparison.html.

Prensky, M. (2001). Digital Natives, Digital Immigrants." *On the Horizon*. MCB University Press, Vol. 9, No. 5, October 2001. Retrieved from http://www.marcprensky.com/writing/prensky%20-%20digital%20natives,%20digital%20immigrants%20-%20part1.pdf.

Stanford (October 17, 2006). Stanford School of Medicine. "Internet addiction: Stanford study seeks to define whether it's a problem." Retrieved from http://med.stanford.edu/news_releases/2006/october/internet.html.

Tapscott, D. (2009). *Grown Up Digital: How the Net Generation Is Changing Your World*. New York: McGraw Hill Professional.

Weinberger, et al. (June 2005).*The Adolescent Brain: A Work in Progress*. The National Campaign to Prevent Teen Pregnancy. Retrieved from http://www.thenationalcampaign.org/resources/pdf/BRAIN.pdf

White House (February 2012). *Consumer Data Privacy in a Networked World: A Framework for Protecting Privacy and Promoting Innovation in the Global Digital Economy*. Washington, D.C.: White House.

Willard, N. (2007). *Cyber-Safe Kids, Cyber-Savvy Teens: Helping Young People Learn to Use the Internet Safely and Responsibly*. San Francisco: Jossey-Bass.

Yahoo/Carat (2003). "Yahoo! and Carat Unveil Research Results Showing Teens Are Truly 'Born to Be Wired.'" Retrieved from http://docs.yahoo.com/docs/pr/release1107.html.

Young, K. (2007). "Cognitive Behavioral Therapy with Internet Addicts: Treatment Outcomes and Implications." *CyberPsychology and Behavior* 10, no. 5 (2007): 671-697.

Young, K. "Addiction to MMORPGs. "Addiction to MMORPGs: Symptoms and Treatment. Retrieved from http://www.netaddiction.com/articles/addiction_to_mmorpgs.pdf.

Zur, O., and Zur, A. (2010). "Psychology of the Web and Internet Addiction." Retrieved from http://www.zurinstitute.com/internetaddiction.html.

Zur, O., and Zur, A. (2011). "On Digital Immigrants and Digital Natives: How the Digital Divide Affects Families, Educational Institutions, and the Workplace." Retrieved from http://www.zurinstitute.com/digital_divide.html.

Chapter 12

Baumrind, D. (1966). "Effects of Authoritative Parental Control on Child Behavior." *Child Development*, 37(4), 887-907.

Reisinger, D. (June 25, 2012). "Those sneaky teens: What they're really up to online." *CNET News*. Retrieved from http://news.cnet.com/8301-1009_3-57459889-83/those-sneaky-teens-what-theyre-really-up-to-online/?tag=mncol;txt.

Sengupta, S. (June 25, 2012, "Big Brother"). "'Big Brother'? No, It's Parents." *New York Times*. Retrieved from http://www.nytimes.com/2012/06/26/technology/software-helps-parents-monitor-their-children-online.html?pagewanted=2&_r=2&ref=technology&src=me.

Sengupta, S. (June 25, 2012, "Tools"). "Tools to Control a Child's Technology. New York Times. Retrieved from http://www.nytimes.com/2012/06/26/technology/tools-to-control-a-childs-technology.html?_r=2&ref=technology.

Willard, N. (2007). *Cyber-Safe Kids, Cyber-Savvy Teens: Helping Young People Learn to Use the Internet Safely and Responsibly*. San Francisco: Jossey-Bass.

Chapter 13

Andrews, L. (2012). *I Know Who You Are and I Saw What You Did*. New York: Free Press.

Center for Democracy and Technology. www.cdt.org.

Electronic Frontier Foundation. www.eff.org.

Engel, C. (March 1999). "The Internet and the Nation State." Retrieved from http://www.coll.mpg.de/sites/www.coll.mpg.de/files/text/engel1.pdf.

EU-U.S. (March 19, 2012). "Joint Statement on Data Protection by European Commission Vice-President Viviane Reding and U.S. Secretary of Commerce John Bryson." PRNewswire via COMTEX.

Fight for the Future. www.fightforthefuture.org

H.Con.Res. 127 (May 30, 2012). "Expressing the sense of Congress regarding actions to preserve and advance the multistakeholder governance model under which the Internet has thrived." Retrieved from http://www.govtrack.us/congress/bills/112/hconres127/text.

Internet Defense League. http://internetdefenseleague.org/.

ITU Constitution Preamble. Retrieved from http://www.itu.int/net/about/basic-texts/constitution/preamble.aspx.

ITU website. http://www.itu.int/en/Pages/default.aspx.

Seidman, A. (July 19, 2012). "Internet Coalition Vows to Stave Off Regulation. Retrieved from http://blogs.wsj.com/washwire/2012/07/19/internet-coalition-vows-to-stave-off-regulation/.

U.N. Charter Preamble. Retrieved from http://www.un.org/en/documents/charter/preamble.shtml.

WCITLeaks.org.

White House (February 2012). *Consumer Data Privacy in a Networked World: A Framework for Protecting Privacy and Promoting Innovation in the Global Digital Economy*. Retrieved at http://www.whitehouse.gov/sites/default/files/privacy-final.pdf.